THE
FOUNDERS'
ALMANAC

George Washington presiding at the signing of the United States Constitution

∽ THE ∽
FOUNDERS'
ALMANAC

A PRACTICAL Guide to the Notable EVENTS, Greatest LEADERS & Most ELOQUENT Words of the AMERICAN FOUNDING

Reference Edition

Edited and with an introduction by
Matthew Spalding

THE HERITAGE FOUNDATION
Washington, D.C.

THIS IS A CENTER FOR AMERICAN STUDIES BOOK
PUBLISHED BY THE HERITAGE FOUNDATION

Copyright © 2002 by The Heritage Foundation
First Published September 2001
All Rights Reserved Under International and Pan-American Copyright Conventions
Published in the United States by The Heritage Foundation, Washington, D.C.

www.heritage.org

Library of Congress Cataloging-in-Publication Data

The founders' almanac : a practical guide to the notable events,
greatest leaders & most eloquent words of the American founding / edited
and with an introduction by Matthew Spalding.-- Library ed.
    p. cm.
Includes bibliographical references
    ISBN 0-89195-104-0 (Lib. ed.) : alk. paper) -- ISBN 0-89195-105-9
(Softcover : alk. paper)
    1. United States--Politics and government--1783-1809--Miscellanea. 2.
United States--Politics and government--1775-1783--Miscellanea. 3.
Constitutional history--United States--Miscellanea. 4.
Statesmen--United States--Biography--Miscellanea. I. Spalding, Matthew.

    E303 .F75 2002
    973.3--dc21
                                    2002004363

Reference Edition

Book Design by Fletcher Design
Cover Design by Woodpile Studios

Printed and bound in the United States by Victor Graphics, Baltimore, Maryland

THE B. KENNETH SIMON CENTER FOR AMERICAN STUDIES

What makes America unique among nations is that it was founded on a common dedication to the principles of liberty, political equality, and self-government. This dedication must be renewed by each generation of citizens and statesmen.

"The preservation of the sacred fire of liberty, and the destiny of the republican model of government," George Washington observed in his First Inaugural Address, "are justly considered as deeply, perhaps as finally, staked on the experiment entrusted to the hands of the American people."

The B. Kenneth Simon Center for American Studies sponsors lectures, organizes seminars, crafts publications and supports scholars with the objective of teaching up-and-coming and current leaders — from student interns and young policymakers to members of Congress and other public officials — about the intellectual underpinnings of American liberty by focusing on the principles of the American Founding and the fundamentals of political and economic freedom.

The purpose of these activities is to promote the ideas and policies that will restore in the United States a limited constitutional government that is guided by the enduring principles of the American Founding.

PROCLAIM LIBERTY THROUGHOUT ALL THE LAND
UNTO ALL THE INHABITANTS THEREOF.

Leviticus 25:10 (Inscription on the Liberty Bell)

CONTENTS

THE PRIMARY DOCUMENTS

ADDITIONAL RESOURCES

Illustrations

All pictures courtesy of the Library of Congress, Washington, D.C.

Acknowledgments

I owe many thanks to The Heritage Foundation and its commitment to conserving the principles of the American Founding. To Adam Meyerson, who supported and encouraged this project from the beginning. To the staff of the Heritage Publishing Department, particularly Daryl Malloy, whose commitment and creativity helped bring the manuscript to life. And to a series of crack research interns — Todd Callais of Notre Dame University, Josh Hawley of Stanford University, Lindol French of the University of Oregon, Nicholas Buccola of Santa Clara University, Jacob Smith of Grove City College, James Swynford of William & Mary College, and Rachel Snodgrass of Bryan College — who did much of the fact-chasing and quote-finding that gives me confidence in the product. I am especially grateful to Kenneth Simon, the entrepreneur and patriot who established The Center for American Studies at Heritage to bolster these principles and renew their influence in our nation. Lastly, I must thank my wife Elizabeth, whose patience and advice was as invaluable at it was generous.

INTRODUCTION

———⟫•◆•⟪———

merica is unique in that its ends are defined by its beginnings. The remarkable generation that founded our great nation led an improbable yet successful revolution against the strongest military power of the time. They declared their independence based on self-evident truths, asserting a new basis of political rule in the sovereignty of the people and launching an experiment in self-government. Through a carefully written constitution that limits power and secures rights while allowing for change through its own amendment, they created an enduring framework of republican government that bestows upon their posterity the same blessings of liberty. Their creed, proclaimed in the Declaration of Independence and promulgated by the United States Constitution, is *our* creed. It instructs us, guides us, and inspires us, still.

Though the United States has become the richest and most powerful nation on the globe, America's primary importance to world history will depend less on the nation's achievements than on its first principles and original foundation.

This nation is still defined by what it embodies. Our highest politics, from Abraham Lincoln's new birth of freedom to Franklin Delano Roosevelt's New Deal to Ronald Reagan's New Beginning, have all been conversations about the meaning of American liberty. The national dialogue — whether on education or social security reform, taxes or national defense — is still best understood within and greatly enriched by the larger context of ordered liberty and constitutional freedom comprehended by the American Founding.

But what the American Founders did not do — could not do — was guarantee the success of their creation. When Benjamin Franklin departed the Constitutional Convention, he was asked if the framers had created a monarchy or a republic. "A republic," he famously replied, "*if you can keep it.*" In the end, Franklin and the other Founders knew that their experiment depended on future generations. Franklin's challenge remains our most important duty.

The self-evident truths and unalienable rights of the Declaration of Independence are increasingly challenged by moral relativism in our culture and by group entitlement in our politics. Throughout the past century the federal government has lost many of its moorings, and today acts with little regard for the principled limits provided in the Constitution. The remarkable ideas and astute warnings from the great statesmen of the American Founding suffer from public neglect, and are more often the subject of parody and farce than of esteem and veneration.

A recent study found that students at the top colleges and universities in America are able to graduate without having taken a single course in American history. That same study also found that while almost every student polled could identify the rap singer Snoop Doggy Dog and cartoon characters Beavis and Butthead, only a third could identify George Washington as the successful general at Yorktown, and less than one student in every four could identify James Madison as the Father of the Constitution.

Meanwhile, American high schools largely ignore or intentionally downplay the American Founding in the classroom because it is thought to be outdated or politically incorrect. The New Jersey Department of Education issued recently history standards that omit any mention of George Washington, Thomas Jefferson, or Benjamin Franklin; and the New Jersey legislature has repeatedly rejected a measure allowing public school students to recite the passage of the Declaration of Independence,

"We hold these truths to be self-evident . . .," because it was deemed insensitive to blacks and women.

This state of affairs demands the renewal of a civic literacy about the principles of the American Founding, particularly among citizens and statesmen intent on reviving those principles as guides for today's confused politics. This literacy is not only about appreciating the extraordinary institutions at the root of our political system — important as that is — but also about understanding the first principles of liberty, the intentions of American constitutionalism, and the sturdy virtues required for self-government. "If a nation expects to be ignorant and free in a state of civilization," Thomas Jefferson once warned, "it expects what never was and never will be."

The tragic events that occurred on September 11, 2001, have focused our national consciousness on those things that matter most — our families, our faiths, and our freedoms. Americans must relearn those things that during peace and prosperity had been forgotten, including the fact that the world can be a dangerous place, and that America is not exempt from its dangers. September 11 provides another lesson: that the patriotism of any one moment must become an informed and long-lasting commitment to America's principles and purposes at home and around the world.

President George W. Bush reminded us of this fact in his remarks at the memorial service for those killed by the terrorist attacks. "In every generation, the world has produced enemies of human freedom," he said. "*They* have attacked America because we are freedom's home and defender, and *the commitment of our fathers is now the calling of our time.*" [italics added]

As we look ahead, we should also look back — not to some mythical moment in America's past — but to the true roots of our national greatness. America needs to transform its resolve into a new era of responsibility in which we, as a nation and as a people, recover our purpose and our spirit. But to do this, we must revive and enliven in ourselves the moral truths and enduring principles of this great experiment in liberty and self-government.

The *Founders' Almanac* is a practical guide to the notable events, eloquent words, and greatest leaders of the American Founding. It is a handbook focusing on information that is especially valuable for our day, intended primarily for policymakers and political leaders but particularly useful for students and teachers as well as activists and citizens.

The book is designed to be used on a regular basis, whether read through, dipped into, or referenced, depending on the reader's circumstances or opportunity. The Calendar of Notable Events is a listing and brief explanation of important events, personages, speeches, and writings from the American Founding. The biographical essays introduce readers to six leading Founders: George Washington, Benjamin Franklin, John Adams, Thomas Jefferson, Alexander Hamilton, and James Madison. Each essay briefly reviews the Founder's life and discusses major themes of his statesmanship that are applicable today. The compilation of quotations, organized by topic and carefully compiled from primary and trustworthy secondary sources, should be especially useful to speakers, writers, and other wits in search of the best words from America's Founders.

The three primary documents — the Declaration of Independence, the United States Constitution, and Washington's Farewell Address — probably familiar to most readers, still invite a re-acquaintance. An introduction precedes each document, and is included to put the document's original meaning in context as well as explain its current relevance. Marginal notes throughout the documents will help guide the eye to pertinent topics, and an extensive index of the Constitution allows quick reference to its key sections and clauses. A brief essay on the signers of the Declaration of Independence is also included, as well as a commentary on how to understand — and answer questions about — the subject of slavery in the context of the American Founding.

Several other resources can be found at the back of the book. An extensive, annotated bibliography will guide additional reading on the subject, whether one is looking for a good biography of James Madison, a popular retelling of the Constitutional Convention, a history of the

Revolutionary War, or a study of the *Federalist Papers*. The bibliography also notes several good sources of information on the Web, focusing on collected documents now available to Internet users. Lastly, there is a list of some practical-minded scholars, experts on the American Founding, who are concerned about reviving its study and popular appreciation. All this information (and in time much, much more) can be found through The Heritage Foundation's Website (*www.heritage.org*) or directly at *www.foundersalmanac.org*, a dedicated source for information concerning the American Founding.

It is important to note that the *Founders' Almanac* is neither comprehensive nor definitive — given the rich history and extensive writings of the time, it is inevitable that some events, quotes, and individuals are not included. This book is both a general introduction and an invitation to learn more about America's origins. Its purpose is to conserve the principles so as to rekindle the spirit of the American Founding in the life of our nation. After all, as James Wilson reminds us, "Law and liberty cannot rationally become the objects of our *love* unless they first become the objects of our *knowledge*."

Matthew Spalding
February 28, 2002
Washington, D.C.

A CALENDAR of
IMPORTANT EVENTS
DURING the
AMERICAN FOUNDING,
WORTHY of NOTE
and SPECIAL
CONSIDERATION

January

2   **Georgia ratifies the Constitution** (1788) by unanimous decision, making it the fourth state to adopt the document. Ratification was advocated by Constitutional Convention delegates William Few (the son of a poor farmer who, after serving as a U.S. senator, becomes a leading philanthropist and banker) and Abraham Baldwin (a chaplain in the Continental army who later serves in the U.S. House of Representatives and the Senate before founding what becomes the University of Georgia).

7   The **first presidential election** (1789). Electors are chosen either by state legislatures or directly by the people. The electors meet on February 4 and select George Washington of Virginia to be the first president (69 votes) and John Adams of Massachusetts to be vice president (34 votes). Washington is the only president ever to be unanimously chosen by presidential electors.

8   George Washington delivers **the first State of the Union address** to Congress (1790). The first president's precedent of speaking to a joint session of the House and Senate in order to fulfill his constitutional duty to give Congress "Information of the State of the Union" is dropped by President Thomas Jefferson (who thought the practice monarchical) but revived by Woodrow Wilson in 1913 and is now a major annual presidential address.

9   **Connecticut ratifies the Constitution** (1788) by a vote of 128 to 40, making it the fifth state — and the first New England state — to adopt the document. Advocating its ratification are William Samuel Johnson (the self-educated lawyer who chaired the Committee on Style and later becomes a U.S. senator) and Roger Sherman (the cobbler who was on the committee that drafted the Declaration of Independence and a prime mover behind the Great Compromise at the Convention, and who will serve as a U.S. representative and a senator).

10 *Common Sense*, the first major American document calling for independence, is published (1776). The author, Thomas Paine, an Englishman, had lived in America for only two years before becoming one of its great patriots and writing this bestseller, which paves the way for the Declaration of Independence six months later. "Everything that is right or reasonable pleads for separation," he writes. "The blood of the slain, the weeping voice of nature cries, 'tis time to part." Samuel Adams will write that Paine's book "awakened the public mind."

11 **Alexander Hamilton** is born on the island of Nevis in the British West Indies (1755). The illegitimate child of a Scottish merchant, Hamilton becomes a military aide and advisor to Washington, and, at age 32, the first U.S. secretary of the treasury. He almost single-handedly transforms the new nation into a commercial republic. The great jurist John Marshall said that next to Hamilton he felt like a candle "beside the sun at noonday." (See biographical essay)

14 Secretary of the Treasury **Hamilton submits his Report on the Public Credit to Congress** (1790). It calls for paying back interest on the national debt and funding of the principal, and proposes that the national government assume the war debts of the individual states. Hamilton's plan, although debated at the time, succeeds in shaping the United States as a major commercial republic.

16 The Virginia House of Burgesses adopts the **Virginia Statute for Religious Freedom** (1786), one of the greatest documents of religious liberty in American history and a philosophical touchstone for the religion clauses of the First Amendment. James Madison introduced the legislation, as its author, Thomas Jefferson, was abroad as minister to France. It opens: "Whereas Almighty God hath created the mind free ... " Jefferson will regard it as one of his greatest accomplishments.

17 **Benjamin Franklin** is born in Boston (1706), the youngest son and 15th child of a soap-maker who had emigrated from England seeking religious liberty. The great social entrepreneur of the era, Franklin established one of the nation's first newspapers (*The Pennsylvanian Gazette*) and first great annuals (*Poor Richard's Almanack*), started a circulating library and a fire company, and founded the American Philosophical Society. He was an accomplished inventor, a significant national leader and the nation's first diplomat. (See biographical essay)

FEBRUARY

2 The **First Session of the Supreme Court** meets in New York City (1790) with John Jay, the secretary of foreign affairs under the Articles of Confederation and co-author of the *Federalist Papers*, as Chief Justice. James Wilson, one of the first American law professors and a crucial figure in the Constitutional Convention, is also on the Court. "The judiciary," Hamilton promises, "is beyond comparison the weakest of the three departments of power." During this and the next two sessions, the Court will hear no cases. It will give its first opinion in 1792.

6 The **Franco-American Alliance,** crucial to the financial and military success of the American Revolution, is established with the first treaty between the United States and a foreign country (1778). The alliance includes a Treaty of Amity and Commerce, which declares most-favored nation status for each country, and a Treaty of Alliance, which promises a military alliance if France and Britain went to war. Formed after four weeks of negotiations by Benjamin Franklin, Arthur Lee, and Silas Deane, the agreements will bring France into the American Revolution in four months on the side of independence.

6 **Massachusetts ratifies the Constitution** (1788) by a close vote of 187 to 168, making it the sixth state — and the first large state after Pennsylvania — to adopt the document. After heated debate several opponents, including Governor John Hancock and Sam Adams, are won over with the promise of amendments. Advocates of ratification include the Constitutional Convention delegates Nathaniel Gorham (who was president of the Continental Congress and a successful businessman before British troops destroyed his property) and Rufus King (the eloquent nationalist who later serves in the Senate for more than 30 years).

22 **George Washington** is born in Westmoreland County, Virginia (1732), eldest son of a well-to-do farmer. A surveyor by trade, Washington will command the Continental forces, chair the Constitutional Convention, and serve as the first president of the United States. Jefferson will write that "never did nature and fortune combine more perfectly to make a man great, and to place him in the same constellation with whatever worthies have merited from man an everlasting remembrance." Although usually referred to as "Presidents' Day," the third Monday in February is still, by law, officially designated "Washington's Birthday." (See biographical essay)

24 The Supreme Court decides the case of *Marbury v. Madison* (1803), which involves a contested appointment by the predecessor of Secretary of State James Madison, thereby establishing the power of judicial review. The Court holds that an act of Congress in conflict with the Constitution is void and that it is the function of the Court to determine whether such a conflict exists. The power of judicial review will not be used again to hold an act of Congress unconstitutional until the historic Dred Scott case of 1857.

MARCH

1 **Ratification of the Articles of Confederation** (1781), the first constitution of the United States until June 21, 1788, when a new (the present) Constitution went into effect. The national government created is so feeble and its powers are so limited, however, that the system proves to be unworkable. And because all thirteen colonies have to ratify amendments, one state's refusal prevented any reform. By the end of the war in 1783, it is widely recognized that the Articles had failed and that a new constitution was needed to assure liberty and the rule of law. (See Introduction to the United States Constitution, p. 233)

4 The **First Congress** under the new Constitution meets in New York (1789) without a quorum — only 8 senators and 13 representatives are present. The House of Representatives convene for the first time on April 1, selecting Frederick Muhlenberg of Pennsylvania (an ordained minister and delegate to the Constitutional Convention) as Speaker. The Senate convene for the first time on April 6, selecting John Langdon of New Hampshire (who had commanded a company at the Battle of Saratoga and was a delegate to the Constitutional Convention) as its temporary presiding officer. Fifty-four members of the new Congress had been delegates to the Federal Convention or the state ratifying conventions and all but seven advocated ratification.

4 **Thomas Jefferson,** who had become a critic of the Washington administration and a leader of the opposition Democratic-Republican Party, is inaugurated as the third president of the United States (1801). Not only is this the first inauguration in Washington, D.C., the newly established nation's capital, but it marks the first peaceful transition of constitutional power between opposing political parties. "A wise and frugal Government, which shall restrain men from injuring one another, shall leave them otherwise free to regulate their own pursuits of industry and improvement, and shall not take from the mouth of labor the bread it has earned," Jefferson notes in his Inaugural Address. "This is the sum of good government." (See biographical essay)

5 The **Boston Massacre** (1770), in which five colonists are killed when British soldiers guarding the State House fire into an angry crowd, is the first serious clash between American colonists and British soldiers. Not only is it an important rallying event for the revolutionary movement but it also demonstrates the American insistence on the rule of law: John Adams will defend the British soldiers in court; seven will be acquitted while the other two will be found guilty of manslaughter and later released. Adams will write that "this was as important a cause as ever was tried in any court or country of the world."

15 General Washington delivers his **Newburgh Address** (1783) in response to disgruntled officers (seeking back pay and pensions) calling for the army to assert itself against Congress. Upholding constitutional law and civilian rule, Washington denounces the use of force against lawful authority and promises redress for their grievances. At the end of the speech, as Washington fumbles for his glasses to read a message from Congress, he remarks: "Gentlemen, you will permit me to put on my spectacles, for I have not only grown gray, but almost blind, in the service of my country." The officers are brought to tears, and the conspiracy collapses. (See sidebar, p. 37)

16 **James Madison** is born in Port Conway, Virginia (1751), the oldest of ten children of an aristocratic family. The brilliant political thinker, who considered entering the ministry, dominated the Constitutional Convention and is known as the "Father of the Constitution," helped frame and ensure the passage of the Bill of Rights, and was the fourth president of the United States. John Marshall said that Madison — who co-authored the *Federalist Papers* — was "the most eloquent man I ever heard." (See biographical essay)

22 The **Stamp Act** is passed by the British Parliament as a means of raising revenue in the American colonies (1765). It requires all legal documents, licenses, commercial contracts, newspapers, pamphlets, and playing cards to carry a tax stamp. The unity of the American colonists in their opposition to the Stamp Act contributes substantially to the rise of nationalist sentiment, and the conflict between the colonists and the British government over the Stamp Act is often considered one of the chief immediate causes of the American Revolution.

23 **Patrick Henry,** one of the most eloquent voices of the independence movement, delivers one of his greatest speeches before the Virginia Convention (1775), arguing in favor of strengthening his state's military preparedness and predicting the outbreak of hostilities in New England. It reportedly ends with these lines: "Is life so dear or peace so sweet as to be purchased at the price of chains and slavery? Forbid it, Almighty God. I know not what course others may take, but as for me, give me liberty or give me death!" Thomas Jefferson describes Henry's speeches as "torrents of sublime eloquence."

28 The **Mount Vernon Conference** convenes at the home of George Washington to consider questions relating to the navigation of the Potomac River and Chesapeake Bay (1785). Commissioners from Virginia and Maryland recommend uniform commercial regulations, a uniform currency, and an annual meeting on commercial problems. The conference is the stimulus for Virginia to organize the Annapolis Conference, which in turn calls for a convention in Philadelphia, thus making it a significant step toward the establishment of the U.S. Constitution.

29 **Congress offers emancipation** to slaves serving in the Continental army from the states of South Carolina and Georgia (1779). The legislation would pay owners for the enlisted slaves, and provides that those "who shall well and faithfully serve as a soldier to the end of the present war, and then shall return his arms, be emancipated." Thus the continental government not only recruited slaves but also financed their freedom. (See Note on Slavery, p. 281)

APRIL

9 In the **first presidential veto,** President Washington strikes down legislation apportioning congressional seats after the first census because he believes it violates Article I, Section 2 of the Constitution (1792). Congress fails to override the veto. Washington's only other veto will be for reasons of policy. John Adams and Thomas Jefferson will not issue any vetoes. It is not until Andrew Jackson (who issues 12 vetoes) and later Andrew Johnson (who issues 29) that the power is used primarily as a policy tool.

12 In the **Halifax Resolves** (1776), North Carolina's Provincial Congress unanimously authorizes its delegates to the Second Continental Congress to vote for separating from Great Britain. The first formal call for independence by a colony not only guides North Carolina representatives but also encourages the Continental Congress to champion the move. A month later, Virginia directs its delegates to submit a resolution for independence.

13 **Thomas Jefferson** is born in Albermarle County, Virginia (1743), the son of a planter and surveyor. Although he will become the first secretary of state and the third president of the United States, Jefferson, one of the most eloquent and influential writers of the American Revolution, wishes to be remembered as the author of the Declaration of Independence and the Virginia Statute for Religious Freedom, and as the founder of the University of Virginia. James Madison called Jefferson "one of the most learned men of the age." (See biographical essay)

18 **Paul Revere** rides from Boston to Concord (1775) to alert the countryside of approaching British soldiers. With tensions rising and the Revolutionary War imminent, British forces have set out to take colonial military supplies at Concord, Massachusetts. Although a British patrol captures him en route, Revere is freed in time to alert John Hancock and Sam Adams and save the secret papers of the Revolution. Although there were other riders, Revere's deed is immortalized by Henry Wadsworth Longfellow's 1861 poem "Paul Revere's Ride."

19 **The Battle of Lexington** (1775), a brief skirmish between some 70 colonial minutemen and about 700 British soldiers marching on Concord, Massachusetts, is the first military clash of the American Revolution. Captain John Parker tells the colonials: "Stand your ground; don't fire unless fired upon, but if they mean to have a war, let it begin here." The Battle of Concord, in which the colonials stopped the British advance and forced their retreat back to Boston, followed later that morning. News of the battles — and what the poet Ralph Waldo Emerson called "the shot heard round the world" — spread quickly throughout the colonies. John Adams later writes that this was the moment that "the Die was cast, the Rubicon crossed."

22 President Washington issues his **Neutrality Proclamation** (which does not include the word "neutrality"), declaring that the United States is at peace with France and Great Britain (1793). The French Revolution, which began in 1789, has developed into a general military conflict throughout Europe. The Hamiltonians generally support Britain while the Jeffersonians side with America's earlier ally, France.

Washington realizes that the United States is still too weak to risk war if it can honorably be avoided, and steers an independent course. "The public welfare and safety," he says, "enjoin a conduct of circumspection, moderation and forebearance."

28 **Maryland ratifies the Constitution** (1788) by a vote of 63 to 11, making it the seventh state to adopt the document. Ratification is advocated by Constitutional Convention delegates James McHenry (an Irish immigrant who was an aide to Washington and the second secretary of war), Daniel of St. Thomas Jenifer (a wealthy bachelor who died soon after the convention), and Daniel Carroll (one of two Roman Catholic signers of the Constitution, who later served in the House of Representatives).

30 The **inauguration of George Washington and John Adams** as the first president and vice president of the United States (1789). As there are no justices of the Supreme Court, the oath of office is administered by Robert Livingstone, chancellor of the State of New York. After the swearing-in ceremony, at Federal Hall on Wall Street in New York, Washington delivers the first inaugural address. "The preservation of the sacred fire of liberty and the destiny of the republican model of government," Washington says, "are justly considered, perhaps, as deeply, as finally, staked on the experiment intrusted to the hands of the American people." Before adjourning the ceremony, Congress proceeds to St. Paul's Chapel for divine services by the Chaplain of the Congress.

MAY

5 The United States Senate passes **the first piece of legislation,** an act to establish and administer an oath of office to support the Constitution (1789). The House of Representatives passes the legislation in June. The Constitution contains an oath of office for the president, but calls for members of Congress and the state legislatures, as well as all executive and judicial officers at the federal and state level, to be bound by oath to support the Constitution. The First Congress passed a simple oath to this effect, while the more extensive oath used today was written to underscore constitutional fidelity during the U.S. Civil War.

10 The **Second Continental Congress** meets in Philadelphia (1775), including new members Benjamin Franklin, James Wilson, John Hancock (who becomes its president), and Thomas Jefferson. The Congress immediately decides to put the colonies in a state of defense, and one year later declares independence. When Washington attends, just after fighting breaks out at Lexington and Concord, he appears in the blue and buff uniform of the Fairfax County militia, the same colors later adopted for the Continental army.

12 The **fall of Charleston, South Carolina** (1780), and the loss of a 5,400 man garrison and several ships, is the heaviest American defeat of the war. British forces under the command of General Henry Clinton force the surrender of General Benjamin Lincoln. Exchanged after the battle, Lincoln later joins Washington's army in time to participate in Cornwallis' defeat at Yorktown; as Washington's second in command, he accepts the British surrender. (See October 19)

22 **George Washington refuses to be king** (1782). One of his officers, Colonel Lewis Nicola, suggests the possibility of making Washington king and establishing an American monarchy, but Washington sternly rebukes him and rejects the idea. Washington writes that there was no "person to whom your schemes are more disagreeable" and that the colonel should "banish these thoughts from your mind, and never communicate, as from yourself or anyone else, a sentiment of the like nature." Nicola is so stung by the rebuke that he writes three letters of apology.

23 **South Carolina ratifies the Constitution** (1788) by a vote of 149 to 73, making it the eighth state to adopt the document. Ratification was advocated by Constitutional Convention delegates John Rutledge (whose property was confiscated by the British during the war; he will later serve on the Supreme Court), Charles Cotesworth Pinckney (an officer during and a diplomat after the Revolution who also becomes a vice-presidential and twice a presidential candidate), Charles Pinckney (a militia officer who becomes governor, representative, and senator of his state, as well as minister to Spain) and Pierce Butler (the Irish immigrant and British officer turned colonial patriot). "The plot thickens fast," Washington writes at this time. "A few short weeks will determine the political fate of America."

25 The **Constitutional Convention** meets in Philadelphia (1787) to create a new constitution for governing the new nation. Not only participating are leaders in the fight for independence, such as Roger Sherman and John Dickinson, and leading thinkers just coming into prominence, such as James Madison, Alexander Hamilton, and Gouverneur Morris, but also legendary figures, such as Benjamin Franklin and George Washington. Jefferson describes it as "an assembly of demigods." John Adams later declares the three-and-a-half month convention "the greatest single effort of national deliberation that the world has ever seen." (See Introduction to the United States Constitution, p. 233)

29 **Rhode Island ratifies the Constitution** (1790), making it the 13th state — and the last of the original colonies — to adopt the document. The only state not to send delegates to the Constitutional Convention, Rhode Island held a popular referendum to decide the matter in 1788, and, the Federalists refusing to participate, initially rejected the Constitution. Rhode Island finally approves the new Constitution two-and-a-half years after the first state ratified.

29 A set of fifteen resolutions known as **the Virginia Plan** is presented at the Constitutional Convention by that state's governor, Edmund Randolph (1787). Largely the work of James Madison, the Virginia Plan abandons the Articles of Confederation and proposes the creation of a supreme national government with separate legislative, executive and judicial branches. The delegates generally agree on the powers that should be lodged in a national legislature, but disagree on how the states and popular opinion should be reflected in it. This plan is often referred to as the large state plan as population would determine representation in both houses of Congress. (See Introduction to the United States Constitution, p. 233)

JUNE

7 Richard Henry Lee calls for independence in the Continental Congress (1776). Lee's resolution, seconded by John Adams, states that "these United Colonies are, and of right ought to be, free and independent states, that they are absolved from all allegiance to the British Crown, and that all political connection between them and the state of Great Britain is, and ought to be, totally dissolved." It also calls for forming foreign alliances and for preparing a plan of confederation. John Adams notes: "Objects of the most stupendous magnitude, and measures in which the lives and liberties of millions yet unborn are intimately interested are now before us."

8 In his final and longest **Circular Address** to the state governors (1783), General Washington announces his military retirement and recommends the policies he considers most conducive to the nation: a permanent union, a proper military establishment, public justice, and the encouragement of the proper dispositions among the citizenry. This was the "moment" that would "establish or ruin the national Character forever," he argues. "It is yet to be decided, whether the Revolution must ultimately be considered as a blessing or a curse: a blessing or a curse, not to the present age alone, for with our fate will the destiny on unborn millions be involved."

12 Congress declares a national day of "public humiliation, fasting and prayer" to occur five weeks later on July 20 (1775). The resolution was communicated to state authorities and then to the churches, a process used for the numerous prayer and thanksgiving days proclaimed by Congress during the Revolutionary War. "Millions will be on their knees at once before their great Creator," John Adams writes, "imploring his smiles on American councils and arms."

12 British General Thomas Gage proclaims marshal law (1775) and offers pardons to any and all rebels who lay down their arms — any and all rebels, that is, except revolutionary leaders Samuel Adams and John Hancock. Rather than surrendering, however, patriots near Boston (where Gage is headquartered) move to occupy Bunker Hill and build fortifications in preparation for British attack (see June 17).

14 The **U. S. Flag,** made up of 13 alternating red and white stripes and 13 white stars in a field of blue, is adopted by the Continental Congress (1777). In the language of the Continental Congress, "White signifies Purity and Innocence; Red, Hardiness and Valor; and Blue, Vigilance, Perseverance and Justice." Tradition has it that George Washington had Philadelphia seamstress Betsy Ross design and make the first flag. The date was designated Flag Day by President Woodrow Wilson in 1916.

15 The Continental Congress appoints **George Washington the general and commander in chief** of the Continental forces by a unanimous vote after a motion by Thomas Johnson of Maryland that is seconded by John Adams of Massachusetts (1775). Two months earlier, fighting broke out in Massachusetts. Washington proceeded to Cambridge and took command of 16,000 men on July 3. In his first orders, he hopes "that all distinctions of colonies will be laid aside so that one and the same spirit may animate the whole."

15 A series of resolutions known as **the New Jersey Plan** is presented at the Constitutional Convention (1787) as an alternative to the Virginia Plan (see May 29). To protect the principle of state equality, William Paterson's plan (often called the small state plan) preserves each state's equal vote in a one-house Congress with slightly augmented powers. (See Introduction to the United States Constitution, p. 233)

17 The **Battle of Bunker Hill** (1775), in which the British attack American fortifications on the Charlestown peninsula, is the first deliberate military engagement of the American Revolution. Following Lexington and Concord, the British army in the colonies are confronted in Boston by an unorganized and inexperienced militia that had assembled from the surrounding towns. The British win this battle, but only after suffering twice as many casualties in numerous assaults and after attacking at bayonet point when the American militia ran out of ammunition but refused to surrender.

20 **Thomas Jefferson hosts a dinner for Hamilton and Madison** (1790). Southern congressmen, led by Madison, who oppose the assumption of state debts by the federal government, are blocking Treasury

Secretary Hamilton's fiscal program in the House of Representatives. In one of the greatest political compromises in American history, Madison agrees to allow Hamilton's program to pass and Hamilton agrees to use his influence to have the permanent seat of government located in the South, on the Potomac River. The new national capital is named Washington in honor of the first president.

20 Congress adopts the **Great Seal of the United States** (1782), the official emblem of the nation. Used to mark official documents, it is found on the back of the dollar bill. Consider its political and theological emblems: on the front is an eagle, holding an olive branch in one talon and thirteen arrows in the other, and a scroll in its beak inscribed with the motto E pluribus unum — "from many, one." The reverse is an unfinished pyramid, the top of which is an eye surrounded by rays of light below the words annuit coeptis — "He approves of what has been started." At the base of the pyramid is the date 1776 and the motto novos ordo seclorum — "a new order of the ages."

21 New Hampshire ratifies the Constitution (1788) by a vote of 57 to 47, making it the ninth state to adopt the document. Nine states are required to establish the Constitution, so the new government can now be put in operation. Ratification was advocated by Convention delegates John Langdon (a businessman who financed 1,500 militia and paid for New Hampshire's delegation to attend the Convention, and later serves in the Senate) and Nicholas Gilman (an officer during the Revolution who later serves in the House and the Senate).

26 Virginia ratifies the Constitution (1788) by a vote of 89 to 79, making it the 10th state to adopt the document. Opinion was closely divided: James Madison, along with George Washington and John Marshall, led the supporters of the Constitution; Patrick Henry, who had refused to attend the Constitutional Convention because he "smelt a rat," and George Mason, who attended but refused to sign the final document, led the opposition. The Federalists won the day after they agreed to support amendments in the First Congress.

JULY

2   Acting in formal session, **Congress votes for independence** (1776) by a vote of 12 to zero (New York will add its favorable vote on July 9). "I am well aware of the Toil and Blood and Treasure, that it will cost us to maintain this Declaration, and support and defend these States," John Adams writes to Abigail the next day. "Yet through all the Gloom I can see the Rays of ravishing Light and Glory."

4   The **Declaration of Independence,** written by Thomas Jefferson pursuant to Richard Henry Lee's resolution, is approved and signed by John Hancock and Charles Thompson (the president and secretary of Congress) and sent to the state assemblies (1776). "There! His Majesty can now read my name without glasses," Hancock declares when he signs the document. "And he can double the reward on my head!" Not proclaimed publicly until July 8 in Philadelphia, Washington will read it aloud to his assembled soldiers on July 9. Madison later calls the Declaration of Independence "the fundamental Act of Union of these States." (See Introduction to the Declaration of Independence, p. 215)

6   The Continental Congress adopts the **Declaration of the Causes and Necessities of Taking Up Arms** (1775). Written by Thomas Jefferson, the proclamation is a formal justification of colonial military resistance and a masterful summary of the American case against Great Britain. "With hearts fortified with these animating reflections, we most solemnly, before God and the world, declare that . . . the arms we have been compelled by our enemies to assume, we will, in defiance of every hazard, with unabating perseverance, employ for the preservation of our liberties; being with our one mind resolved to dye Free-men rather than live Slaves."

9   In his Last Will & Testament, **George Washington frees his slaves** (1799). Washington earlier wrote of slavery that "there is not a man living who wishes more sincerely than I do, to see a plan adopted for the abolition of it." He had devised a plan to rent his lands and turn his slaves into paid laborers, and at the end of his presidency he quietly left several of his own household slaves to their freedom. In his will, after caring for his beloved wife Martha, his first item is that his slaves would become free upon her death. The old and infirm were to be cared for while they lived, and the children were to be taught to read and write and trained in a useful skill until they were twenty-five. Washington's estate paid for this care until 1833. (See Note on Slavery, pg. 281)

13 The Confederation Congress adopts the **Northwest Ordinance** (1787), the historic legislation that provides for the administration of land in the Northwest Territories and, in general, the peaceful admission of new states into the American nation. Territories will become states, not colonies, on an equal footing with the original thirteen. It forbids slavery in the territories and provides a bill of rights for the inhabitants of the territories, including the famous provision: "Religion, morality and knowledge, being necessary to the good government and the happiness of mankind, schools and the means of education shall forever be encouraged." Re-affirmed two years later under the new Constitution, it (along with the Declaration of Independence) is an organic law of the United States.

16 The **Constitutional Convention adopts the Great Compromise** (1787) between the Virginia Plan (see May 29) and the New Jersey Plan (see June 15), under which the House of Representatives would be apportioned based on population and each state would have two votes in the Senate. As a precaution against having to assume the financial burdens of the smaller states, the larger states exacted an agreement that revenue bills could originate only in the House, where the more populous states would have greater representation. (See Introduction to the United States Constitution, p. 233)

20 The **first national day of public humiliation, fasting and prayer,** as proclaimed by Congress on June 12 (1775). Congress attended religious services at an Anglican church in the morning, and a Presbyterian church in the afternoon so as not to show any religious favoritism. On later occasions, for the same reasons, Congress also attended Roman Catholic and Dutch Lutheran churches.

26 **New York ratifies the Constitution** (1788) by a close vote of 30 to 27, making it the 11th state to adopt the document. Governor George Clinton led those opposed to ratification. New Yorkers Alexander Hamilton and John Jay are strong supporters of the Constitution and (along with James Madison) wrote the *Federalist Papers* to support the new government. With the ratification of large states, Virginia and New York, the only holdouts are Rhode Island and North Carolina.

27 The first executive department, **Department of Foreign Affairs,** which is soon renamed the Department of State, is created under the new government (1789). The first secretary of state, Thomas Jefferson, will not take office for another six months, until he has completed his tour as minister to France, so John Jay handles foreign affairs while also serving as the first chief justice of the United States.

AUGUST

2 The **Declaration of Independence is formally signed** by fifty members of the Continental Congress (1776). The document was officially signed by John Hancock and Charles Thompson (the president and secretary of Congress) on July 4, but most signed their names later. George Wythe signed August 27. Richard Henry Lee, Elbridge Gerry and Oliver Wolcott signed September 4, Matthew Thorton on November 19 and Thomas McKean (who had been with Washington's army) did not sign until 1781.

7 President Washington issues a proclamation concerning the **Whiskey Rebellion** (1794). It is the first serious test of the new government's prerogatives and law enforcement power. Organized resistance to an excise tax on whiskey by grain farmers in western Pennsylvania led to riots and the death of a federal officer. Washington, concerned about the rule of law and social order in the new Republic, calls forth the militia for the "suppression of so fatal a spirit" and "to cause the laws to be duly executed."

7 The original **Purple Heart** (1782), called the Badge of Military Merit, is instituted by George Washington to reward troops for "unusual gallantry" and "extraordinary fidelity and essential service." The award is a purple cloth heart edged in silver braid, and the honoree's name is inscribed in a Book of Merit. "The road to glory in a patriot army and a free country," Washington writes in his orderly book on this day, "is thus open to all." The honor will be revived by General Douglas MacArthur for the bicentennial of Washington's birth in 1932.

18 In his **letter to the Hebrew Congregation** at Newport, Rhode Island (1790), President George Washington, on behalf of the new nation, guarantees to one of the most persecuted peoples of the world an equal claim to the exercise of their inherent natural rights. The United States, Washington writes, "gives to bigotry no sanction, to persecution no assistance." Part of a series of letters to various religious congregations after his inauguration as the first president, the letter is one of the most eloquent and powerful statements of religious liberty in American history.

23 King George III, in a **Royal Proclamation of Rebellion** (1775), declares the American colonies — "misled by dangerous and ill designing men" — to be in a state of rebellion and instructs his officers "to exert their utmost Endeavors to suppress such Rebellion, and to bring the Traitors to Justice." Issued in light of the costly British victory at Bunker Hill, the proclamation effectively stifles moderate voices, and makes the rejection of peaceful reconciliation and the outbreak of armed conflict inevitable.

31 Known as **Shays' Rebellion** (1786), a mob of debt-ridden farmers in Massachusetts led by Daniel Shays rise up to prevent the sitting of courts of law that might foreclose on their properties; the farmers also threaten the Continental arsenal at Springfield. While the insurrection quickly collapses, it highlights the fears of skeptics and many political leaders that popular government is not possible. "Influence is no Government," Washington would later write. "Let us have one by which our lives, liberties and properties will be secured; or let us know the worst at once. Under these impressions, my humble opinion is, that there is a call for decision."

[?] In *A Summary View of the Rights of British America* (1774), a set of proposed instructions to the Virginia delegates to the First Continental Congress, Thomas Jefferson argues that Parliament has "no right to exercise authority" over the colonies and that their actions prove "a deliberate and systematical plan of reducing us to slavery." He argues further that kings were "the servants, not the proprietors of the people" and implies that the colonists might be driven to a separation. Considered too radical at the time, the prophetic document, nevertheless, brings Jefferson's pen notice and will eventually epitomize American thinking.

SEPTEMBER

3   The **Treaty of Paris** (1783), formally ending the American Revolution almost three years after the Battle of Yorktown, is signed in Paris. In it "His Britannic Majesty acknowledges the said United States . . . to be free, sovereign and independent states." "The times that tried men's souls are over," Thomas Paine proclaims, " — and the greatest and completest revolution the world ever knew, gloriously and happily accomplished."

5   The **First Continental Congress** convenes in Carpenters Hall, in Philadelphia (1774), with all of the colonies represented except Georgia. Members include Sam Adams, Patrick Henry, and Richard Henry Lee. The purpose of the meeting, which lasts until October 27, is to consider and act on the situation arising from the so-called Intolerable Acts, passed by the British Parliament in retaliation to the Boston Tea Party.

7   The **First Continental Congress gathers in prayer** as its first order of business (1774), led by the Reverend Jacob Duche, an Anglican priest of Philadelphia. John Adams recorded that Duche read several prayers, including the Thirty-fifth Psalm and an extemporaneous prayer. "I must confess that I have never heard a better prayer or one so well pronounced . . . with such fervor, such ardor, such earnestness and pathos, and in language so eloquent and sublime — for America, for the Congress, for the Province of Massachusetts Bay, and especially for the Town of Boston. It has had an excellent effect upon every body here."

10 The **first English-language Bible** published on the North American continent (1782) is approved by congressional resolution and recommended "to the inhabitants of the United States." Congress has been concerned about a shortage of Bibles during hostilities with Great Britain and, based on the recommendation of its chaplains, endorses an edition prepared by Philadelphia printer Robert Aitken.

14 The **Annapolis Convention** meets to discuss interstate commercial relations (1786) and calls for a new convention in May 1787 at Philadelphia to discuss all matters necessary "to render the constitution of the Federal Government adequate to the exigencies of the Union." Alexander Hamilton and James Madison both attend, playing key roles in this important step toward the creation of a new constitution.

17 The new **United States Constitution** is signed and sent to Congress (1787), which will send it to the states for ratification. The Committee on Style, under the direction of Gouverneur Morris, created the final draft of the document in two days at the end of the Constitutional Convention. Thirty-nine of the delegates (along with Convention Secretary William Jackson) sign the document, thus closing the convention. This date is now commemorated as "Constitution Day." (See Introduction to the United States Constitution, p. 233)

19 George Washington's **Farewell Address** (1796) is printed in the *Daily American Advertiser* of Philadelphia. Written with the help of James Madison and Alexander Hamilton, the document explains why Washington will not seek a third term, asserts the importance of religion and morality, and warns of partisan spirit and the dangers of foreign influence and permanent alliances. John Quincy Adams hoped that it would "serve as the foundation upon which the whole system of [America's] future policy may rise, the admiration and example of future time." (See Introduction to Washington's Farewell Address, p. 293)

22 **Lieutenant Nathan Hale,** a schoolteacher from Connecticut on an intelligence mission for General Washington, is executed by the British for espionage (1776). One of six brothers who served in the Continental army, Hale volunteered for the job behind enemy lines. A

British officer later delivers an account of Hale's heroic last words from the gallows: "I only regret that I have but one life to lose for my country."

23 **John Paul Jones,** commanding an old French merchant ship refitted and renamed the *Bonhomme Richard* (after Benjamin Franklin's Poor Richard), engages a British warship in the North Sea (1779). During the naval battle, 300 of 375 Americans are killed or wounded. Jones's ship sustains such heavy damage that it sinks the next day, but he forces the surrender of the British ship, which he will use to raid British home waters. During the battle, when the British ask if the Americans would surrender, Jones defiantly replies: "I have not yet begun to fight."

24 Congress, by the **Judiciary Act** (1789), in accordance with Article III, Section I of the Constitution — which states that "The judicial power of the United States shall be vested in one Supreme Court, and in such inferior courts as the Congress may from time to time ordain and establish" — organizes the federal judiciary. Congress approved a Supreme Court with a chief justice and five associates, and created 13 district courts, three circuit courts, and the Office of the Attorney General.

29 The **first appropriation bill,** passed by Congress to fund the budget for 1789, is signed by President Washington (1789). The legislation — which is the shortest of its kind in American history — takes up 13 lines in the Statutes at Large and uses only four categories: $216,000 for the civil list, $137,000 for the War Department, $190,000 to discharge warrants issued by the previous Board of Treasury, and $196,000 for pensions to disabled veterans. Senator William Maclay of Pennsylvania nevertheless objected vehemently that the appropriations "were all in gross, to the amount of upwards of half a million."

OCTOBER

17 **British General John Burgoyne surrenders** his army of almost 7,000 men following the American victory at the Battle of Saratoga (1777). Outmaneuvered and outnumbered by colonial forces under the command of General Benedict Arnold, the loss destroys British plans to cut off New England from the other colonies. The defeat was critical in convincing the French that the fighting was more than an uprising — and that the Americans could eventually win the war.

19 Following the Battle of Yorktown, **Lord Cornwallis surrenders** his army to General Washington (1781), effectively ending the American Revolution. Allied forces under the command of Washington successfully besieged the British across the narrow peninsula in southeastern Virginia, while the French navy attacked by sea. (Lieutenant Colonel Alexander Hamilton led the war's last infantry assault on October 14, which successfully captured two British redoubts.) Since Cornwallis, pleading illness, sends a subordinate to give up his sword, Washington sends General Benjamin Lincoln (see May 12) to accept the surrender. A British military band plays "The World Turned Upside Down."

20 The **First Continental Congress** abolishes the slave trade as part of the Articles of Association (1774). The several colonies agree that they will "neither be concerned in it ourselves, nor will we hire our vessels, nor sell our commodities or manufactures to those who are concerned in it." The ban is reaffirmed by the Second Continental Congress in April 1776. Thus the first national governmental body acts to disfavor slavery by blocking its expansion.

27 The first of the *Federalist Papers* appears in New York City newspapers under the pseudonym Publius (1787). Alexander Hamilton, in an effort to win support for the new Constitution in his home state, writes many of what becomes a series of 85 essays (including contributions by James Madison and John Jay) focusing on the inadequacies of the Articles of Confederation, the need for an energetic national government, and the conformity of the Constitution with the principles of republicanism. Jefferson would proclaim the work to be "the best commentary on the principles of government which ever was written." (See sidebar, p. 99)

NOVEMBER

2 In his **final orders to the Continental army** (1783), George Washington wishes "an affectionate, a long farewell" to the rag-tag army that had become what he called a "patriotic band of Brothers." The general hopes that "they should carry with them into civil society the most conciliating dispositions; and that they should prove themselves not less virtuous and useful as Citizens, than they have been persevering and victorious as Soldiers." Washington resigns his military commission a month later.

19 **The Jay Treaty** between the United States and Great Britain is signed in London (1794). In 1794, when war with Britain threatened due to controversies over the Treaty of Paris (see September 3), President Washington appointed Chief Justice John Jay to negotiate a settlement. The Jay Treaty brings about the withdrawal of the British from the northwest posts — putting an end to the foreign occupation of American territory north of the Ohio River — and places British trade with the United States on a most favored nation status. Although controversial, causing the first clear party divisions in Congress, Washington supports the treaty because it will prevent war at a point when the nation is weak and buys time for the growth of American strength and prosperity.

21 Ten months after the first presidential elections, **North Carolina ratifies the Constitution** (1789), making it the 12th state to adopt the document. The decision was delayed until proposed amendments had been submitted to the states for their approval. Ratification was advocated by Constitutional Convention delegates William Blount (who has the dubious distinction of being the first member ever expelled from the Senate), Richard Dobbs Spaight (one of the youngest signers, who later becomes governor and also serves in the House of Representatives), and Hugh Williamson (a preacher, a surgeon in the Revolutionary War, and a member of the House of Representatives).

25 Although not called for in the Constitution, the **first presidential cabinet** meets for the first time to discuss foreign and military matters

(1792). When Congress authorized the creation of the first executive departments, Washington appointed Alexander Hamilton to head the Treasury Department, a move urged by James Madison. He reappointed Henry Knox as secretary of war, the job he held during the Confederation. John Jay was Washington's first choice to head the State Department, but Jay preferred to be chief justice of the United States so Washington turned to the next highest official in the foreign service, Thomas Jefferson. Washington completed his "cabinet" by appointing Samuel Osgood to be postmaster general, and Edmund Randolph as the first attorney general.

26 The first **National Day of Thanksgiving,** as legislated by Congress and proclaimed by President Washington (1789). "Whereas it is the duty of all nations to acknowledge the providence of Almighty God, to obey his will, to be grateful for his benefits and humbly to implore his protection and favor," Washington calls on all Americans to devote themselves "to the service of that great and glorious Being, who is the beneficent Author of all the good that was, that is or that will be."

DECEMBER

7 **Delaware ratifies the Constitution** (1787), by a unanimous vote, making it the first state to adopt the document. Ratification was promoted by Delaware signers Richard Bassett (who will serve as a senator and then governor of his state), George Read (who signed both the Declaration of Independence and the Constitution), Gunning Bedford Jr. (James Madison's college roommate who served in the Continental army and was a federal district judge) and John Dickinson (who voted against the Declaration of Independence as a delegate from Pennsylvania but strongly advocated the new Constitution).

7 **John Adams is elected** as the second president of the United States (1796). Adams had been Washington's vice president for eight years. According to the Constitution at that time, the candidate receiving the most votes (in this case Adams, a Federalist) becomes president and the runner-up (Thomas Jefferson, a Democratic-Republican) becomes vice president. This procedure is changed in 1804, when the 12th Amendment is ratified.

12 **Pennsylvania ratifies the Constitution** (1787) by a vote of 46 to 23 after a bitter debate, making it the second state to adopt the document. The convention was barely able to maintain a quorum, and did so only after two anti-Federalists were carried in and forced to sit in their seats and the doors barred behind them. The case for ratification was made by Thomas Fitzsimons (one of two Roman Catholic signers, who also led a company of militia in the Revolutionary War and later serves in the House of Representatives), Benjamin Franklin (the oldest and, next to Washington, the most famous signer), Thomas Mifflin (who served as a brigadier general under Washington), Gouverneur Morris (who actually drafted the Constitution), and James Wilson (one of Washington's first appointments to the Supreme Court).

14 **George Washington dies** at Mount Vernon (1799). John Marshall writes the words of the official eulogy, which is delivered in Congress by Representative "Lighthorse Harry" Lee: "First in war, first in peace, and first in the hearts of his countrymen, he was second to none in humble and enduring scenes of private life. Pious, just, humane, temperate, and sincere; uniform, dignified, and commanding; his example was as edifying to all around him as were the effects of that example lasting." (See biographical essay)

15 The **Bill of Rights,** as the first 10 amendments to the Constitution are now called, becomes effective after the ratification of three-fourths of the states (1791). In October, President Washington had submitted 12 possible amendments for consideration, but the first two — concerning the number of constituents for each representative and compensation for members of Congress — were rejected. The latter amendment was finally ratified in 1992 as the 27th Amendment. (See sidebar, p. 114)

16 In the **Boston Tea Party** (1773), a group of citizens, many disguised as Indians, swarm over British ships and dump 342 chests of tea into Boston Harbor. Led by Samuel Adams, the American colonists had refused to buy the English tea to protest the violation of their consti-

tutional right not to be taxed without representation. John Adams later writes that the "destruction of the tea is so bold, so daring, so firm, intrepid and inflexible, and it must have important consequences." In debating how to punish the Americans, Edmund Burke warned Parliament that "a great black book and a great many red coats will never be able to govern it."

17 **France formally recognizes the independence of the United States** (1777). The French had been secretly supporting the American war effort since May 1776, but when victory at the Battle of Saratoga proved the Americans' staying power, the French decided to officially recognize and open treaty negotiations with the new nation.

18 **New Jersey ratifies the Constitution** (1787) by a unanimous vote, making it the third state to adopt the document. Ratification was encouraged by signers David Brearly, (a colonel in the New Jersey militia who later serves as a federal district judge), William Paterson, (who introduced the New Jersey plan for equal state representation at the Convention and later serves in the Senate, the governor of New Jersey, and a justice of the U.S. Supreme Court), Jonathan Dayton (at 26, the youngest of the signers, he later serves in both the House and the Senate), and William Livingston (brigadier general in the New Jersey militia and the first governor of his state).

19 **The Continental army arrives at Valley Forge** — a place ever to be synonymous with hardship — for winter quarters (1777). As they cannot seek comfort in the cities and leave the countryside to be ravaged by the British, they build crude huts on the snowy hillsides near Philadelphia. Supplies are virtually nonexistent, food is scarce and typhus is common. Twenty-five hundred soldiers will die; some two thousand will desert. "These are the times that try men's souls," Thomas Paine wrote. "The summer soldier and the sunshine patriot will, in this crisis, shrink from the service of his country; but he that stands it now, deserves the love and thanks of man and woman."

23 Having won the American Revolution, **General Washington resigns** as commander in chief of the army (1783) — a move unknown in the annals of history. Washington addresses Congress at Annapolis, Maryland: "Having now finished the work assigned me, I retire from the great theatre of action; and bidding an affectionate farewell to the august body under whose orders I have so long acted, I here offer my commission, and take my leave of all employments of public life." This scene is depicted in one of the great paintings in the U.S. Capitol Rotunda. Upon hearing of this, King George III remarked that Washington would be "the greatest man in the world."

26 In a daring move, **Washington crosses the Delaware River** and attacks the British encampment at Trenton, New Jersey (1776). The American cause was at a low ebb, the Continental army having suffered numerous defeats, retreated all the way from New York, until Washington decided to regain the initiative by recrossing the Delaware River on Christmas night and capturing 1,000 Hessians in the Battle of Trenton. One week later Washington defeats the British at Princeton, forcing the British to withdraw, thus preventing their advance on Philadelphia.

᪥

INTRODUCTORY
ESSAYS on LEADING
STATESMEN of the
AMERICAN
FOUNDING
TO CONSIDER WHAT
THEY TEACH AMERICA
TODAY
᪥

GEORGE WASHINGTON
1732 - 1799

"First in war, first in peace, and first in the
hearts of his countrymen, he was second to none in
humble and enduring scenes of private life. Pious,
just, humane, temperate, and sincere; dignified, and
commanding; his example was as edifying to all
around him as were the effects of that example
lasting.... Correct throughout, vice shuddered in
his presence and virtue always felt his fostering
hand. The purity of his private character gave
effulgence to his public virtues."

Official eulogy of Washington, written by John Marshall,
delivered by Rep. Richard Henry Lee
December 26, 1799

Born
February 22, 1732, near Popes Creek, Westmoreland County, Virginia; first child of Augustine Washington (landowner, part owner of an iron-works and county justice of the peace) and Mary Ball [Washington].

Childhood
Attended local schools, but received little formal education; farmed his father's land; trained and worked as a surveyor.

Religion
Episcopalian

Family
At the age of 26 married Martha Dandridge Custis on January 6, 1759; fathered no children, but raised two of Martha's children from her previous marriage (John Parke Custis and Martha Parke Custis) and two step grandchildren (George Washington Parke Custis and Eleanor Parke Custis) as his own.

Accomplishments
Surveyor of Culpeper County, Virginia (1749-1750)
Major, Southern District, Virginia militia (1753)
Lieutenant Colonel in the French and Indian Wars (1754)
Colonel and Commander, Virginia Forces (1755-58)
Virginia House of Burgesses (1758-1774)
Justice of the Peace, Fairfax County (1768-1774)
First Continental Congress (1774)
Second Continental Congress (1775)
Commander of the Continental army (1775-1783)
President of the Constitutional Convention (1787)
First President of the United States (1789-1796)

Died
December 14, 1799, at his home Mount Vernon, in Virginia, where he is buried.

Last Words
" 'Tis well."

FATHER OF OUR COUNTRY

George Washington was by all accounts "the indispensable man" of the American Founding. He was the military commander who led a ragtag Continental army to victory against the strongest and best trained military force in the world. Crucial to the success of the Constitutional Convention, his personal support of the new Constitution, more than anything else, assured its final approval. His election to the presidency — the office having been designed with him in mind — was essential to the establishment of the new nation.

"Be assured," James Monroe reminded Thomas Jefferson, "his influence carried this government."

A soldier by profession and a surveyor by trade, Washington was first and foremost a man of action. He never learned a foreign language or traveled abroad, and never wrote a political tract or a philosophical treatise on politics. Like Abraham Lincoln, Washington had received little formal education. And yet his words, thoughts, and deeds as a military commander, a president, and a patriotic leader make him one of the greatest — perhaps the greatest — statesman of our history.

The Life of Washington

BORN IN VIRGINIA IN 1732, the descendant of English farmers, young Washington learned the surveying trade and traveled extensively in the area west of the Appalachian Mountains. At just 21, he was appointed a major in the Virginia militia. Later, as a lieutenant colonel, he was sent to the Ohio Valley to challenge a French expedition; the resulting skirmishes marked the opening battles of the French and Indian War.

After resigning from the British military, he served as a volunteer aide-de-camp to Major General Edward Braddock. In 1755 he was appointed colonel and commander in chief of Virginia's forces, which made him the highest-ranking American military officer, and, for the next three years, he struggled with the endless problems of frontier defense.

From 1758 to 1774 he was a member of the House of Burgesses, the lower chamber of the Virginia legislature. In 1769 he introduced a series of resolutions (drafted by his colleague George Mason) denying the right of the British parliament to tax the colonists, and in 1774 introduced the Fairfax Resolves, which closed Virginia's trade with Britain.

He was elected to the First Continental Congress and spent the winter of 1774 organizing militia companies in Virginia; he attended the Second Continental Congress in military uniform. In 1775, just after the battles of Lexington and Concord, he was appointed general and commander in chief of the Continental army. For the next eight and a half years, Washington led the colonial army through the rigors of war, from the daring attack on Trenton from across the Delaware River to the trying times of Valley Forge and then the triumph of Yorktown in 1781. Through force of character and brilliant political leadership, Washington transformed an underfunded militia into a capable force that, although never able to take the British army head-on, outwitted and defeated the mightiest military power in the world.

After the War of Independence was won Washington played a key role in the formation of the new nation. He was instrumental in bringing about the Constitutional Convention. A conference at Mount Vernon was the stimulus for Virginia to organize the Annapolis Conference, which in turn called for a convention in Philadelphia. Having been immediately and unanimously elected president of the convention, Washington worked actively throughout the proceedings and an examination of his voting record shows his consistent support for a strong executive and defined national powers. His widely publicized participation gave the resulting document a credibility and legitimacy it would have otherwise lacked. The vast powers of the presidency, as one delegate to the Constitutional Convention wrote, would not have been made as great "had not many of the members cast their eyes towards General Washington as president; and shaped their ideas of the powers to be given to a president, by their opinions of his virtue."

As our first president, Washington set the precedents that define what it means to be a constitutional executive. He was a strong, energetic president, but always aware of the limits on his office; he deferred to authority when appropriate but aggressively defended his prerogatives when necessary. His first term as the first president of the United States was dominated by the creation of the new government and the debate over Alexander Hamilton's plan to build a national economy; his second by foreign affairs — mainly the French Revolution, which he wisely avoided, and the debate over his support of the Jay Treaty with Great Britain. Each of these events divided opinion and contributed to the rise of the first political parties.

Washington wanted to retire after his first term, but the unanimous appeals of his colleagues induced him to serve again. Four years later — the situation stabilized, two important treaties concluded and the republic strengthened — he finally decided to step down from the presidency, quit the political scene, and return to private life.

In 1796, on the anniversary of the Constitution, Washington released his Farewell Address, one of the greatest documents of the American political tradition. Best remembered for its counsel concerning international affairs, it also gives Washington's advice concerning federal union and the Constitution, faction and political parties, the separation of powers, religion and morality, knowledge and public credit.

During his lifetime, there was hardly a period when Washington was not in a position to bring his deep-seated ideas and the lessons of his experience to fruition, influencing not only events but also, as his writings attest, the men around him. Four great themes of Washington's life — individual character, religion and religious liberty, the rule of law, and the defense of national independence — are particularly reflective of the objectives of his statesmanship and suggest why his example is a prime model for today's confused politics.

Character

That Washington is known for his character is no accident. One of his earliest writings was an adolescent copybook record of one hundred and ten "Rules of Civility and Decent Behavior in Company and Conversation." Drawn from an early etiquette book, these social maxims taught lessons of good manners concerning everything from how to treat one's superiors ("In speaking to men of Quality do not lean nor look them full in the face") to how to moderate one's own behavior ("Let your recreations be manful not sinful"). Simple rules of decent conduct, he always held, formed the backbone of good character.

In his later letters Washington constantly warned young correspondents of "the necessity of paying due attention to the moral virtues" and avoiding the "scenes of vice and dissipation" often presented to youth. Because an early and proper education in both manners and morals would form the leading traits of one's life, he constantly urged the development of good habits and the unremitting practice of moral virtue. "To point out the importance of circumspection in your conduct, it may be proper to observe that a good moral character is the first essential of man, and that the habits contracted at your age are generally indelible, and your conduct here may stamp your character through life," he advised one correspondent. "It is therefore highly important that you should endeavor not only to be *learned* but *virtuous*."

Washington's own moral sense was the compass of both his private and public life, having become for him a "second" nature. The accumulation

The Crisis at Newburgh

The victorious conclusion of the Revolutionary War left many questions unanswered concerning American governance, not the least of which was the relationship between the military and the nation's elected civilian leadership. The correct answer to this question was necessary for the successful establishment of republican government.

At the end of the war, army officers had several legitimate grievances: Congress was in arrears with the military's pay, and had not settled the officer's food and clothing accounts or made provision for military pensions. In March 1783, an anonymous letter circulated at Washington's main camp near Newburgh, New York, calling on the officers to take an aggressive tone, draw up a list of demands, and possibly defy the new government. Washington acted quickly to blunt the movement; he called a meeting of all the officers for March 15. Although he was not expected to attend, Washington came in at the last moment and delivered one of the most eloquent and important speeches of his life.

While pledging himself in "the most unequivocal manner" to argue the soldiers' cause to Congress, Washington implored them "not to take any measures, which, viewed in the calm light of reason, will lesson the dignity, and sully the glory you have hitherto maintained." He appealed to "the name of our Common Country ... your sacred honor ... the rights of humanity" and "the Military and National Character of America." He concluded in great rhetorical fashion, telling them that if they stood with him to uphold the rule of law:

> you will, by the dignity of your Conduct, afford occasion for Posterity to say, when speaking of the glorious example you have exhibited to Mankind, had this day been wanting, the World had never seen the last stage of perfection to which human nature is capable of attaining.

After the speech, Washington drew a letter from his pocket expressing Congress's efforts at redressing the army. He hesitated and then, as he fumbled in his pockets, remarked: "Gentlemen, you will permit me to put on my spectacles, for I have not only grown gray, but almost blind, in the service of my country." By all accounts, the officers were brought to tears, and the conspiracy collapsed immediately.

—MS

of the habits and dispositions, both good and bad, that one acquired over time defined one's character. In the 18th century "character" was also shorthand for the persona for which one was known and was tied to one's public reputation. Washington knew that the best way to establish a good reputation was to be, in fact, a good man. "I hope I shall always possess firmness and virtue enough to maintain (what I consider the most enviable of all titles) the character of an honest man," he told Hamilton, "as well as prove (what I desire to be considered in reality) that I am."

Republican government, far from being unconcerned about questions of virtue and character, was understood by Washington to require self-government. In his First Inaugural, Washington spoke of "the talents, the rectitude, and the patriotism, which adorn the characters selected to devise and adopt" the law. It was here, and not in the institutional arrangements or laws themselves, that Washington ultimately saw the "surest pledges" of wise policy and the guarantee that "the foundation of our national policy will be laid in the pure and immutable principles of private morality."

Religion and Religious Liberty

Religion and morality are the most important sources of character, Washington advises us, as they teach men their moral obligations and create the conditions for decent politics. They are necessary for the maintenance of public justice. A sense of individual religious obligation, Washington notes in his Farewell Address, is needed to support the oaths necessary in courts of law. But it goes beyond that: "Of all the dispositions and habits which lead to political prosperity, religion and morality are indispensable supports. In vain would that man claim the tribute of Patriotism, who should labor to subvert these great Pillars of human happiness, these firmest props of the duties of Men and citizens."

This holds true despite the theories of academic elites, then or now, who argue that religion is not required to support the morality needed for free government. "And let us with caution indulge the supposition, that morality can be maintained without religion." Washington conceded some ground to rationalists — like Benjamin Franklin and Thomas Jefferson — who seem to have had less personal use for religion. Nevertheless, he insisted on the general argument. "No matter what might be conceded to the influence of refined education on minds of peculiar structure, reason and experience both forbid us to expect that National morality can prevail in exclusion of religious principle." While there might be particular cases where morality did not depend on religion, this was not the case for the morality of the nation.

Washington's statements about the importance of religion in politics must be understood in light of his equally strong defense of religious liberty. In a letter to the United Baptists, for instance, he writes that he will be a zealous guardian against "spiritual tyranny, and every species of religious persecution," and that under the federal Constitution every American would be protected in "worshiping the Deity according to the dictates of his own conscience." Perhaps Washington's most eloquent statement is found in his letter to the Hebrew Congregation of Newport, Rhode Island:

> It is now no more that toleration is spoken of as if it were the indulgence of one class of people that another enjoyed the exercise of their inherent natural rights, for, happily, the Government of the United States, which gives to bigotry no sanction, to persecution no assistance, requires only that they who live under its protection should demean themselves as good citizens in giving it on all occasions their effectual support.

While it is often thought that the separation of church and state marks the divorce of religion and politics in America, Washington's conception of religious liberty was almost exactly the opposite. His understanding of free government requires the moralization of politics, which includes — and requires — the expansion of religious influence in our politics. For Washington, religious liberty meant that religion, in the form of morality and the moral teachings of religion, was now free to exercise an unprecedented influence over private and public opinion by shaping mores, cultivating virtues, and, in general, providing an independent source of moral reasoning and authority.

The Rule of Law

WASHINGTON LED A REVOLUTION to root out monarchical rule in America and establish a republican government based on the rule of law. In 1776 and again in 1777, when Congress was forced to abandon Philadelphia in the face of advancing British troops, General Washington was granted dictatorial powers to maintain the war effort and preserve civil society; he gave the authority back as soon as possible. At the end of the war, at the moment of military triumph, one of his colonels raised the possibility of making Washington an American king — a proposal he immediately repudiated. Likewise, Washington rejected the option of using military force (with or without his participation) to take control of the Congress and force upon it a new national administration. Instead, when the task assigned him was complete, General Washington resigned his military commission and returned to private life.

We take for granted the peaceful transferal of power from one president to another, but it was Washington's relinquishing of power in favor of the rule of law — a first in the annals of modern history — that made those transitions possible. "The moderation and virtue of a single character," Thomas Jefferson tellingly noted, "probably prevented this Revolution from being closed, as most others have been, by a subversion of that liberty it was intended to establish." His peaceful transfer of the presidency to John Adams in 1797 inaugurated one of America's greatest democratic traditions. King George III wrote that Washington's retirement, combined with his resignation fourteen years earlier, "placed him in a light the most distinguished of any living man" and made him "the greatest character of the age."

George Washington was a strong supporter of the Constitution: it established a limited but strong national government, created an energetic executive, and formed the legal framework necessary for a commercial republic. By the Constitution our government is limited and structured to prevent encroachment, with "as much vigour as is consistent with the perfect security of Liberty" yet strong enough "to maintain all in the secure and tranquil enjoyment of the rights of person and property." As a result, it is our strongest check against tyranny and the best guardian of our freedoms. Washington reminds us that it deserves our support and fidelity. Until it was formally changed "by an explicit and authentic act of the whole People," he wrote, the Constitution is "sacredly obligatory upon all."

Ignoring the Constitution and allowing the rule of law to be weakened, Washington sternly warns us, is done at our own peril. Americans must always guard against "irregular oppositions" to legitimate authority and "the spirit of innovation" that desires to circumvent the principles of our Constitution. Nor should we overlook Washington's abiding concern about the corrupting power of the state. He warns us that government tends to encroach on freedom and consolidate power: "A just estimate of that love of power, and proneness to abuse it, which predominates in the human heart is sufficient to satisfy us of the truth of this position." In the long run, disregard for the rule of law allows "cunning, ambitious and unprincipled men" to subvert the people and take power illegitimately by force or fraud. This, he reminds us, is "the customary weapon by which free governments are destroyed."

National Independence

IN THE MOST QUOTED — AND MISINTERPRETED — PASSAGE of the Farewell Address, Washington warns against excessive ties with any country: "'Tis our true policy to steer clear of permanent Alliances, with any portion of the foreign world." He recommends as the great rule of conduct that the United States primarily pursue commercial relations with other nations and have with them "as little political connection as possible."

Although this statement is often cited to support isolationism, it is difficult to construe Washington's words as strict noninvolvement in the political and military affairs of the world. The activities of his administration suggest no such policy; the warning against "entangling alliances," often attributed to Washington, is to be found in the 1801 Inaugural Address of Thomas Jefferson. President Washington warned against political connections and permanent alliances with other nations. And he added the hedge "So far, I mean, as we are now at liberty to do." In order to maintain a strong defensive posture, the nation could depend on "temporary alliances for extraordinary emergencies."

The predominant motive of all of Washington's polices, both foreign and domestic, was to see America "settle and mature its yet recent institutions" so as to build the political, economic and physical strength — and the international standing — necessary to give the nation "the command of its own fortunes." Rather than a passive condition of detachment, Washington describes an active policy of national independence as necessary for America, at some not too distant period in the future, to determine its own fate.

Commerce, not conquest or subservience, was to be the primary means of America for acquiring goods and dealing with the world. Commercial policy should be impartial, neither seeking nor granting favors or preferences, and flexible, changing from time to time as experience and circumstances dictate. But even under the best circumstances economic and trade policy should be conducted in ways that maintain American independence.

To be sure, Washington's intent was to establish a strong, self-determined and independent foreign policy. But this idea also encompasses a sense of moral purpose and well being — sovereignty in the fullest and most complete sense. For America this means a free people governing themselves, establishing their own laws, and setting up a government they think will best ensure their safety and happiness. Or as the Declaration of Independence says: "to assume among the powers of the earth, the sepa-

rate and equal station to which the Laws of Nature and Nature's God entitle them" and obtain the full power to do the "Acts and Things which
Independent States may of right do."

In the end, to have the command of its own fortunes means that
America has the full use of its independence — not to impose its will on
other nations but to prove without help or hindrance from other nations
the viability of republican government. Washington's wish, as explained to
Patrick Henry, was that the United States "*may be* independent of all, and
under the influence of *none*. In a word, I want an American character, that
the powers of Europe may be convinced we act for *ourselves* and not for
others; this in my judgment, is the only way to be respected abroad and
happy at home."

First in War, First in Peace

THE LAST JOURNEYS OF WASHINGTON'S LIFE were to the army camp at
Harper's Ferry, Virginia (now West Virginia), and to Philadelphia to con-
sult on military matters. That same year President Adams appointed
Washington head of a provisional army during a period of tensions with
France. But Washington was happily retired at his beloved home, Mount
Vernon. A sore throat, the result of inspecting his farm during a snow-
storm, quickly worsened and he died on December 14, 1799.

The news of Washington's death spread quickly throughout the
young nation. Every major city and most towns conducted official obser-
vances. Churches held services to commemorate his life and role in the
American Revolution. Innumerable pronouncements, speeches, and sermons were delivered to lament the event. From the date of his death until
his birthday in 1800, some 300 eulogies were published throughout the
United States, from as far north as Maine and as far south as Georgia to
as far west as Natchez on the Mississippi River.

Congressman Richard Henry Lee delivered the official eulogy, which
was written by John Marshall. Although we only remember a few phrases

today, it included these memorable words:

> First in war, first in peace, and first in the hearts of his coun-
> trymen, he was second to none in humble and enduring scenes
> of private life. Pious, just, humane, temperate, and sincere; uni-
> form, dignified, and commanding, his example was as edifying
> to all around him as were the effects of that example lasting. .
> . . Correct throughout, vice shuddered in his presence and
> virtue always felt his fostering hand. The purity of his private
> character gave effulgence to his public virtues.

"Let his countrymen consecrate the memory of the heroic general,
the patriotic statesman and the virtuous sage," read the official message of
the United States Senate. "Let them teach their children never to forget
that the fruit of his labors and his example are their inheritance."

President John Adams was more to the point: "His example is now
complete, and it will teach wisdom and virtue to magistrates, citizens, and
men, not only in the present age, but in future generations, as long as our
history shall be read."

—MATTHEW SPALDING

Benjamin Franklin

1706-1790

"Well known to be the greatest phylosopher
of the present age; — all the operations of nature he
seems to understand, — the very heavens obey him,
and the Clouds yield up their Lightning to be
imprisoned in his rod."

Delegate William Pierce, Farrand's Records
of the Federal Convention
1787

Born
January 17, 1706, in Boston, Massachusetts; son of Josiah Franklin (tallow chandler and soap boiler who immigrated from England in 1683 to escape religious persecution) and Abiah Folger [Franklin] of Nantucket.

Childhood
Attended one year of grammar school and briefly had a private tutor; apprenticed at father's tallow shop and later learned the printing trade; started his first newspaper (New England Courant in 1721) before moving to Philadelphia to open a print shop.

Religion
Raised Presbyterian, but did not actively practice in adult life.

Family
At the age of 24 married Deborah Read on September 1, 1730; they had three children: William Franklin (1729 or 1730), Francis Folger Franklin (1732), and Sarah "Sally" Franklin (1743).

Accomplishments
Purchased the *Pennsylvania Gazette* (1729)
Published *Poor Richard's Almanack* (1732-57)
Clerk of the Pennsylvania Assembly (1736-51)
Deputy Postmaster of Philadelphia (1737-53)
Invented the Franklin stove (1741)
Founded the American Philosophical Society (1743)
Pennsylvania Assembly (1751-64)
Founded what became the University of Pennsylvania (1751)
Deputy Postmaster General for the colonies (1753-74)
Commissioner, Albany Congress (1754)
Agent in England for Pennsylvania (1764-75), Georgia (after 1768), New Jersey (after 1769), and Massachusetts (after 1770)
Second Continental Congress (1775-76)
Postmaster General of the United States (1775-76)
Agent of the United States to France (1776-85)
President of the Executive Council of Pennsylvania (1785-88)
President, The Pennsylvania Society for Promoting the Abolition of Slavery (1787-90)
Delegate, Constitutional Convention (1787)

Died
April 17, 1790, Philadelphia, Pennsylvania, where he is buried at Christ Church.

Last Words
"A dying man can do nothing easy."

THE SAGE OF AMERICA

There was a time, not too long ago, when every school child in America learned about Benjamin Franklin and his exploits; a great many read his brief *Autobiography*. Unfortunately, that time has passed. None of the American Founders is the icon he once was of course, but in the case of Franklin this is especially lamentable because Franklin addressed himself more to the common man, and to the young, than did his colleagues. He directed his writing largely to the formation of popular character, and had a very salutary effect on that character for as long as he was widely read.

The Life of Franklin

BORN IN BOSTON IN 1706, Franklin was older by a generation than most of his fellow-Founders. The youngest son of youngest sons for five generations back, as he tells us with pride, Franklin necessarily made his own way in the world. He tried several trades before settling on printing, the one mechanical trade that suited his bookish and searching mind. While still very young, he read books of "polemic Divinity," mostly attacks on Deism that he found in his father's library. As a result, Franklin tells us, he became "a thorough Deist" by the time he was 15. His unconventional religious beliefs, together with his fondness for disputing with his fellow Bostonians, contributed to his eventual need to depart for Philadelphia.

When only 16 and a printing apprentice to his brother James, he penned a series of essays under the pseudonym Silence Dogood, devoted to chiding the faults and encouraging the virtues of his fellow Bostonians. It was a device he returned to again and again. In Philadelphia, he wrote as the Busy-Body, a self-proclaimed censor morum, and at other times as Alice Addertongue, Obadiah Plainman, Homespun, and of course Poor Richard, whose sententious proverbs (many gleaned from other sources) remain part of our heritage. Franklin considered newspapers (as well as almanacs) to be "another Means of communicating Instruction" to the wider public, and filled his out with small, edifying pieces. It was part of a larger educational project, to which his *Autobiography* also belongs.

Franklin's curiosity extended not only to politics, morality, and theology, but also to science. He investigated natural phenomena from weather patterns to the Gulf Stream to electricity. He founded the American Philosophical Society to advance the cause of science in the New World. His research in electricity led to the discovery of the polarity of electrical current; his invention of the lightning rod, and many other advances, brought him international renown. He was admitted to the Royal Society of London and other European learned societies. Franklin was the only one of the Founders with an international reputation before independence, and that reputation was scientific.

After he became wealthy enough to retire from business (in his early forties), Franklin often expressed the desire to devote himself wholly to science. But the public would not let him. His reputation for selfless public service resulted in continual calls for more. His principle was "I shall never ask, never refuse, nor ever resign an office," and he was asked again and again. He was elected to the Pennsylvania Assembly repeatedly, beginning in 1750. He was appointed deputy postmaster for the colonies in 1753, and in 1754 was a delegate to a intercolonial congress that met in Albany to discuss dealing with the French and Indian War. Although it was rejected, he presented his Albany Plan for local independence within a framework of colonial union.

In 1757, he was made colonial agent for Pennsylvania in London. He lived in England for all but two of the years from 1757 to 1775, representing one or more of the colonies. These were the years when differences between the Americans and the mother country ripened into an open breach. Franklin strove mightily to prevent the rupture, but it proved impossible. He returned to Philadelphia in 1775, only to be sent to Paris by the Continental Congress in 1776, as representative of the new United States to the French court. There he negotiated a treaty of commerce and a defense alliance with France, which proved vital to the success of the American Revolution. Franklin also was a negotiator of the final peace treaty with Great Britain, which was signed in Paris in 1783.

Franklin returned home in 1785, and participated in the Constitutional Convention of 1787. Public knowledge that he and George Washington supported the proposed Constitution was perhaps as important as any other factor in securing its acceptance. One of his last public acts was to sign a petition to Congress, as president of the Pennsylvania Society for Promoting the Abolition of Slavery, urging emancipation and the end of the slave trade. He died not long after the Constitution's ratification, in April 1790.

Although he was at the center of some of the most momentous episodes of the American Founding, Franklin's thoughts and writings are devoted more to matters of culture and popular morality than to laws and institutions. In the end, he held that institutions matter less than the character of the people who sustain them. Thus his famous response to one who inquired what government the framers had given the Americans: "a republic, if you can keep it." Only a populace with the proper temper can support a free government, making it the task of a Founder not only to shape institutions, but character as well.

Democratic Virtues

A FREE, EGALITARIAN, AND DEMOCRATIC SOCIETY requires certain virtues in its citizens, virtues different from those that sustained the feudal and aristocratic societies of Europe. These are the virtues that Franklin aims to identify and cultivate. Compared to feudal virtue — or the classical virtues of Aristotle or Cicero — Franklin's virtues appear so humble as to invite ridicule. The two he praises most, Industry and Frugality, would scarcely be regarded as virtues by aristocratic traditions. But Franklin's morality is designed for the common man, a new common man who must be self-reliant, a lover of liberty, and responsible in its exercise. The question Franklin had to ponder, which we still must ponder, is what virtues does the common man need?

In his *Autobiography*, Franklin gives us a list of thirteen virtues, along with a brief gloss on each:

1. TEMPERANCE (Eat not to Dulness. Drink not to Elevation)
2. SILENCE (Speak not but what may benefit others or your self. Avoid trifling conversation)
3. ORDER (Let all your Things have their Places. Let each Part of your Business have its Time)
4. RESOLUTION (Resolve to perform what you ought. Perform without fail what you resolve)
5. FRUGALITY (Make no Expence but to do good to others or yourself: i.e. Waste nothing)
6. INDUSTRY (Lose no Time — Be always employ'd in something useful — Cut off all unnecessary Actions)
7. SINCERITY (Use no hurtful Deceit. Think innocently and justly; and, if you speak, speak accordingly)
8. JUSTICE (Wrong none, by doing Injuries or omitting the Benefits that are your Duty)
9. MODERATION (Avoid Extreams. Forbear resenting Injuries so much as you think they deserve)
10. CLEANLINESS (Tolerate no Uncleanness in Body, Cloaths or Habitation)
11. TRANQUILITY (Be not disturbed at Trifles, or at Accidents common or unavoidable)

12. CHASTITY (Rarely use Venery but for Health or Offspring; Never to Dulness, Weakness, or the Injury of your own or another's Peace or Reputation)
13. HUMILITY (Imitate Jesus and Socrates)

This is a homely list, to be sure, but remarkably similar to the curriculum urged today by those who want to revive basic moral instruction in schools. Franklin shares with them the project of laying a solid foundation for democratic citizenship. The first building blocks of that foundation are not less important for being so humble.

It is important to bear in mind that the audience for whose edification Franklin proposed his list was the common folk of America, not its elite. These were the people on whose virtues a prosperous democracy would be built, or on whose vices it would founder. Franklin recognized two distinctive features of American society. First, Americans began life with little, and needed to make their own way. Second, America provided sufficient opportunity that prosperity was within the reach of almost anyone who was willing to work for it. This is a recipe for tremendous economic development and social happiness, but only if the human soil is properly prepared.

Our contemporaries have rediscovered the truth that even capitalism depends upon certain virtues that do not appear spontaneously. Curiously, the incentive of personal prosperity is insufficient, without a willingness to pursue prosperity honestly and industriously. Not only work and postponed gratification, but trust and trustworthiness are necessary to commerce, and these traits do not come into being on their own. Franklin's writing emphasizes both the importance of these virtues and the obstacles to their development. In his 1758 *Almanack,* Franklin strung together many of Poor Richard's proverbs on economy as a harangue on "The Way to Wealth," by one Father Abraham. Poor Richard listens to the speech, then observes that "The People heard it, and approved the Doctrine, and immediately practiced the contrary." A premature taste for luxury, the allure of get-rich-quick schemes (Philadelphians were digging up the riverbanks on rumors of pirate treasure), and idle or self-destructive amusements, all may seduce people from the straight and narrow (if not short) path to prosperity. In so doing, they may even derail general economic health.

Franklin could be quite strict toward those who turned their back on his exhortations. Despite his affinity with the common man, he had little patience for the folly that led people astray. His reflections on the English poor laws, based upon his years in London, are remarkably harsh by today's standards. Poor laws, he thought, risked falling into that species of misdirected charity that "tends to flatter our natural indolence, to encourage idleness and prodigality, and thereby to promote and increase poverty." Legitimate relief is one thing, but in excess, "may it not be found fighting against the order of God and Nature, which perhaps has appointed Want and Misery as the proper Punishments for, and Cautions against as well as necessary consequences of Idleness and Extravagancy." Franklin earnestly wished the well being of the common man, but was firm in his insistence that that well being be earned. Only in this way would the social, as well as the individual, good be served.

Social Entrepreneurship

THE ECONOMIC VIRTUES ARE SO PROMINENT in Franklin's writing because of their importance to his audience. But they are the foundation, or beginning, not the whole, of his moral teaching. He does not consider prosperity the only purpose in life, or the only requisite of a healthy republic. Economic self-reliance is in reality only one aspect of the sturdy individualism that democracy requires. It is only a precondition of the other-regarding virtues of citizenship proper.

For Franklin, the heart of morality is doing good to one's fellow man. His mature theology was a providential Deism whose fundamental principle was that "the most acceptable Service of God is doing Good to

Poor Richard's Almanack

Ben Franklin's famous *Poor Richard's Almanack* was an annual calendar and datebook that included practical suggestions, astrological signs, and weather predictions. One of the most popular and influential works in colonial America (John Paul Jones, for instance, named his ship the *Bonhomme Richard*, after Poor Richard), Franklin started the almanac in 1731, when he was 26, and continued to publish it until 1757. Franklin wrote under the pseudonym of Richard Saunders — hence Poor Richard — a simple-minded astronomer and hen-pecked country husband who filled the almanac with common-sense advice and homespun stories. Each edition offered several witty but practical aphorisms, many now famous, such as:

"Early to bed, early to rise, makes a man healthy, wealthy, and wise"

"Never leave that till to-morrow which you can do to-day"

"Penny wise, pound foolish"

"God helps them that help themselves."

The famous phrase "A penny saved is a penny earned" is actually a popularization of Franklin's original "A Penny sav'd is Twopence clear," which better reflects Franklin's encouragement of accumulated saving.

Over time Poor Richard became a significant voice for, and a popular teacher of, Franklin's philosophy that thrift, duty, hard work, and simplicity are not only good qualities but also lead to success. But it is incorrect to assume that Franklin's message is merely utilitarian. Many of his best proverbs on business and public life were collected in the preface to the 1757 final edition called "The Way to Wealth," which ends with this advice: "Do not depend too much upon your own industry, and frugality and prudence, though excellent things, for they may all be blasted without the blessing of Heaven; and therefore ask that blessing humbly, and be not uncharitable to those that at present seem to want it, but comfort and help them."

—MS

Man." In Franklin's own life, this service took many forms. His legendary ingenuity was an exhaustless source of ideas for public benefit. His scientific observations produced the lightning rod and the Franklin stove. He conceived the American Philosophical Society as an instrument for the spread of "Useful Knowledge," to the benefit of mankind. His *Autobiography* presents for our imitation his efforts to improve night watches, streetlights and street cleaning, and his organizing of fire and civil defense brigades. He mustered support for the first public library, hospital, and school in Philadelphia. In each of these cases, the initiative was his, but the organized efforts of many were required to bring them to fruition.

In relating these episodes, Franklin wishes to draw our attention not to the individual improvements, but to the model of public-spirited social entrepreneurship they represent. Franklin is firmly of the opinion that "one Man of tolerable Abilities may work great Changes" for the good, if he forms a plan and pursues it diligently. Not exceptional ability, but a devotion to the public good, and the discipline to pursue it, are the qualities Franklin relies on. These are qualities many can share in, and Franklin wishes as many as possible to share them.

Franklin was not against government taking over many of the tasks he describes, but he saw that the health of a democratic society rests on individuals' willingness to devote time to the public good. Poor Richard once counseled, "The first Mistake in publick Business, is the going into it," but there are many opportunities for public-spirited action outside of politics, and as Tocqueville was to argue later, a successful democracy must have citizens able and willing to seize those opportunities. Poor Richard, like Silence Dogood and the Busy-Body before him, insistently, if gently, pushes his readers to good citizenship. Franklin's *Autobiography* does the same, while showing the way to higher forms of public service, even politics, for those with the talent and leisure.

Education to Liberty

ECONOMIC SELF-RELIANCE and public-spirited citizenship presuppose the political liberty that is necessary for both to flourish. Political liberty in turn requires free institutions, and a public character that will sustain them. Franklin's attempt to secure this character is best seen in a set of proposals he penned for a public school in Philadelphia. "Genius without Education is like Silver in the Mine," wrote Poor Richard. Franklin proposes to "mine" this genius with a new approach to education. Rejecting the European model, which emphasized classical learning and catered to the needs and tastes of a privileged class, Franklin wishes his students to learn principally what they will need to be efficient tradesmen, and vigilant democratic citizens. For trade, his pupils learn basic mathematics and accounting, clear writing, and living rather than dead languages.

His education for democratic citizenship is more complex. Franklin conveys this education principally through the study of history. The vividness of historical example drives home the advantages of virtue and the disadvantages of vice, illustrates the importance of public religion and, says Franklin, reveals the superiority of Christianity in this role.

History also teaches the great advantages of society, how it serves the security and property of men as well as the advancement of arts and human comforts. Finally, it makes students sensible of "The Advantages of *Liberty*, Mischiefs of *Licentiousness*, Benefits arising from good Laws and a due Execution of Justice, &c. Thus may the first Principles of sound *Politicks* be fix'd in the Minds of Youth."

Franklin educates his pupils to a sage and vigilant citizenship. Thomas Jefferson reflected the same aspiration in his educational writings: Democratic citizens must cultivate certain personal virtues to be sure, but they must also become aware of the social preconditions of liberty, and learn to recognize the threats to it. This requires a fairly sophisticated political education. In his *Autobiography*, Franklin suggests that the spread of public libraries in the colonies, a trend begun by him in Philadelphia, played a role in the vigilance of the colonists on behalf of their liberties, and their willingness to stand "in Defense of their Privileges."

The sturdy individualism that begins with economic self-reliance culminates for Franklin in an enlightened jealousy for political liberty. His political curriculum aims to fix this vigilance and pugnacity in the American character.

Democracy and Leadership

THOUGH FRANKLIN'S PRIMARY CONCERN was the diffusion of enlightenment and democratic virtues throughout the populace, he was concerned also with leadership. While many in the "neo-classical" 18th century were inspired by ancient models of leadership, by Cato or Brutus or Publius, Franklin undertook the project of devising a new type of leadership appropriate for the coming democratic age. To be sure, leadership is a less pressing need in a healthy democratic society, one where the public-spirited virtues Franklin describes have wide currency. These in a sense spread leadership, in the form of citizen initiative, across the population. But that does not eliminate entirely the need for great leadership from the best citizens. Paradoxically, the very virtues of democracy make such leadership more difficult.

Aristocratic societies have a norm of deference, a recognition of superiority, and a presumption of its right to lead. In an egalitarian society, the reverse is almost true: pretensions to superiority are resented and leadership itself typically called into question. This is partly a consequence of democracy's insistence on the equality of men, its individualism, and its self-reliance. One can see both the pride, and the resentment, of democracy in Poor Richard's dictum, "A Plowman on his Legs is higher than a Gentleman on his Knees." Franklin developed a style of leadership to deal with this prickly, and on the whole admirable, individualism.

The mode of democratic leadership is persuasion, not coercion. One of Franklin's earliest lessons, he tells us in his *Autobiography*, was that a contentious or imperious style is self-defeating. Rather than persuading men, it offends their pride, and accomplishes nothing. When dealing with pugnacious egalitarians, a more humble presentation is more effective, and creates more pleasant social relations in the bargain.

Franklin discovered that his public-spirited proposals often encountered resistance rooted in envy. No matter how beneficial the project, some would refuse to follow if they thought it would elevate the leader above the rest. Franklin therefore began presenting projects as the initiative of "a number of friends" or "publick-spirited Gentlemen," even if the initiative was wholly his. This greatly smoothed the way by removing the issue of personal credit or honor. Besides, Franklin wryly notes, if someone else tried to take credit for the project, envy itself unmasked the pretender and returned the credit to him.

This method of leadership by stealth, as it were, is one of Franklin's most important lessons to those who would advance the public good in a democratic milieu. He himself applied it systematically. He formed one group, the Junto, as a private forum for discussion and as a surreptitious instrument for leading public opinion. One of the functions of the group was to brainstorm publicly beneficial ideas. If the group found one, its members were to drum up wider support without revealing their cabal of a few as the source. We find in Franklin's writings more than one blueprint for such secret societies of virtuous men, who would use their collective but hidden influence to move public affairs toward the good.

It is not that Franklin was secretive or conspiratorial by nature, or that he had a fundamental distrust of the democratic public. But he did believe that that public could be led effectively only by those who respected its pride, and realized that its resentments needed to be taken into account. He often exerted leadership through alter egos — Silence Dogood, the Busy-Body, Poor Richard — who were disarming in their ordinariness. Franklin himself eventually became one of the most trusted and heeded men in America, partly because of his reputation for humility. Yet humility, he tells us in the *Autobiography*, is a virtue he possessed only by appearance. He also tells us that in such matters appearance is enough. It was by a kind of benevolent deceit (see his gloss on the virtue of Sincerity) that he became such an effective servant of the public good. He counsels us to do likewise.

Franklin found this approach congenial partly because, however exceptional he was, his background was thoroughly common. He had great patience with the oft-unjustified resentments of the common man, because he knew the pride from which it stemmed was one of the signature traits of the new democratic culture, and was on the whole a salutary thing.

American Sage

FRANKLIN WAS MORE INTERESTED in democratic culture and its health than many in the founding generation. His thoughts on the subject are most timely today, when we are wondering afresh what are the underpinnings of a healthy democratic culture, and whether we still possess them. Franklin, writing at a time when American democracy was just maturing from its colonial roots, had much the same perspective. It led him to a concern for certain key virtues that his countrymen needed to develop or solidify.

First were economic virtues like Industry and Frugality. These are the virtues Poor Richard emphasizes most, the virtues with which Franklin is typically identified. The reason is that economic independence, honestly come by, is the precondition of all else in a nation where inherited wealth is a rarity, and self-reliance a trait with more than economic implications. The sturdy individualism it fosters is the backbone of the American political system. But this individualism too must be led in the proper direction. It must be wedded to a love of liberty; pride is here its ally. It must also become sage, recognizing the social preconditions of liberty, its beneficial effects, and the threats to it. This is the portion of his project that Franklin most entrusted to schooling, for these are lessons taught by history.

Finally, our self-reliant individualists must become public-spirited citizens. Democracy requires a concern for the common good, and an initiative for advancing it, to be diffused throughout the populace. Some of Franklin's most vigorous efforts were devoted to cultivating this in his fellow-citizens. His greatest monument is an *Autobiography* which shows us how a life dedicated to all these virtues, public-spiritedness above all, can be supremely happy and supremely enviable.

—STEVEN FORDE

JOHN ADAMS
1 7 3 5 – 1 8 2 6

"The man to whom the country is most
indebted for the great measure of independence is
Mr. John Adams ... I call him the Atlas of
American independence. He it was who sustained
the debate, and by force of his reasoning
demonstrated not only the justice, but the
expediency of the measure."

Richard Stockton (attributed), New Jersey delegate
to the Second Continental Congress
circa 1776

Born
October 19, 1735, Braintree (now Quincy), Massachusetts, son of John
Adams and Susanna Boylston [Adams].

Education
Attended Dame and Latin School, graduated from Harvard College
(1755); studied law and was admitted to the Massachusetts bar (1758).

Religion
Unitarian

Family
At the age of 28 married Abigail Smith on October 25, 1764; they had
five children: Abigail Amelia Adams (1765), John Quincy Adams (1767),
Susanna Adams (1768), Charles Adams (1770), and Thomas Adams
(1772).

Accomplishments
School Master (1755-58)
Law practice (1758-1771)
General Court [Massachusetts House
of Representatives] (1770-71)
Continental Congress (1774-1777)
Chairman of the Board of War and Ordnance (1775-1777)
Commissioner to France (1778-1779)
Minister to the Netherlands (1780-1783)
Minister to Great Britain (1785-88)
Vice President of the United States (1789-97)
President of the United States (1797-1801)

Died
July 4, 1826, Quincy, Massachusetts, where he is buried.

Last Words
"Thomas Jefferson still lives."

ATLAS OF AMERICAN INDEPENDENCE

J ohn Adams is often overlooked as one of America's greatest statesmen. Yet he was widely regarded as the most learned and penetrating
thinker of his generation and played a central role in the American
Founding. "The man to whom the country is most indebted for the
great measure of independence is Mr. John Adams," one delegate to the
Second Continental Congress wrote. "I call him the Atlas of American
independence."

Adams witnessed the American Revolution from beginning to end:
In 1761 he assisted James Otis in defending Boston merchants against
enforcement of Britain's Sugar Act, and he participated in negotiating the
peace treaty with Britain in 1783. He was a key leader of the radical political movement in Boston and one of the earliest and most principled voices for independence at the Continental Congress. Likewise, as a public
intellectual, he wrote some of the most important and influential essays,
constitutions, and treatises of the Revolutionary period. If Revolutionary
leaders like Samuel Adams and Patrick Henry represent the *spirit* of the
independence movement, John Adams exemplifies the *mind* of the
American Revolution.

Of his many significant contributions to the American Founding,
three are most important — concerning his own character, constitutional
development, and the principles of political architecture.

The Life of Adams

JOHN ADAMS WAS BORN ON OCTOBER 19, 1735, in Braintree, Massachusetts. His life and moral virtues were shaped early by the manners and mores of a New England culture that honored sobriety, industry, thrift, simplicity, and diligence.

After graduating from Harvard College, Adams taught school for three years and began reading for a career in the law. He was admitted to the Boston bar in 1758 and soon settled into a flourishing law practice. In 1764, he married Abigail Smith, to whom he was devoted for 54 years. Together they had five children, including John Quincy Adams, who became the sixth president of the United States.

The passage of the Stamp Act in 1765 thrust Adams into the public affairs of colony and empire. In that year, he published his first major political essay, *A Dissertation on the Canon and the Feudal Law*, attacking the Stamp Act for depriving the American colonists of two basic rights guaranteed to all Englishmen by Magna Carta: the right to be taxed only by consent and to be tried only by a jury of one's peers.

Between 1765 and 1776, Adams's involvement in radical politics ran apace with the escalation of events. He was a leader of the radical political movement in Boston, and his Novanglus letters are generally regarded as the best expression of the American case against parliamentary sovereignty. By the mid-1770s, Adams had distinguished himself as one of America's foremost constitutional scholars.

The year 1774 was critical in British–American relations, and it proved to be a momentous one for John Adams. With Parliament's passage of the Coercive Acts, Adams realized that the time had now come for the Americans to invoke what he called "revolution-principles." Later that year, he was elected to the First Continental Congress. Over the course of the next two years, no man worked as hard or played as important a role in the movement for independence. His first great contribution to the American cause was to draft in October 1774 the principal clause of the

Declaration of Rights and Grievances. He also chaired the committee that drafted the Declaration of Independence, he drafted America's first Model Treaty, and, working eighteen-hour days, he served as a one-man department of War and Ordnance. In the end, he tirelessly worked on some thirty committees.

Shortly after the battles at Lexington and Concord, Adams began to argue that the time had come for the colonies to declare independence and to constitutionalize the powers, rights, and responsibilities of self-government. In May 1776, in large measure due to Adams's labors, Congress passed a resolution recommending that the various colonial assemblies draft constitutions and construct new governments. At the request of several colleagues, Adams wrote his own constitutional blueprint. Published as *Thoughts on Government,* the pamphlet circulated widely and constitution-makers in at least four states used its design as a working model for their state constitutions.

Adams's greatest moment in Congress came in the summer of 1776. On July 1, Congress considered final arguments on the question of independence, and John Dickinson, a delegate from Pennsylvania, argued forcefully against it. When no one responded to Dickinson, Adams rose and delivered a rhetorical tour-de-force that moved the assembly to vote in favor of independence. Years later, Thomas Jefferson recalled that so powerful in "thought & expression" was Adams's speech, that it "moved us from our seats." He was, Jefferson said, "our Colossus on the floor."

In the fall of 1779, Adams drafted the Massachusetts Constitution, which was the most systematic constitution produced during the Revolutionary era. It was copied by other states in later years, and it was an influential model for the framers of the Federal Constitution of 1787.

Adams spent much of the 1780s in Europe as a diplomat and propagandist for the American Revolution. He succeeded in convincing the Dutch Republic to recognize American independence and he negotiated critical loans with Amsterdam bankers. In 1783 he joined Benjamin Franklin and John Jay in Paris and played an important role in negotiating a Treaty of Peace with England. Adams completed his European tour of duty as America's first minister to Great Britain.

It was during his time in London that Adams wrote his great treatise in political philosophy, the three-volume *A Defence of the Constitutions of Government of the United States of America*. Written as a guidebook for American and European constitution-makers, the Defence was influential at the Constitutional Convention in 1787, and it was used by French constitution-makers in 1789 and again in 1795.

After his return to America in 1788, Adams was twice elected vice president of the United States. His election to the presidency in 1796 was the culmination of a long public career dedicated to the American cause. Unfortunately, the new President inherited two intractable problems from the Washington administration: an intense ideological party conflict between Federalists and Republicans, and hostile relations with an increasingly belligerent French Republic. This last, known as the Quasi-War, became the central focus of his administration. Consistent with his views on American foreign policy dating back to 1776, Adams's guiding principle was "that we should make no treaties of alliance with any European power; that we should consent to none but treaties of commerce; that we should separate ourselves as far as possible and as long as possible from all European politics and war." The crowning achievement of his presidency was the ensuing peace convention of 1800 that re-established American neutrality and commercial freedom. When Adams left office and returned to Quincy in 1801, he could proudly declare that America was stronger and freer than the day he took office.

The bitterness of his electoral loss to Thomas Jefferson in 1800 soon faded as Adams spent the next twenty-five years enjoying the scenes of domestic bliss and a newfound philosophic solitude. During his last quarter century he read widely in philosophy, history, and theology, and in 1812 he reconciled with Jefferson and resumed with his friend at Monticello a correspondence that is unquestionably the most impressive in the history of American letters.

John Adams died on July 4, 1826, fifty years to the day after the signing of the Declaration of Independence.

Character Matters

DESPITE HIS EXTRAORDINARY ACHIEVEMENTS, Adams has always posed a genuine problem for historians. From the moment he entered public life, he always seemed to travel the road not taken. Americans have rarely seen a political leader of such fierce independence and unyielding integrity. In debate he was intrepid to the verge of temerity, and his political writings reveal an utter contempt for the art of dissimulation. Unable to meet falsehoods halfway and unwilling to stop short of the truth, Adams was in constant battle with the accepted, the conventional, the fashionable, and the popular.

When Adams spoke of moral goodness and right conduct, he most often had in mind the ordinary virtues associated with self-rule. Mastery of oneself for Adams was the indispensable foundation of a worthy life and the end to which virtues like moderation, frugality, fortitude, and industry are directed.

As a young man, John Adams was always looking inward — surveying, evaluating, and judging the state of his soul. He imposed on himself a strict daily regimen of hard work and spartan austerity. He constantly cajoled and implored himself to rise early, to apply himself to a rigid system of work and study, to conquer his passions, and to ferret out any weaknesses in his character. A 21-year-old Adams resolved:

> to rise with the Sun and to study the Scriptures, on Thursday, Fryday, Saturday, and Sunday mornings, and to study some Latin author the other 3 mornings. Noons and Nights I intend to read English Authors. This is my fixt Determination, and I will set down every neglect and every compliance with this Resolution. May I blush whenever I suffer one hour to pass unimproved.

But he did not always succeed. In order to bolster and inflame his flagging spirit after an extended period of lethargy and weakness, Adams sketched a fable of Hercules, adapting the story to his own situation. "Let Virtue Address me — ," Adams wrote.

> Which, dear Youth, will you prefer? a Life of Effeminacy, Indolence and obscurity, or a Life of Industry, Temperance, and Honour? Take my Advice . . . Let no trifling Diversion or amuzement or Company decoy you from your Books, i.e., let no Girl, no Gun, no cards, no flutes, no Violins, no Dress, no Tobacco, no Laziness, decoy from your Books.

The goal of self-knowledge and self-rule for Adams was rational independence in the fullest sense. He was always demanding of himself that he return to his study to tackle the great treatises and casebooks of the law:

> Labour to get Ideas of Law, Right, Wrong, Justice, Equity. Search for them in your own mind, in Roman, grecian, french, English Treatises of natural, civil, common, Statute Law. Aim at an exact Knowledge of the Nature, End, and Means of Government. Compare the different forms of it with each other and each of them with their Effects on Public and private Happiness. Study Seneca, Cicero, and all other good moral Writers. Study [Montesquieu], Bolingbroke [Vinnius?], &c. and all other good, civil Writers, &c.

Like many great-souled men, John Adams was ambitious and desiring of fame, but unlike most such men he spent a good deal of time thinking about his ambition and its relationship to his moral and political principles. The passion for fame was both an intellectual and a personal problem for Adams because it cut two ways. On the one hand, there is a kind of fame that is benevolent and noble in purpose — the kind associated with Pericles, Cato, and Washington. On the other hand, there was a passion for fame that could also serve malevolent and base ends — the kind associated with Alcibiades, Caesar, and Napoleon.

Adams understood benevolent fame to be motivated by a desire to promote the public good, and is achieved either by performing some great deed or through an act of unusual genius that benefits the common weal.

But he did not take the well-being or the opinion of others as his Pole Star. Ultimately, benevolent fame is connected to higher principles that the honorable man seeks for selfish reasons. Such men act because they love that which is noble, good, and just for its own sake.

Never the hypocrite, Adams lived by his own words and avowed principles. He always chose to act in ways he thought right or just, regardless of reward or punishment. The linchpin that united theory and practice in Adams's moral universe was the virtue of integrity. Success, reputation, and fame were not ends in themselves for Adams; they had to be attached to a noble end and to some virtuous action. He would not violate his strict code of character to achieve the favorable opinion of posterity. Above all else, John Adams was a man of strict principle, a man of unyielding integrity, a man of firm justice.

The Principles of Liberty

DURING HIS RETIREMENT YEARS, John Adams was fond of saying that the War of Independence was only a consequence of the American Revolution. The real revolution, he declared, began, 15 years before any blood was shed at Lexington, as an intellectual and moral revolution in the minds and hearts of the American people. Adams played an important role in shaping this intellectual and moral revolution by articulating in his many writings a new theory of constitutional development.

In 1765 Adams responded to the Stamp Act with *A Dissertation on the Canon and Feudal Law,* which was primarily an essay in moral education. Its purpose was to rekindle the American "spirit of liberty." But what did Adams mean by a "spirit of liberty"? Spiritedness for Adams united in body and soul certain *"sensations* of freedom" and certain *"ideas* of right."

Adams meant to inspire the colonists' *sensations* of freedom, and thus guarantee present freedoms, by calling for a remembrance of things past: He implored all patriots to recall the hardships endured by the first settlers and to honor their heroic deeds. On a deeper level, however, the revolution for Adams was about certain *ideas* of right, and so he appealed to the colonists' reason, imploring them to study the philosophical foundations of their rights and liberties. The Americans, he wrote, have a "habitual, radical Sense of Liberty, and the highest Reverence for Vertue" that can and must be appealed to in the face of British tyranny.

Liberty, for Adams, meant freedom from foreign domination, freedom from unjust government coercion, freedom from other individuals, and freedom from the tyranny of one's passions. A free people ought to be jealous of their rights and liberties, and they must always stand on guard to protect them. Adams knew that genuine freedom is fragile, fleeting, and rare; few people have it and those who do must fight to keep it. Ultimately, the spirit of liberty for Adams was a certain kind of virtue: it "is and ought to be a jealous, a watchful spirit." The maxim that he chose to define the spirit of liberty was "Obsta Principiis," meaning, to resist first beginnings. He implored his fellow citizens to resist the "first approaches of arbitrary power."

By 1774, when Parliament passed the Coercive Acts, Adams thought that tyranny no longer threatened America from a distance — it had arrived. But how should the Americans respond? During the 1760s Adams had attempted to foster an enlightened "*spirit* of liberty" as an antidote to the "*spirit* of subservience." By 1774, however, the time had come for the Americans to invoke what he called "revolution-principles." In that moment, Adams ceased to be a conservative defender of colonial rights and liberties and he became a revolutionary republican.

Adams's revolution-principles were guided by principles of justice and virtue that he learned from "Aristotle and Plato, ... Livy and Cicero, and Sydney and Harrington and Locke." They were, he said, "the principles of nature and eternal reason." But revolutions should not be undertaken for light and transient reasons; they must be pursued with caution, moderation, and prudence. There must be objectively definable principles and observable conditions that justify such a momentous step.

For Adams, the boundary line between resistance and revolution was

John and Abigail: An Affair to Remember

One of the most well known courtships and marriages of the early American Republic was that of John and Abigail Adams. After a courtship of three years, John Adams married Abigail Smith in 1764. The marriage lasted 54 years, until Abigail's death in 1818. They had five children, one of whom, John Quincy Adams, became the sixth president of the United States.

Before they were married, and anytime they were apart thereafter, they wrote letters to each other. Between 1774 and 1784 the Adamses saw very little of each other because John was continuously serving the young nation, first in the Continental Congress and later abroad. During that time alone, they exchanged some 300 letters. Their voluminous writings not only present a vivid picture of the day, but also — filled with affection and marital devotion — form one of the greatest correspondences of all time.

As was the common practice of the day, they took literary pennames: Abigail was *Diana,* the Roman goddess of purity and love, and John was Lysander, the great Spartan general. John wrote about the "noisy, dirty town of Boston" and the "soul-confounding wrangles of the law," but also how his future wife had "always softened and warmed my heart [and] shall polish and refine my sentiments of life and manners." Abigail's letters — remember she was the one who was in America during the Revolutionary War — blend stories about the children and the difficulties of managing the family farm with descriptions of battles and the domestic production of saltpeter (potassium nitrate), used to make gunpowder. They also talked politics: she advocated independence early ("Shall we not be despised," she wrote, "for hesitating so long at a word?") and he wrote her about "the Toil and Blood and Treasure, that it will cost us to maintain this Declaration" but that "through all the Gloom I can see the Rays of ravishing Light and Glory." Abigail told John that their hearts were "cast in the same mould." John told Abigail that her letters make "my heart throb like a cannonade."

In one famous exchange, Abigail playfully told John to "remember the ladies, and be more generous than your ancestors" when the new laws of the nation were written. John replied in kind that "in practice you know that *We* are the subjects" and that he did not want to "completely subject *Us* to the despotism of the petticoat." But then Abigail revealed her true feelings: "all my desires and all my ambition is to be esteemed and loved by my partner, to join with him in the education and instruction of our little ones, [and] to sit under our own vines in peace, liberty and safety."

— MS

the constitution. He always sought constitutional solutions to constitutional problems, but when that was no longer possible, a "recourse to higher powers not written" was entirely justified. But he defended the resort to what he called "original power" only when fundamental constitutional principles were at stake. By 1776, the British constitution was broken, unable to accommodate the new demands of empire. Eventually Adams saw it as fundamentally flawed. In the end, the conflict between the center and the peripheries of the British empire could not be resolved precisely because there was no standard, no higher law, no written constitution by which to sort out the conflicting claims of Parliament and the colonies.

During the years of the imperial crisis, Adams developed a radically new theory that sought to identify, protect, and enshrine certain basic rights and liberties — revolution principles — from the intrusions of government through written constitutions. As early as 1775, notably in his *Thoughts on Government*, Adams was advocating that new constitutions be drafted and governments established on the basis of the consent of the governed. For Adams, a written constitution was the product not of history, custom, usage, or the "artificial reasoning" of common-law lawyers, as it was in England, but rather of philosophy and free will, reason and choice, deliberation and consent. What was radically new in all this — which today we take for granted — was that the people's will was to be captured by special conventions to create and then ratify written constitutions. By lifting the Constitutional Convention above ordinary acts of legislation, Adams and his fellow Revolutionaries created a process by which written constitutions could be sanctified, and come to be respected and defended, as fundamental law. Elaborating the stages of constitutional development — from the spirit of liberty to the principles of the revolution to a supreme written constitution as fundamental law — may very well be Adams's greatest contribution to America.

The Principles of Political Architecture

AT THE CORE OF ADAMS'S POLITICAL THEORY, elaborated in his great treatise, *A Defence of the Constitutions of Government of the United States of America*, were three basic but essential principles of political architecture: first, representation instead of direct democracy; second, a separation of the legislative, executive, and judicial powers; and third, a mixture and balance in the legislature between the one, the few, and the many — that is, a mixing of the monarchic, aristocratic, and democratic passions that Adams thought natural to all societies. The combination of these three elements was a true innovation in the history and practice of western constitutionalism.

Adams's three principles of political architecture were the foundation and framework on which he thought all constitutions must be constructed. The first two, representation and separation of powers, were distinctly new: both were logically derived from Lockean natural-rights theory and its corollary theory of consent. Legitimate political power for Adams rested on the principle of representation which in turn rested on the more fundamental principles of consent, equality, and self-government. The purpose of political representation is to serve as a guardian of the people's rights and liberties without being subject to their immediate passions. Separation of powers for Adams is the architectonic principle that defined, shaped, and constitutionalized the republican form of government. The purpose of the separation of powers is to dilute the inherent tendency of all governments — including republics — to centralize political power in the hands of one man or a group of men.

The last principle, however, was hardly a new idea. With its roots in the theory and practice of classical antiquity, the so-called mixed regime rested on an entirely different theoretical foundation. The theory of mixed government was a peculiarly classical notion necessarily related to the question of who should rule, while the separation of powers was a uniquely modern idea connected to the question of the *limits* or *extent* of rule.

From Adams's perspective there were two critical problems that must be addressed by all republican constitution-makers. The first was the tendency of democracies to democratize. The great danger associated with the doctrine of equality is that it can generate a downward psychological and moral momentum that is hard to resist or control, destroying old manners and mores and transforming the soul in profound ways. Adams feared that unchecked democratization would eventually liberate passions dangerous to democratic government.

The second problem is the ambition of the exceptional few. Adams was particularly fearful of those men whom Abraham Lincoln later referred to as the "tribe of the eagle and the family of the lion" — that is, those talented men consumed with political ambition. But he also understood that a healthy democratic regime must be able to recognize and appreciate the truly great individuals who elevate and ennoble self-government by reminding us of democratic greatness.

Adams's solution was to constitutionalize the naturally occurring conflict between the exceptional few and the many of any given society by incorporating what he called the "triple equipoise" — a mixing and balancing of the one (a president with a legislative veto), the few (a senate) and the many (a house of representatives) — into the legislative branch. His mixed government theory would harness, channel and balance the naturally occurring conflict between the few and the many in politically useful ways, forcing the competing social orders to moderate their passions, to look beyond their immediate self-interest, and to compromise with competing interests.

The mixed regime attempted to harmonize the competing and ineradicable notions of justice held by different social orders (i.e., the few and the many), while the separation of powers was about preventing the centralization of government's coercive power. Adams thought that mixed government and separation of powers could be employed together as overlapping and mutually reinforcing principles. Each order, with its incomplete view of justice, and each branch, with its separate powers, would be forced to moderate and elevate it partial claims, thereby producing and necessitating laws that were just, equitable, and, ultimately, for the common benefit.

Independence Forever

JOHN ADAMS HAD AN ENORMOUS INFLUENCE on the outcome of the American Revolution. He dedicated his life, his property, and his sacred honor to the cause of liberty and to the construction of republican government in America. The force of his reasoning, the depth of his political vision, and the integrity of his moral character are undeniable. From the beginning of his public career until the very end, he always acted on principle and from a profound love of country.

We may take the following words that he wrote to a friend during some of the darkest days of the Revolution as a kind of motto to describe who he was as a man and as a patriot: "Fiat Justitia ruat Coelum" — let justice be done though the heavens should fall. To live by such words, though, requires a kind of moral independence that honors doing only what is right and just at all times. "I must think myself independent, as long as I live," he wrote to his son John Quincy in 1815. "The feeling," he said, "is essential to my existence."

As the 50th anniversary of the Declaration of Independence approached, a 91-year-old Adams was asked to provide a toast for the upcoming celebration in Quincy, Massachusetts. He offered as his final public utterance this solemn toast: "INDEPENDENCE FOREVER." These last words stand as a signature for his life and principles. At a time in our nation's history when most Americans cynically assume that their political leaders are dishonest, corrupt, and self-serving, we might do well to recall the example of John Adams and restore to posterity the respect and admiration that he so richly deserves.

—C. BRADLEY THOMPSON

THOMAS JEFFERSON
1743 – 1826

"Jefferson will live in the memory and gratitude
of the wise & good, as a luminary of Science, as
a votary of liberty, as a model of patriotism, and
as a benefactor of human kind."

James Madison, letter to Nicholas P. Trist
July 6, 1826

Born
April 13, 1743, Shadwell, Albemarle County, Virginia; the son of
Peter Jefferson (a planter who died when Jefferson was 14) and Jane
Randolph [Jefferson] (a first generation immigrant from England).

Childhood
Attended a preparatory school and was graduated from William and
Mary College (1762); studied law and was admitted to the Virginia
bar (1767).

Religion
Known but to God.

Family
At the age of 28 married Martha Wayles Skelton on January 1, 1772;
they had six children: Martha Washington Jefferson (1772), Jane
Randolph Jefferson (1774), an unnamed son, who died soon after
childbirth (1777), Mary Jefferson (1778), an unnamed daughter who
died soon after childbirth (1780), and Lucy Elizabeth Jefferson (1782).

Accomplishments
Virginia House of Burgesses (1769-74)
Second Continental Congress (1775-76)
Primary Author of Declaration of Independence (1776)
Virginia House of Delegates (1776-1779)
Governor of Virginia (1779-81)
Confederation Congress (1783-1784)
Minister to France (1785-88)
Secretary of State (1789-1793)
Vice President of the United States (1797-1801)
President of the United States (1801-09)
Founded the University of Virginia (1819)

Died
July 4, 1826 at his home, Monticello, Virginia, where he is buried.

Last Words
"Is it the Fourth?"

APOSTLE OF DEMOCRACY

————⋙◆⋘————

F rom the beginning, Americans have looked with special favor on Thomas Jefferson, who penned the immortal words of our Declaration of Independence. With great eloquence, he dedicated our nation to the proposition that all men are created equal, endowed with unalienable rights to life, liberty and the pursuit of happiness. In doing so, he transformed what would have been a mere political document to a proclamation of America's highest ideals. "The principles of Jefferson," Abraham Lincoln reminds us, "are the definitions and axioms of free society." Indeed, few words have been as influential in spreading the growth of freedom throughout the world as those of Jefferson. Alexis de Tocqueville pronounced him "the most powerful apostle of democracy there has ever been."

Jefferson once wrote that in drafting the Declaration of Independence, he meant simply to furnish an "expression of the American mind." Yet, Jefferson did more than just articulate the moment. This nation was founded not on blood or ethnicity, but on an idea. The writings and deeds of Jefferson gave life to that idea and shaped the American mind. His legacy is our dedication to individual rights, religious liberty, and the importance of education.

The Life of Jefferson

BORN ON APRIL 13, 1743, in Albermarle County, Virginia, Jefferson was to become many things: a great visionary, a radical reformer, a farmer, a philosopher, a writer, a scientist, an educator, an architect, a musician, and a statesman. His father, Peter Jefferson, was a land surveyor, and his mother, Jane Randolph, came from a well-established Virginia family. When he was sixteen, he began his studies at William and Mary College. After two years, Jefferson entered the law office of his professor, George Wyeth, where he remained for five years, attending not only to his legal studies but also a rigorous program of self-education that ranged from ethics and politics to mathematics and rhetoric. Jefferson was known for being an assiduous student — family legend was that during college he followed a strict regimen of studying fifteen hours a day.

In 1769, the same year he began building Monticello, Jefferson was elected to the Virginia House of Burgesses, where he served for five years. He soon became caught up in the anti-British sentiments sweeping the colonies, playing a central role in the Virginia Committee of Correspondence and supporting measures urging resistance to British authority. Among his more important writings was a set of proposed instructions to the Virginia delegates to the First Continental Congress, *A Summary View of the Rights of British America*, which called for the king to recognize the colonists' natural rights.

In June of 1775, Jefferson arrived in Philadelphia to serve as a delegate in the Second Continental Congress, bringing with him "a reputation for literature, science, and a happy talent of composition." Never much of a public speaker (John Adams claimed that he never heard Jefferson "utter three sentences together" while they both sat in Congress), Jefferson made his mark behind the scenes. His most important appointment was in June of 1776 to serve on a committee along with John Adams, Benjamin Franklin, Robert Livingston, and Roger Sherman to write the Declaration of Independence. Only 33 years old, Jefferson was selected to draft what he later called "the declaratory charter of our rights." (See Introduction to the Declaration of Independence, p. 215)

When Jefferson returned to Virginia and re-entered the House of Delegates (where he first met James Madison), he turned his attention to revising the laws of the state of Virginia to make them more democratic. Jefferson proposed legislation to abolish primogeniture (a law giving the first-born son exclusive right of inheritance) and entail (a law limiting inheritance to a lineal descent of heirs), and to establish religious liberty and a means for the general diffusion of knowledge. The first two bills became law in 1777 and the third passed in 1786, but his plan for establishing a broader educational system was defeated. Madison called Jefferson's efforts "a mine of legislative wealth."

Jefferson was elected governor of Virginia in 1779 and spent the bulk of his two-year term dealing with the various exigencies arising from the Revolutionary War. He resigned after one term and happily returned "to my farm, my family and books." He declined a seat in the House of Delegates as well as a diplomatic post to negotiate peace with Great Britain, resuming work instead on *Notes on the State of Virginia*. It was a book that he had never intended to publish, probably because it contained a severe condemnation of slavery.

The Statesman

IN NOVEMBER 1782, shortly after the untimely death of his wife Martha, Jefferson was again appointed to the peace commission to Great Britain, and this time he accepted. But before he set sail for England, he received word that the peace treaty had already been concluded. In 1783, he served as a Virginian delegate to Congress, drafting the resolves that served as a model for the famous Northwest Ordinance of 1787. In 1785, he was appointed by Congress to succeed Benjamin Franklin as minister to France. Although Jefferson's achievements overseas were limited by the Articles of Confederation (which gave individual states the power to authorize treaties with foreign powers), his diplomatic responsibilities kept him from attending the Constitutional Convention in Philadelphia.

Jefferson played a decisive role, albeit from afar, in persuading Madison of the need to add a bill of rights. While in France, Jefferson received a copy of the new Constitution and, in a famous letter to Madison, gave his general approval to it. But Jefferson had an important objection: "Let me add that a bill of rights is what the people are entitled to against every government on earth, general or particular, and what no just government should refuse, or rest on inference." Madison, who had been against a bill of rights, became a firm advocate, and made it the first order of business to pass a bill of rights when he served in the First Congress.

When Jefferson returned to America in 1789, he had every intention of returning to France, but President Washington appointed him as the first secretary of state, a position that Jefferson reluctantly accepted. In Washington's administration, Jefferson came into conflict with the brash and brilliant secretary of the treasury, Alexander Hamilton. Jefferson believed that Hamilton harbored aristocratic sentiments and desired to put America on a course toward monarchy. Hamilton wanted a strong national government, whereas Jefferson favored strong state authority; Hamilton was pro-British, while Jefferson was pro-French. Jefferson envisioned America as a land of small landholders, the "chosen people of God ... whose breasts he has made his peculiar deposit for substantial and genuine virtue." Hamilton, on the other hand, favored an economy based on manufacturing, viewing America as a land of limitless commercial possibilities. The antagonism between Hamilton and Jefferson became increasingly fierce and partisan, and Jefferson left the administration at the end of 1793.

The rivalry between Hamilton and Jefferson ultimately led to the development of America's first political parties, the Federalists and the Republicans. In fact, Jefferson's defeat of John Adams for the presidency in 1800 was the first national election in which two organized political parties vied for office. In his inaugural address, Jefferson laid out his vision of limited government, dedicated to religious toleration and "equal and exact justice to all men" no matter their religious or political background.

The highlight of Jefferson's two terms as President was undoubtedly the purchase of the Louisiana Territory from France, which nearly doubled the size of the United States and gave it control of the Mississippi River. However, Jefferson was reluctant to trumpet this great accomplishment in part because he feared it violated the Constitution. A strict constructionist, Jefferson knew that the Constitution did not give the federal government the power to purchase territory. He supported passing a constitutional amendment to render the purchase legitimate, but was advised that any delay might jeopardize the agreement. Jefferson ultimately found the constitutional authority for purchasing Louisiana under the presidential power to make treaties.

After the presidency, Jefferson eagerly left the world of politics and returned to Monticello, where he gave "up newspapers in exchange for Tacitus and Thucydides, for Newton and Euclid; and I find myself much the happier." Jefferson's retirement was a time for reflection on matters of philosophy and theology, letter writing (his broken correspondence with John Adams was renewed), farming experiments, and most important, establishing the University of Virginia.

Individual Rights

THOMAS JEFFERSON WAS a child of the Enlightenment, and considered three English philosophers of the 17th century — Isaac Newton, John Locke, and Francis Bacon — to be "the three greatest men that have ever lived, without any exception…." He took the ideas of equality and liberty — ideas that had merely been abstractions in aristocratic times — and put them into practice, enshrining them in our Declaration of Independence.

Today, many Americans take their rights for granted. We fail to

Jefferson's Wall of Separation

The "wall of separation" metaphor of the relationship between church and state is taken from an 1802 letter President Thomas Jefferson wrote to the Danbury Baptist Association of Connecticut. Jefferson wrote:

> Believing with you that religion is a matter which lies solely between Man & his God, that he owes account to none other for his faith or his worship, that the legitimate powers of government reach actions only, & not opinions, I contemplate with sovereign reverence that act of the whole American people which declared that their legislature should 'make no law respecting an establishment of religion, or prohibiting the free exercise thereof,' thus building a wall of separation between Church & State.

The metaphor had previously been used by Puritan clergyman Roger Williams and the Whig writer James Burgh. Jefferson's purpose was to explain why he opposed proclaiming national days of public fasts and thanksgivings, as had Washington and Adams. He thought the policy suggested a uniform religious exercise by the nation. Jefferson did not intend the letter to mean that the government should be completely secular or antireligious. So to demonstrate his symbolic friendliness to religion,

Jefferson attended church services in the House of Representatives two days after he wrote the letter — a practice he regularly continued throughout his presidency. It is important to note that Jefferson was writing the letter — which he first ran by key New England political advisors — to a group of his own party supporters living under the Congregationalist establishment of Connecticut (which had opposed him in the election of 1800).

Although the letter was highly political, and continues to spark controversy about what precisely Jefferson meant by the metaphor, most scholars generally argue that it should be read from the perspective of federalism, illuminating the meaning of the First Amendment, which Jefferson understood to apply only to — and thus limit — the national government. It was the Supreme Court that later transformed the letter into a doctrine of religious jurisprudence. In *Reynolds v. United States* (1876) the Supreme Court said the letter may be seen as "an authoritative declaration of the scope and effect" of the First Amendment, and in *Everson v. Board of Education* (1947) went further to declare that the wall "must be high and impregnable. We could not approve the slightest breach."

—MS

realize that when Jefferson was propounding the self-evident truth of human equality (and hence the equal rights and dignity of individuals), the rest of the world believed that the "favored few" — monarchs, aristocrats, despots — should have dominion over the many. But Jefferson, writing fifty years after the Declaration, in the last letter he ever wrote, was convinced that the world was beginning to embrace the idea that all people had a right to liberty: "All eyes are opened, or opening, to the rights of man. The general spread of the light of science has already laid open to every view the palpable truth, that the mass of mankind has not been born with saddles on their backs, nor a favored few booted and spurred, ready to ride them legitimately, by the grace of God."

Of course, the question must be raised: How could a man so dedicated to safeguarding individual rights be a slave owner? A look at Jefferson's public statements and legislative proposals on the issue of slavery reveals a man dedicated to the abolition of slavery. During his first term in the Virginia House of Burgesses, a young Jefferson advocated legislation to make it easier for Virginians to free individual slaves. In *A Summary View of the Rights of British America* Jefferson called for an end to the slave trade: "The abolition of domestic slavery is the great object of desire in those colonies where it was unhappily introduced in their infant state."

Two years later, in his draft of the Declaration of Independence, Jefferson used the strongest language to condemn George III for promoting an untrammeled slave trade in the colonies: "He has waged cruel war against human nature itself, violating its most sacred rights of life and liberty in the persons of a distant people who never offended him, captivating & carrying them into slavery in another hemisphere, or to incur miserable death in their transportation thither.... Determined to keep open a market where MEN should be bought & sold, he has prostituted his negative for suppressing every legislative attempt to prohibit or to restrain this execrable commerce." (See Note on Slavery, p. 281)

In revising the laws of Virginia in the late 1770s, Jefferson took up the cause of emancipation. He submitted a proposal urging his fellow legislators to end slavery gradually in Virginia and to return the freed slaves to their native lands. As Jefferson recounted in his *Autobiography*, his reform would have granted "freedom to all [slaves] born after a certain day, and deportation at a proper age…. Nothing is more certainly written in the book of fate than that these people are to be free."

Nevertheless, Jefferson was a slave owner, and never freed more than a few of his slaves. He struggled throughout his life with the glaring contradiction between the principles of equality and the existence of slavery: "The love of justice and the love of country plead equally the cause of these people, and it is a moral reproach to us that they should have pleaded it so long in vain." "We have the wolf by the ears, and we can neither hold him, nor safely let him go," Jefferson lamented in 1820. "Justice is in one scale, and self-preservation in the other." He had hoped that "the younger generation" moved by "the generous temperament of youth" and shaped by the "flame of liberty" that his generation had kindled would end slavery.

Yet it was Jefferson's words and ideas that led to the abolition of slavery. Abraham Lincoln would constantly refer back to the principles of Jefferson — to his "abstract truth, applicable to all men and all times" — in his effort to end slavery. And a century later, Martin Luther King Jr. understood Jefferson's words in the Declaration to be a "promissory note" that would inspire the struggle for civil rights. By enshrining the idea "that all men are created equal" and the primacy of individual rights in the Declaration of Independence (and also by playing an important role in adding a Bill of Rights to the Constitution), Jefferson committed America to upholding its first principles.

Indeed, in this task, Jefferson might have been too successful. Today we are saturated with what some have called "rights-talk." Few Americans pay any attention to the Constitution except for the Bill of Rights. As a result, some have argued that Americans have become too zealous in defending their individual rights and have lost a national sense of community. Thus, it is important to pay attention to the closing lines of the Declaration of Independence, where the signers pledged "our lives, our fortunes and our sacred honor" to the cause of liberty. For Jefferson, rights were to be secured by individuals who were animated by a sense of patriotism, duty, and honor. In a letter of advice to a young boy, Jefferson told him: "Love your neighbor as yourself and your country more than yourself." To be sure, Jefferson's first principle was that governments were formed, based on the consent of the governed, to protect the individual rights of their citizens. At the same time, Jefferson was well aware that the principles of liberty and equality would best flourish among a citizenry dedicated not only to maintaining their rights, but also to appreciating the nation instituted to secure those rights.

Religious Liberty

THE HISTORY OF THE WORLD IS REPLETE with examples of religious persecution. Our earliest settlers came to America to escape the religious intolerance that was then prevalent in England and Europe. Even today, in most parts of the world, from Ireland, to China, to Africa, there are still religious hostilities and persecution. America is a wonderful exception to these trends. So committed were Americans to the idea of religious liberty that during the Constitutional Convention there was simply no debate on the issue of the right of conscience.

Nevertheless, our Founders were not willing to take our religious liberty for granted. They were all too aware of the danger of mixing political power with religious authority. The First Amendment, of course, recognizes the right to the free exercise of religion and prohibits the national government from making laws respecting an establishment of religion. Jefferson and Madison were perhaps the most vigilant of the Founders when it came to safeguarding religious liberty.

Jefferson's warnings on the danger of church establishments were often blistering and always provocative. He didn't mince words when it came to attacking would-be tyrants. In the "Preamble to his Bill for Religious Freedom," Jefferson singled out "the impious presumption of legislators and rulers, civil as well as ecclesiastical, who, being themselves but fallible and uninspired men, have assumed dominion over the faith of others, setting up their own opinions and modes of thinking as the only true and infallible, and as such endeavoring to impose them on others, hath established and maintained false religions over the greatest part of the world and through all time." In his *Notes on the State of Virginia,* Jefferson extended the widest scope of toleration to atheists and pagans: "The legitimate powers of government extend to such acts only as are injurious to others. But it does me no injury for my neighbour to say there are twenty gods, or no god. It neither picks my pocket nor breaks my leg."

For Jefferson, religious belief was a matter of individual conscience and thus "a matter which lies solely between man and his God." In his famous and often quoted letter to the Danbury Baptist Association (see sidebar, p. 84), Jefferson used this now-familiar analogy to discuss the First Amendment: "I contemplate with sovereign reverence that act of the whole American people which declared that their legislature should 'make no law respecting an establishment of religion, or prohibiting the free exercise thereof,' thus building a wall of separation between Church and State." He considered religious liberty to be the cornerstone of every other liberty, and its defense crucial to the maintenance of free government. As he wrote to his friend Benjamin Rush, "I have sworn upon the altar of God eternal hostility against every form of tyranny over the mind of man."

Many Americans have taken those statements to mean that there should be a strict divide between the state and religion generally. Yet Jefferson's stance on religious liberty is more nuanced than that. At the same time that he drafted his "Bill for Establishing Religious Freedom" in the late 1770s, he also proposed a "Bill for Punishing Disturbers of Religious Worship and Sabbath Breakers" and a "Bill for Appointing Days of Public Fasting and Thanksgiving." As governor of Virginia he issued a proclamation of "solemn thanksgiving and prayer to Almighty God."

As president, Jefferson did not proclaim national days of fasting and thanksgiving because he feared that such proclamations had the effect of imposing uniform religious practices on all citizens. Yet (beginning two days after issuing the Danbury letter) Jefferson regularly attended church services held in Congress during his presidency, well aware that the symbolic gesture of his attendance would likely offset any perception of his hostility toward religion. He also gave generously to several churches and ministers while in office, and allowed religious services in public facilities of the executive branch. And although he seems untroubled in *Notes on the State of Virginia* if his neighbor believes in many or no gods, in that same work Jefferson also implores: "And can the liberties of a nation be thought secure when we have removed their only firm basis, a conviction in the minds of the people that these liberties are of the gift of God? That they are not to be violated but with his wrath? Indeed I tremble for my country when I reflect that God is just...."

Thus, while it might seem that Jefferson advocates a radical separation between church and state, he considers liberty a gift of God and posits a firm reliance on God for protecting our natural rights — with which all men "are endowed by their Creator." Jefferson believed in unrestrained religious expression in an open marketplace of ideas, and thought that religious establishments threatened religious liberty. At the same time, he had little problem with government supporting voluntary, non-sectarian religious activity, including the use of public property for religious purposes, if that cooperation was necessary for the cause of religious expression and the flourishing of the good effects of religion generally.

Education

JEFFERSON'S LOVE OF LEARNING was boundless, and it informed his priorities as legislator, reformer, president, and later as a retired statesman. His vigilance against political tyranny and religious fanaticism was matched by what he foresaw as a more formidable enemy of self-government: ignorance. Part and parcel of his trenchant defense of individual rights and religious liberty was his understanding that free citizens, in order to remain free, must be educated.

Of all the bills Jefferson submitted to the revisal committee when he was a legislator in Virginia, Jefferson wrote "by far the most important bill in our whole code is that for the diffusion of knowledge among the people. No other sure foundation can be devised for the preservation of freedom, and of happiness." For Jefferson, education protected "individuals in the free exercise of their natural rights, and ... against degeneracy." So vital was the role of education to "guard the sacred deposit of [our] rights and liberties" that Jefferson proposed what was at the time a very radical plan to extend a free education to all children of elementary school age in the state of Virginia. Jefferson believed that gifted children come from all walks of life. As he put it, "talents are sown as liberally among the poor as the rich." It was in the public interest for the state to seek out and educate all children "whom nature hath fitly formed and disposed to become useful instruments of the public" rather than confine education "to the weak or wicked." Jefferson's scheme provided a free education to all at the elementary level, and encouraged the best students, whom Jefferson called the "natural aristocracy," to pursue higher education.

The importance of education to Jefferson can also be seen in one of the central policies of his presidential administration. In 1803, Jefferson persuaded Congress to appropriate $2,500 for the first scientific expedition of the United States, which sent Meriwether Lewis, his private secretary, and William Clark on one of America's most famous exploratory missions. Jefferson instructed Lewis that his "observations are to be taken with great pains and accuracy, to be entered distinctly, and intelligibly for others as well as yourself." He was especially interested in what they might observe of the American Indians ("the names of the nations and their numbers; the extent and limits of their possessions; their language, traditions, monuments, the state of morality, religion and information among them") and singled out a few other "objects worthy of notice" such as "the soil, vegetation, animals, mineral productions, climate." Jefferson's love of natural history was in part fueled by his patriotism. He wanted to show the world that America was geographically the equal of, if not the superior to, Europe.

Jefferson spent the bulk of his retirement years working on the ambitious project of establishing what would become the University of Virginia. The Virginia Assembly appropriated funds to charter the university in 1819, and Jefferson set about at once to attract the best faculty from abroad and to amass a vast catalogue of books for the library. He designed not only a curriculum but also the architecture of the entire campus, which the American Institute of Architects has praised as "the proudest achievement of American architecture in the past 200 years."

The University of Virginia was perhaps Jefferson's proudest accomplishment. As much as Jefferson admired our political institutions, he put his greatest faith in the virtue of a free people, educated to uphold self-government: "Above all things I hope the education of the common people will be attended to; convinced that on their good sense we may rely with the most security for the preservation of a due degree of liberty."

Jefferson's educational aims were three-fold. One was simply to provide all children with the skills — reading, writing, arithmetic, geography, and history — necessary to live free and independently as adults. Second, all children must be given a civic education that instructs them in "their rights, interests and duties, as men and citizens." Jefferson stressed the importance of educating Americans in the science of politics — in the axioms of free government. Finally, and perhaps most important for Jefferson, education was meant to cultivate virtue. Jefferson believed educators should "cultivate [children's] morals and instill into them the precepts of virtue and order." He optimistically believed that education "engrafts a new man on the native stock, and improves what in his nature is vicious and perverse into qualities of virtue and social worth." Perhaps this is Jefferson's greatest lesson to us, that rights and democracy are nothing without an education in virtue.

Is it the Fourth?

JEFFERSON'S DEATH IS AN EXTRAORDINARY, almost mythical ending to a patriotic life. In February of 1826, Jefferson became ill and, by the spring of that year, he knew he was dying. He wrote a new will, and in mid-June he called for his physician to stay with him at Monticello as he slowly began slipping away. By July 2, Jefferson began falling in and out of consciousness, and on July 3 he fitfully awoke to speak his last words: "Is it the Fourth?" Jefferson held onto life until the afternoon of July 4, 1826, the 50th anniversary of the adoption of the Declaration of Independence. His great friend and fellow revolutionary John Adams passed away a few hours later.

This extraordinary life would furnish the most impressive of epitaphs. But Jefferson left behind explicit instructions to his grandson to note only three achievements on the obelisk at his Monticello grave, which reads: "Here was buried Thomas Jefferson, Author of the Declaration of American Independence, of the Statute of Virginia for Religious Freedom, and Father of the University of Virginia; because by these, as testimonials that I have lived, I wish most to be remembered." And it is precisely Thomas Jefferson's achievements in the areas of individual rights, religious liberty, and education that explain to a large extent the success of our American democracy and that still define our national character.

—DOROTHEA WOLFSON

ALEXANDER HAMILTON
1757 – 1804

"He smote the rock of national resources
and abundant streams of revenue
gushed forth; he touched the dead corpse of
public credit and it sprang upon its feet."

Daniel Webster, speech in New York City
March 10, 1831

Born
January 11, 1757, Nevis, St. Croix, British West Indies; the son of James
Alexander Hamilton (a Scottish merchant) and Rachel Fawcett Lavien.

Childhood
Worked as a clerk for a St. Croix trading post; immigrated to America in
1772; attended grammar school in Elizabethtown, N.J., and was graduated
from Kings College (now Columbia University) in 1775.

Religion
Presbyterian

Family
At the age of 25 married Elizabeth Schuyler on December 14, 1780; they
had eight children: Philip Hamilton (1782), Angelica Hamilton (1784),
Alexander Hamilton Jr. (1786), James Alexander Hamilton (1788), John
Church Hamilton (1792), William Stephen Hamilton (1797), Eliza
Hamilton (1799), and Phillip Hamilton (1802).

Accomplishments
Captain, New York Artillery Company (1776)
Lt. Colonel and aide de camp to George Washington (1777-81)
Practiced law in New York (1783-1804)
Delegate to the Continental Congress (1782-83 and 1788)
Commanded infantry brigade at the Battle of Yorktown (1781)
Founder and Director, Bank of New York (1784)
Delegate to the Annapolis Convention (1786)
Member, New York State Assembly (1787)
Delegate to the Constitutional Convention (1787)
Co-author, the *Federalist Papers* (1787-88)
Secretary of the Treasury (1789-95)
Inspector General of the Army (1798)
Founder, New York Evening Post (1801)

Died
July 12, 1804, New York City (after being fatally wounded in a duel with
Aaron Burr); buried at Trinity Churchyard in Manhattan.

Last Words
"Remember, my Eliza, you are a Christian."

CHAMPION OF AMERICAN ENTERPRISE

O f all the Founders of the American Republic, Alexander Hamilton has fluctuated the most in reputation. During his own lifetime, Hamilton had committed defenders as well as passionate detractors. During the antebellum period, his reputation declined, but after the Civil War, with the triumph of neo-Federalism, he was accorded the highest honors in the national pantheon.

Today, Hamilton's reputation is ambiguous. Liberals consider him too elitist, a mouthpiece for the rich and well-born (despite Hamilton's humble origins), and a militarist. Conservatives often dismiss him as an anti-free-trade protectionist and the forefather of national industrial policy, or the idea that government can do a better job than markets at picking eventual winners and losers in the economy. Both sides are wrong, however. Hamilton is to be honored for the critical role he played in three important areas: constitutional government, political economy and public finance, and national defense.

The Life of Hamilton

HAMILTON PROBABLY WAS BORN IN 1757 — the record is not clear — on the Dutch West Indian island of St. Eustatius. As a teenager, the precocious Hamilton favorably impressed his employer Nicholas Cruger and the Reverend Hugh Knox, a Presbyterian minister, who in 1772 conspired to send the 15-year-old to North America for an education. Hamilton matriculated at King's College (now Columbia University) in New York.

Hamilton became involved in the pre-Revolutionary politics of King's College in particular and of New York in general. In the winter of 1774-75, Hamilton wrote anonymously two pamphlets, *A Full Vindication of the Measures of Congress from the Calumnies of Their Enemies* and *The Farmer Refuted*, in response to popular Loyalist writings. As the patriot cause spread, Hamilton joined a drill company, and in March 1776 was made captain of a New York artillery battery. He served in this capacity through the summer and fall as the British maneuvered George Washington's Continental army out of New York and pursued it south across New Jersey. His artillery saw action at both Trenton and Princeton. Two months after Princeton, Hamilton was promoted to lieutenant colonel and became an aide to George Washington. He served in this role for four years, forging a relationship with Washington that would have immense consequences for the new nation.

In the summer of 1781, Washington gave Hamilton command of an infantry brigade. He saw action at Yorktown, including leading his brigade in a nighttime attack on a British trench line. Washington praised Hamilton and his men for "intrepidity, coolness and firmness" during the action.

The British surrendered at Yorktown on October 19, 1781. Although the war would not officially end for another two years, Hamilton was able to return to his family in New York and take up the study of law in Albany. In November 1782 the New York assembly chose Hamilton to be a delegate to Congress, where he first met James Madison, who would be both ally and adversary over the next two decades. A series of events (which culminated with Congress fleeing to New Jersey when a group of disaffected soldiers marched on Philadelphia) convinced Hamilton that the national legislature was a weak and debilitated body. Hamilton resigned from Congress and returned to his family and to the law.

Nevertheless, the New York assembly chose Hamilton as a delegate to the Annapolis Convention in September 1786 and later to the

Constitutional Convention in Philadelphia. His contributions to the actual drafting of the Constitution were fairly limited and far less important than his truly Herculean efforts to gain New York's ratification of the final document.

Hamilton turned first to the press, collaborating with John Jay and James Madison to write the *Federalist Papers*, a series of newspaper essays under the Plutarchian pseudonym of Publius (see sidebar, p. 99). Of the 85 essays comprising the *Federalist Papers*, Hamilton wrote over two-thirds, mostly on war and foreign policy, the law, executive power, and the administration of government. During the New York Ratifying Convention, Hamilton was virtually a one-man show, making numerous, powerful speeches over the course of the convention that successfully swayed many anti-Federalist opponents to support the new government. By a close vote, New York agreed to ratification in July 1788, making it the 11th state to adopt the new Constitution.

When the new government met in New York City during the spring of 1789, President Washington chose Hamilton as the first secretary of the treasury. The Senate confirmed his nomination in September 1789 and Hamilton immediately set to work to establish America's credit by resolving the problem of the country's outstanding debt. As secretary of the treasury, Hamilton presented three important reports to the new Congress on behalf of the Washington administration. His *Report on the Public Credit* provided for funding the national and foreign debts of the United States, as well as for federal assumption of the states' Revolutionary War debts. Hamilton's next major project was to establish a national bank, a means for fulfilling the government's powers in the event of an emergency such as war. His *Report on a National Bank* was delivered in December 1790 and a bill passed through Congress fairly quickly. James Madison questioned the constitutionality of an act chartering a national bank but Hamilton made a powerful argument for the bank's constitutionality — based on the "implied powers" of the Constitution — and Washington signed the bank bill into law in early 1791. He immediately set to work on his third great project, a *Report on the Subject of Manufactures,* which he delivered to Congress at the end of that year.

Hamilton's financial program caused Thomas Jefferson and his allies great concern. They saw it as an instrument of monarchy and corruption, at odds with the yeoman virtues necessary for the young Republic. Disputes between Hamilton and Jefferson exploded into public view in the "Newspaper War" of 1792. Their quarrel over finances was exacerbated by a difference of opinion regarding the French Revolution. Jefferson thought the United States should assist France against Britain out of "gratitude" for its assistance to America during its own revolution while Hamilton favored closer ties with Great Britain and believed America should remain neutral. Washington concurred with Hamilton and issued his Neutrality Proclamation.

Jefferson left the cabinet at the end of 1793, frustrated by Hamilton's influence. Following the crisis of the Whiskey Rebellion of 1794 (see p. 17), Hamilton also left to return to private life, but the furor over the Jay Treaty (see p. 23) led Hamilton to enter the fray once more in a series of newspaper essays entitled "The Defence" under the pen name of Camillus. Hamilton's final service to Washington was his assistance in drafting his Farewell Address, the outgoing President's call on America to preserve the Union.

In the election of 1796, Hamilton worked assiduously to prevent Jefferson from becoming president by attempting to ensure that federal electors in New England cast their votes for Thomas Pinckney as well as John Adams. Adams interpreted this strategy as an attempt to influence the election in favor of Pinckney rather than him. This episode, along with Hamilton's influence over Adams's cabinet led to a falling out between the two that would severely weaken the Federalist Party and contribute to its defeat in the election of 1800.

Although Hamilton would never hold public office again, he remained politically active. He returned to New York to practice law and found the *New York Evening Post.*

The Federalist Papers

In the fall of 1787, Alexander Hamilton enlisted the support of James Madison and John Jay to write a series of essays to refute the arguments of the opponents of the proposed Constitution. Seventy-seven of the essays were originally published in the New York City newspaper the *Independent Journal* between October 17, 1787, and April 12, 1788. Those and eight additional essays soon appeared in book form as the *Federalist Papers*. The essays were largely responsible for the ratification of the Constitution by New York in 1788.

The initial essays (Nos. 2-14) stress the inadequacy of the Confederation and the advantages of a national union. In his famous essay, Federalist No. 10, James Madison addresses the problem of majority faction and argues that republics would thrive best in large territories that encompassed many diverse and competing factions. The middle essays (Nos. 15-36) argue for an energetic government, in particular the need for the government to be able to tax and provide for the national defense. The last essays (Nos. 37-84) explain the "conformity of the proposed Constitution to the true principles of republican government." This section includes important articles (Nos. 47-51) explaining the leading "auxiliary precaution" of the Constitution, namely, the separation of powers and the resulting system of checks and balances.

The original essays where written under the pen name Publius, a statesman of ancient Rome who had been important in establishing the Roman republic and then warned its citizens of threats to their freedom. Today we know that Hamilton wrote 51 essays, Madison 26, and Jay five, and that Hamilton and Madison wrote three jointly.

The *Federalist Papers* is a brilliant set of essays on American political theory, and remains an enduring source of incisive and authoritative commentary on the Constitution. In recommending the *Federalist Papers,* George Washington wrote that they "have thrown a new light upon the science of government, they have given the rights of man a full and fair discussion, and explained them in so clear and forcible a manner, as cannot fail to make a lasting impression." Thomas Jefferson proclaimed the work to be "the best commentary on the principles of government which ever was written."

— MS

Constitutional Order

HAMILTON, LIKE JEFFERSON and most of the founding generation, saw the American Revolution as an act of deliberation designed to secure the natural rights enumerated in the Declaration of Independence — "life, liberty, and the pursuit of happiness." However, a revolution is inherently lawless. Men must "dissolve [existing] political bands" before they can establish a new form of government more congenial to rights and liberty. But revolutionary fervor is inappropriate for living in a stable political society, even one that is intended to protect individual rights.

Hamilton understood that a passion for liberty was necessary if the cause of American independence was to succeed, but that ultimately it had to be tempered by the rule of law. As he said during the New York Ratifying Convention in 1788,

> In the commencement of a revolution ... nothing was more natural than that the public mind should be influenced by an extreme spirit of jealousy ... and to nourish this spirit, was the great object of all our public and private institutions. Zeal for liberty became predominant and excessive. In forming our confederation, this passion alone seemed to actuate us, and we appear to have had no other view than to secure ourselves from despotism. The object certainly was a valuable one. But Sir, there is another object, equally important, and which our enthusiasm rendered us little capable of regarding. I mean the principle of strength and stability in the organizing of our government, and of vigor in its operation.

The problem is that the passions released in the fight for one's rights can in the end destroy those rights. Ultimately, individual rights can be preserved only when there exists in society a strong sense of "law-abidingness." Hamilton was appalled at the call for "permanent revolution" that characterized Jefferson's rhetoric. He believed that Jefferson's complacent and bookish reaction to Shays' Rebellion and the French Revolution ("I hold it that a little rebellion now and then is a good thing" and "the Tree of Liberty must be watered from time to time with the blood of tyrants") was a recipe for disaster, an approach that would ensure "frequent tumults" instead of good government. The answer was to make Americans law-abiding by attaching them to their Constitution, which, although their own creation, binds them by its constraints while it is in force.

Attaching the people to the Constitution's rule of law would preserve the new government as if it were an ancient establishment, promoting the stable administration of justice without which the protection of our rights — the object of the Revolution — could not be assured. Hamilton sought by speech and deed to moderate the passions of the people and attach them first to their state constitutions and then to the federal Constitution. Examples of how Hamilton sought to build this attachment included his legal defense of New York Loyalists after the Revolution (along with his Phocion letters on the same topic), his defense of the new Constitution during the ratification debates of 1787-1788, his activities as secretary of the treasury to teach Americans the necessity of paying their debts and keeping contracts, and his efforts as a member of Washington's cabinet to subordinate American gratitude to France and the passion of Americans for the French Revolution to the dictates of international law. Nothing indicates Hamilton's purpose in moderating revolutionary passions better than a letter he wrote to John Jay at nearly the same time as he was writing his own revolutionary pamphlets:

> The same state of passions which fits the multitude ... for opposition to tyranny and oppression, very naturally leads them to contempt and disregard of all authority.... When the minds of those are loosed from their attachments to ancient establishments and course, they seem to grow giddy and are apt more-or-less to turn into anarchy.

Political Economy

ALEXANDER HAMILTON PLAYED AN IMPORTANT ROLE in laying the foundation for America's young market economy and encouraging the entrepreneurship that would be at the forefront of America's economic growth. As the first secretary of the treasury, Hamilton set the conditions for the United States' future prosperity and economic success by establishing the nation's credit, which provided an incentive for individuals and nations alike to invest in America.

In 1790, the United States faced what seemed to be insuperable barriers to financial stability. The new nation owed vast sums to both its citizens and foreign creditors. It was behind in its payment of both principal and interest, and lacked the means to raise the necessary revenues. As a result, the credit of the United States was held in low esteem, which meant that no one would be willing to lend money to America unless there was added a substantial "risk premium." The American economy was weak and its financial future unclear, making large-scale investment and long-term prosperity unlikely.

Some called for the repudiation of the domestic portion of the debt; some called for a scaled down version of repudiation — "discrimination" between original holders and present holders of debt, which would punish "speculators." Others demanded that the government pay its debt precisely according to the terms set down. Hamilton proposed that the federal government "assume" the debts of the previous government (as well as the war debts of the individual states) and pay them over time. Such a course would lead to the eventual retirement of the debt in an orderly manner and in such a way that it would be "monetized," making significant additional capital available for new investment. "The proper funding of the present debt [would] render it a national blessing," said Hamilton. Allowing for the regular payment of interest while keeping the principal more or less intact would serve as the basis for a uniform and elastic currency. This would make future credit available as quickly as possible, facilitating economic growth and stability. Hamilton knew that a creditworthy America would generate vast quantities of capital from both domestic and foreign investors. Credit, as the word itself indicates, depends on trust and faith, which must be earned in the marketplace. In order to earn credit, a country must show that it will honor long-term commitments and keep its financial obligations — both necessary for stable economic transactions.

His financial plan also reinforced his goal of making Americans law-abiding; by emphasizing that the country must pay its own debt, he was reminding citizens of the moral importance of paying theirs. And the assumption of the states' debts by the national government had the additional benefit of strengthening ties to the new government, and thereby further cementing the Union. Hamilton believed that the establishment of justice and the creation of a law-abiding and virtuous people required habituation to virtue and that paying one's debts, both private and public, played an important role in achieving such a habituation. As he wrote in Federalist No. 72, "the best security for the fidelity of mankind is to make their *interests* coincide with their *duty*."

The second element of Hamilton's grand plan was to stimulate the growth of domestic manufactures. Rejecting the common assumption that America could prosper with just an agricultural base, he argued that the new nation should concentrate on developing the nation's small business entrepreneurs. But his strategy was not to assist domestic industry through state control of the market. Hamilton was neither a mercantilist nor a protectionist. He envisioned the role of government as using limited bounties or subsidies (contingent on a surplus of revenue) to help infant American industries overcome barriers to entry erected by the existing terms of trade. His advocacy of limited tariffs was not to advantage particular manufactures but to yield customs revenues, then the leading source of government funds. In general, Hamilton maintained that trade was directed by its own natural rules and was, for the most part, best left alone. He considered it the role of government to create a stable framework that would allow the free market to prosper.

Hamilton wanted to affect the very nature of the American economy, and arouse a dynamic liberty of industriousness, enterprise, and innovation. He envisioned a nation in which citizens of differing aptitudes could achieve happiness, and he saw commerce as a positive good that would make citizens more fully human and would perfect human nature by stimulating the intellect, the most characteristic possession of man. Manufactures would give "greater scope for the diversity of talents and dispositions, which discriminate men from each other."

In his *Report on the Subject of Manufactures,* Hamilton argues that a diverse economy develops society:

> The spirit of enterprise ... must be less in a nation of mere cultivators, than in a nation of cultivators and merchants; less in a nation of cultivators and merchants than in a nation of cultivators, artificers, and merchants .... Every new scene which is opened to the busy nature of man to rouse and exert itself, is the addition of a new energy to the general stock of effort.

Rather than based on conventional distinctions such as birth or wealth, the United States would distribute its rewards in accordance with ability and republican virtue. To do this it was necessary to create a free nation — a commercial republic — that rewarded merit and ambition.

Hamilton understood that commerce and a market economy provide prosperity and growth without which, as history has shown, there can be no free government. Prosperity is necessary to create the military and naval power necessary to sustain a regime capable of protecting the natural rights of its citizens. He also knew that liberty — and the economic diversity and human excellence that would flourish as a result — depended on a government strong enough to protect it and confident enough to allow each individual to flourish. Hamilton wrote:

> It is a just observation, that minds of the strongest and most active ... fall below mediocrity, and labor without effect, if confined to uncongenial pursuits. And it is thence to be inferred, that the results of human exertion may be immensely increased by diversifying its objects. When all the different kinds of industry obtain in a community, each individual can find his proper element, and can call into activity the whole vigor of his nature.

Such an environment is hospitable to great men, to captains of industry, to seekers after honor and fame. A great nation based on equal political rights in which merit, as opposed to status, is to be the basis for reward

provides the greatest opportunities for those actuated by the "love of fame
… the ruling passion of the noblest minds."

National Defense

THROUGHOUT HISTORY, WAR has been the great destroyer of free
government: it seems always to have been the case that the necessities,
accidents, and passions of war undermine liberty. The unprecedented ability of the United States to wage war while still preserving liberty is a legacy of Alexander Hamilton, who deserves much of the credit for the
institutions that have enabled the United States to minimize the inevitable
tension between the necessities of war and the requirements of free government. This, of course, was not the conventional view of Hamilton.
Contemporaries such as Thomas Jefferson, James Madison, and John
Adams saw Hamilton as a Caesar or a Bonaparte, bent on tyranny at home
and conquest abroad. Unfortunately, many of today's historians also accept
this false view.

Hamilton was a soldier-statesman who could be trusted with the
sword of his country. Rejecting the utopian vision of Thomas Jefferson and
many of his allies, Hamilton understood that war was a fact of international life, and that the survival of the infant Republic depended on developing and maintaining the potential to make war. But Hamilton was not
a militaristic state-builder along the lines of Frederick the Great or
Bismarck. He was an advocate of limited government and therefore always
understood the necessity of remaining within the legal bounds established
by the Constitution. "Let us not establish a tyranny," he wrote in 1798.
"Energy is a very different thing from violence." Hamilton's goal was to
establish a republican regime both fit for war and safe for freedom. He was
a strategist before the word was coined, and his strategic objectives were to
enable the American Republic to avoid war when possible and to wage it
effectively when necessary, all the while preserving both political and civil
liberty.

Hamilton had to contend with several popular views that tended to denigrate foreign affairs and national security, views that have their counterparts today. The first was the uncritical belief that economic progress and commerce would not only lead to improvements in the material conditions of life, but would also change human nature sufficiently to make war a thing of the past. The second was a corollary of the first — that a focus on domestic affairs alone was the key to peace and prosperity. Being realistic, Hamilton knew that force ruled relations among nations; this was as true in the New World as it had been in the Old. He hoped that if America could survive its infancy as an independent nation, consent might replace force in the New World. But for the foreseeable future the volatile and uncertain geopolitical situation required that America take steps to defend itself, its rights, and its national honor.

The first step in making the United States secure was to create a powerful and indissoluble Union that would greatly discourage war on the North American continent, thus avoiding the militarization that had led to the downfall of earlier free governments. Indeed, Hamilton's support for the Constitution was based largely on his belief that only such a Union could ensure American security at home and project unity abroad.

The second step was to ensure that the nation had the means to defend itself in a hostile world. These included the establishment of credit and a national bank, and the encouragement of manufactures, and also the creation of a strong standing army and an ocean-going navy. Even more so, Hamilton emphasized being able to defend the constitutional order itself, the necessary instrument for protecting the liberty, happiness, and prosperity of its citizens. When it came to national defense, as Hamilton wrote in Federalist No. 23, the powers necessary to defend the Constitution "ought to exist without limitations, because it is impossible to be foreseen or define the extent and variety of the means which may be necessary to satisfy them. The circumstances that endanger the safety of nations are indefinite and for this reason, no constitutional shackles can wisely be imposed on the power to which the care of it is committed."

Hamilton's concern for national defense, and his desire to provide for the national strength that would make the use of national power less necessary (he was an early advocate of peace through strength), goes far in explaining why he supported a broad rather than a narrow construction of the Constitution, a strong rather than a weak executive, a standing army rather than a militia, and commerce and manufactures over an agricultural economy. In most of these controversies, Hamilton's strategic sobriety prevailed, and that accounts in large measure for the unprecedented ability of the United States to combine great power and an unprecedented degree of liberty.

Hamilton's Character

TWO EVENTS IN PARTICULAR CAPTURE the essence of Hamilton's character. The first is especially instructive to our day and the second, though less immediately applicable, shows how Hamilton's life ended.

While serving as secretary of the treasury, Hamilton had an affair with Maria Reynolds, a married woman, whose husband proceeded to blackmail him. When his political enemies accused Hamilton of serious financial improprieties, Hamilton wrote a pamphlet in which he admitted to the extramarital affair, for which he expressed remorse, in order to refute the far more dangerous charge that he was accepting bribes. Hamilton understood the extent to which his political reputation was tied into the success of his financial plan, and thus the early success of the new nation, but was willing to sacrifice his private reputation for the public good.

In 1800, an electoral tie between two Republican candidates, Thomas Jefferson and Aaron Burr, threw the election to the House of Representatives. With John Adams out of the picture, several Federalists made clear their intention to vote for Burr in order to deny Jefferson the presidency. But Hamilton wrote a series of letters to several Federalists urging them to support Jefferson because he considered Burr to be a dangerously unprincipled adventurer. "In a word," Hamilton wrote, "if we have an embryo-Caesar in the United States, 'tis Burr." The representatives in the House voted 35 times, and after each ballot the votes were equally split between Jefferson and Burr. On the 36th ballot, one of the recipients of Hamilton's letter-writing blizzard abstained, handing the election to Jefferson.

In 1804, disaffected New England Federalists hatched a plan to secede from the Union, and convinced Burr to run for governor of New York and persuade his state to support their cause. Hamilton again did his best to thwart Burr's ambitions. After this defeat, Burr challenged Hamilton to a duel, which Hamilton — like Cato, willing to die for the republic to prevent the triumph of a Caesar — felt obliged to accept. Although Hamilton was opposed to dueling — his eldest son Phillip had died in a duel — he met Burr at Weehawken, New Jersey, on the morning of July 11, 1804. Hamilton was mortally wounded and died the next day.

—MACKUBIN OWENS

JAMES MADISON
1751–1836

"Eloquence has been defined to be the art of
persuasion. If it included persuasion by convincing,
Mr. Madison was the most eloquent man
I ever heard."

Patrick Henry, letter to an unidentified correspondent
November 12, 1790

Born
March 16, 1751, Port Conway, King George County, Virginia; son of
James Madison Sr. (family emigrated to Virginia in 1653) and Nelly
Conway [Madison].

Education
Studied under private tutors and was graduated from the College of
New Jersey, now Princeton) in 1771.

Religion
Episcopalian

Family
At the age of 43 married Dolley Payne Todd on September 15, 1794;
they had no children.

Accomplishments
Committee of Safety for Orange County, Virginia (1774)
General Assembly of Virginia (1776)
Virginia Council of State (1778-79)
Continental Congress (1780-83; 87-88)
Virginia House of Delegates (1784-86)
Annapolis Convention (1786)
Constitutional Convention (1787)
Co-author, the *Federalist Papers* (1787-88)
United States House of Representatives (1789-97)
Secretary of State (1801-09)
President of the United States (1809-17)
Rector of the University of Virginia (1826-36)

Died
June 28, 1836, at his home, Montpelier, in Virginia, where he is buried.

Last Words
"Nothing more than a change of mind, my dear."

FATHER OF THE CONSTITUTION

J ames Madison is generally regarded as the Father of the United States Constitution. No other delegate was better prepared for the Federal Convention of 1787, and no one contributed more than Madison to shaping the ideas and contours of the document or to explaining its meaning. In 1787 and 1788 Madison authored, with Alexander Hamilton and John Jay, the *Federalist Papers*, a penetrating commentary on the principles and processes of the proposed Constitution. In 1789, as a member and leading voice in the House of Representatives in the new Republic, Madison introduced a series of constitutional amendments that would form the basis of the Bill of Rights. A few years later, he and Thomas Jefferson organized the opposition to Alexander Hamilton's administrative policies, thereby founding the first political party in America.

Winston Churchill once said that a man must choose either a life of words or a life of action. Like Churchill, Madison demonstrated that rare individuals could be both scholars and statesmen. His scholarly quest to discover the means by which popular government could also be just government was not merely academic; his dedication to finding a "republican remedy" to the problems that had always plagued popular government was meant to answer the "sighs of humanity" throughout the ages. Madison believed that he and his generation of American Founders had discovered the way to rescue popular government from its past failures, but that its ultimate success depended on the great experiment in self-government entrusted to the hands of future generations. The destiny of republican government, Madison believed, is staked on the vigilance of the American people to tend "the sacred fire of liberty."

The Life of Madison

JAMES MADISON JR. WAS BORN IN 1751 in Port Conway, Virginia. At the age of 18 he entered the College of New Jersey, now Princeton University, where he studied history, classics, moral philosophy, politics, and law. Called by some of his friends "Jemmy," he was five foot six, of slight build, quiet voice, serious demeanor, and scholarly habits. He was, unfortunately, plagued with ill health in his youth and intermittently throughout his life. This notwithstanding, on more than one occasion Madison worked himself to exhaustion despite the protests of his dearest friends.

During the revolutionary years Madison served in the general assembly of Virginia, the Continental Congress, and the Congress under the Articles of Confederation. In the mid 1780s he served in the Virginia House of Delegates, and in 1786 he attended the Annapolis Convention, the precursor to the Federal Convention. Soon thereafter he began preparing for the Federal Convention, to be held in Philadelphia the following summer, by combing ancient and modern texts that might contribute to an understanding of stable and effective federal government and to solutions to the problems faced by popular government over the ages.

Madison arrived early at Philadelphia and used the time before the Convention commenced to meet with fellow delegates from Virginia and Pennsylvania to formulate the opening agenda. Though introduced by Madison's friend and then governor of Virginia, Edmund Randolph, the "Virginia Plan" was largely the brain child of James Madison. Calling for a stronger central government and a bicameral legislature, the Virginia Plan became the basis for subsequent discussions and debate at the Convention and laid the groundwork for the Constitution of 1787. Throughout the long, hot summer at Philadelphia, Madison took extensive notes on the proceedings, and it is primarily this record that has provided us with a knowledge of the speeches and debates of that propitious gathering. During the New York ratification debates he collaborated with Hamilton and Jay on a series of essays in support of the proposed Constitution. Their combined efforts produced the *Federalist Papers,* which is generally considered the most definitive exposition of the tenets of American republicanism.

In the late 1780s and 1790s Madison served four terms in the House of Representatives, and then served as secretary of state under President Thomas Jefferson. Madison succeeded Jefferson in the office of the chief executive, serving two terms as the fourth president of the United States. During the War of 1812, sometimes called "Mr. Madison's War," he and his wife Dolley were forced to flee the White House in Washington, D.C., as the British destroyed it and its contents in a devastating fire.

Following his presidency, Madison retired to his family estate at Montpelier, only a partial day's ride from his closest friend's residence at Monticello. The road between the homes of James Madison and Thomas Jefferson is today fittingly named "Constitution Way," linking the two friends and their greatest achievements in an uninterrupted ribbon leading from the ideas of the Declaration of Independence to the principles of the American Constitution. Together Jefferson and Madison worked on founding the University of Virginia, where, they hoped, the "true doctrines of liberty" might be inculcated into future statesmen.

During his twilight years, in which he was "the last of the founders" remaining on the American scene, Madison became increasingly disturbed by the secessionist theories of Senator John C. Calhoun of South Carolina. Though Calhoun attempted to defend his theories with the political thought and writings of Jefferson and Madison, Madison clarified his position that the union of the states was justly founded on the consent of the people of the several states, and as such can only be altered through the prescribed constitutional processes. There is no constitutional basis, he argued, for the right of secession in the compact of a free

A Bill of Rights

The Constitutional Convention unanimously defeated a motion to draw up a bill of rights for the new Constitution. Why did the framers reject this added protection?

First, the Constitution did contain numerous guarantees, such as trial by jury and habeas corpus, and prohibitions, such as those against religious tests and the impairment of contracts. Second, a national bill of rights was thought to be unnecessary because a bill of rights was already included in most state constitutions. Third, and most important, the framers created a government of specific, limited powers. "Why declare that things shall not be done," Alexander Hamilton asked, "which there is no power to do?"

Nevertheless, the lack of a formal bill of rights became a rallying cry during the ratification debate and the advocates of the Constitution agreed to add one.

When the First Congress convened in March 1789, Representative James Madison took charge of the process and quickly got 17 amendments passed through the House of Representatives, a list that was trimmed to 12 in the Senate. President Washington sent each of the states a copy of the 12 amendments adopted by the Congress. The first two proposed amendments, concerning the number of constituents for each Representative and the compensation of congressmen, were not ratified. (The second proposed amendment was eventually ratified as the 27th Amendment in 1992.) By December 15, 1791, three-fourths of the states had ratified the 10 amendments now known as the Bill of Rights.

Based largely on George Mason's "Declaration of Rights" written for the Virginia Constitution of 1776, but framed in its final form by Madison, the clear purpose of the Bill of Rights was to restrict the federal government. The First Amendment guarantees substantive rights involving religion, speech, press, assembly and petition, while the next seven deal with more procedural rights, such as protections against searches and seizures and double jeopardy and the guarantees of due process and the right to bear arms. The Ninth Amendment notes that the listing of rights in the Constitution does not deny or disparage others retained by the people, and the 10th Amendment notes that the powers of the national government are limited to only those delegated to it by the Constitution on behalf of the people.

—MS

people. Madison's last public writing— the "advice to my country" nearest to his heart and deepest in his convictions — was that the American union be cherished and perpetuated.

Having served his country for more than forty years and taken part in the founding "epochs of its destiny," Madison had throughout his life dedicated himself "to the cause of liberty." He died "as quietly as the snuff of a candle goes out" on the morning of June 28, 1836, at the age of 85.

The Extended Republic and Representation

MADISON BELIEVED ALONG WITH his contemporaries that the great danger to popular government is faction. A faction, Madison explained in Federalist No. 10, is a number of citizens "united and actuated by some common impulse of passion, or of interest, adverse to the rights of other citizens, or to the permanent and aggregate interests of the community." In a free society, factions that consist of a minority of the citizens are not constitutionally dangerous because, given the principle of majority rule, they cannot legally gain their ends. However, if a majority composes a faction, might pretends to determine right and the very purpose of government and the fabric of freedom are threatened with destruction. The problem is that the causes of faction and injustice are "sown in the nature of man."

Factions stem from self-interest and prejudice, which in turn tend to influence people's opinions and views. Since the causes of a faction cannot be removed without coercing people's minds and destroying liberty, Madison advocated a system of government that could control the effects of faction and deter the formation of an unjust majority. His proposed remedy included establishing a popular government over a large territory and instituting the principle of representation.

The size of the territory matters, Madison argued, because in a small republic it is easy for a majority to communicate and unite on the basis of selfish interest or prejudice and thereby oppress the minority. In an extensive republic, however, there will be more people, a greater diversity of interests and views, and a greater distance over which their views must be communicated. This will make it more difficult for a majority to form on the basis of a narrow interest or harmful passion. In a large society a *coalition* of the majority will be necessary in order to achieve an authoritative status, and its demands will have to pass muster with a great variety of economic, geographical, religious, and other groups in society. In effect, Madison was the first in America to celebrate the benefits of a diverse population, welcoming the differences that freedom of conscience, freedom of thought, freedom of choice of occupation, and display of talents bring forth.

This did not mean for Madison, however, that the American people have no need to be guided by a common purpose. Dedication to the principles of freedom also meant a common commitment to the idea of responsibility and the practice of self-government. As we shall see, this is the cornerstone of Madison's vision of the "new and more noble course" of free government in the modern world. The purpose of the principle of representation, Madison argued, is to "refine and enlarge the public views, by passing them through the medium of a chosen body of citizens, whose wisdom may best discern the true interest of their country, and whose patriotism and love of justice, will be least likely to sacrifice it to temporary or partial considerations." Like the effects of the extended republic, representation is another crucial factor intended to prevent narrow interests and unjust views from determining public decisions. The job of the representative is not to follow daily polls or raise a finger to the wind to decide how to vote; sudden breezes in popular opinion, Madison taught, are too often the result of prejudice and partial interests. Rather, the task of the representative is to promote a consensus grounded in justice and the common good.

The achievement of this consensus requires deliberation within the legislature as well as a two-way process of communication between the representatives and their constituents. When the people are "stimulated by some irregular passion, or some illicit advantage," the good representative will place duty above personal ambition. Rather than flattering the people's prejudices in order to curry their immediate favor, he will check their misguided demands, so that "reason, justice, and truth, can regain their authority over the public mind." The goal, Madison argued, is to achieve public decisions based on the "cool and deliberate sense of the community." Accordingly, the duty of the representative is both to listen to the concerns of his constituents and to promote among them an enlarged view of the public interest. Within this milieu of public communication and deliberation a kind of civic education takes place. It contributes to forming and settling public opinion on the basis of right, and it justifies "the respect due from the government to the sentiments of the people."

The Madisonian process of refinement and enlargement of the public views can be seen throughout the broad workings of the legislative process today, from public hearings on political matters in home districts to the deliberative proceedings on the House or Senate floor; from the contest and compromise of interests in legislative committees to the representatives' open newsletters to their constituents; from the necessity to defend their public stances and votes during re-election campaigns to the honor felt by those representatives whose "faithful discharge of their trust shall have established their title to a renewal of it."

Separation of Powers and Checks and Balances

THOUGH MADISON HOPED the representatives of America would be wise and virtuous, he was not naive about the temptations of power and the charms of ambition that accompany political office. He well knew that "enlightened statesmen will not always be at the helm." Some representatives will be weak of mind or lacking in backbone. Some may possess the ambition and political skills of a demagogue, and be able to work their wiles on less clever and weaker colleagues. Even the most philosophic and patriotic representatives, Madison warned, should not be given a blind trust, for the political scenes in which they must operate often distract their reasoning "and expose it to the influence of the passions." In essence, Madison advised his fellow citizens to be wary of the heat generated by politics and the allurements of political power.

"The accumulation of all powers [of government] ... in the same hands ... [is] the very definition of tyranny," Madison wrote in the *Federalist Papers*. To guard against the danger of governmental tyranny, Madison endorsed a system of prudential devices, including separation of powers, checks and balances, bicameralism, and federalism, which are intended to divide and channel the self-interest and ambitions of office holders and enable government to control itself. Accordingly, the Constitution separates the government into three distinct branches: legislative, executive, and judicial. However, Madison argues, it is not sufficient to establish separation of powers on parchment only. Because men are not angels — because they are so often actuated by private interest and ambition — these very motives themselves must be employed to keep the departments of government within their limited, constitutional boundaries. "Ambition must be made to counteract ambition. The interest of the man must be connected with the constitutional rights of the place."

Madison thus proposed a system of checks and balances that would incorporate the less than sterling side of human nature into the very workings of government. To accomplish this, the powers of the three branches of government are partially blended, enabling each branch to guard against usurpations of power by the others and safeguard its own constitutional province. Examples of constitutional checks and balances include the executive veto of legislative bills, the legislative override of the executive veto, the required Senate confirmation of presidential appointments to the Supreme Court, and judicial review. In essence, Madison wanted the different branches of government, as well as the two houses of Congress, and the national and the state governments, to check each other in the exercise of power, thereby guaranteeing the diffusion of governmental power and the protection of the people's rights and liberties.

Madison termed these safeguards against governmental tyranny "auxiliary precautions." The primary control on the government, he emphasized, remains always with the people. In the final analysis, governmental decisions depend on the will of the society. If liberty is to be preserved, the will of the people must be grounded in the principles of justice and informed by the precepts of moral responsibility. In arguing for constitutional and institutional safeguards for liberty, Madison never lost sight of the fact that the preservation of freedom ultimately depends on the citizens and their exercise of personal and political responsibility.

Freedom and Responsibility

MADISON'S CONTRIBUTIONS TO THE American Republic are best summarized by his lifelong dedication to the principles of freedom and responsibility. These principles go hand in hand and constitute the cornerstone of republican self-government. Together they protect the citizens in the free exercise of their faculties. The individual's free exercise of his or her mind and talents is the most basic of all rights, from which all our civil rights and liberties are derived. These include freedom of conscience, freedom of speech, freedom of assembly, freedom of the press, and the rights of property.

A staunch supporter of the separation of church and state, Madison argued that the religion of every person must be left to his own conscience and cannot rightly be forced by the dictates of other human beings. In promoting the doctrine of religious freedom, his intent was not to privilege the secular over the religious or in any way to diminish the realm of the latter, but rather to protect men's religious convictions against the intrusion of the state. The obligation of every human being to God, Madison argued, is higher than his duty to country. Freedom of conscience is an inalienable right because "what is here a right towards men, is a duty towards the Creator."

Before human beings are members of civil society, they are subjects of the "Governor of the Universe," and not even a majority in society has the legitimate right to interfere with a man's allegiance to divine authority. Madison's claim for religious freedom is thus an aspect of his understanding of the hierarchy of obligations and responsibilities of human beings. "A just government," Madison wrote, will protect "every citizen in the enjoyment of his Religion with the same equal hand which protects his person and his property."

When government interferes with the freedom to derive the fruits of one's talents and labors, it violates the principle of human equality by subjecting some to peculiar burdens and others to particular exemptions. When government dictates arbitrary taxation or the taking of property from one class of citizens to benefit another, freedom is assailed. This is because the right of property is simply the natural and necessary extension of the free use of one's faculties. A just government, Madison teaches, will protect the citizens in both their rights of property and their property in rights. A person's "opinions and the free communication of them" is a no less sacred form of property, from which freedom of speech, assembly and press are derived. "Government is instituted to protect property of every sort," Madison asserts, "as well that which lies in the various rights of individuals, as that which the term particularly expresses. This being the end of government, that alone is a just government, which *impartially* secures to every man, whatever is his *own*."

We are all familiar with the Bill of Rights as a document listing our protected freedoms. Madison hoped it would in time become much more than a parchment barrier against oppressive acts. Over time a bill of rights becomes sanctified and incorporated in public opinion, and its principles exert an influence on the actual views and sentiments of the people. The guardianship of our constitutional rights is immeasurably strengthened when those rights, and the responsibilities that flow from them, are written not just on paper, but on the minds and hearts of the citizens.

In all free governments, Madison claimed, public opinion is sovereign. Public opinion is the authority that ultimately determines governmental measures; it is the spirit behind the laws. The arena of public opinion is the sphere in which a coalition of the majority takes place on any given issue. Majority opinion in a republican polity is constantly in the process of constructing itself within an intellectual, moral, and psychological milieu larger than itself. Consequently, the things that influence public opinion are of critical importance to those concerned with the stability, character, and future of the political order. To foster the formation of a citizenry who will respect the rights of others and exercise the responsibilities that come with freedom, Madison promoted a national bill of rights, a free press circulating throughout the land, educational establishments to encourage learning and cultivate public manners, and representatives who take seriously their duty to encourage the enlargement of the public viewpoint. His aim was to construct a society in which the people are truly capable of governing themselves.

Madison's advocacy of the formation of a deliberative and just public opinion was his sustained attempt to solve the problem of majority opinion in a manner fully consistent with the form and spirit of popular government. Three quarters of a century later Abraham Lincoln would echo Madison's republican convictions. On the brink of civil war Lincoln reminded the American people that "a majority, held in restraint by constitutional checks, and limitations, and always changing easily, with deliberate changes of popular opinions and sentiments, is the only true sovereign of a free people."

Self-Control

Robert Frost, perhaps the greatest of American poets, captured in homely phrases the simple charms of the American countryside. His poems are landscapes of snowy lanes and winter's quiet, of uncharted paths through amber woods, of fences of privacy that promote neighborly bonds and mutual respect. Even more than the actual land Americans inhabit, Frost's words capture the tenor and timbre of the American way of life. They are quiescent reminders of the resounding majesty of the American dream. "I wonder what the dream is, or why.... I wonder who dreamed it," Frost once wrote. "Did Tom Paine dream it, did Thomas Jefferson dream it, did George Washington dream it? Gouverneur Morris?" After putting the question down, and then picking it up again, and leaving it and returning to it yet again and again, Frost thought he had come to understand the dream. He decided, "the best dreamer of it was Madison." "Now I know — I think I know ... — what Madison's dream was," Frost wrote. "It was just a dream of a new land to fulfill with people in self-control. That is all through his thinking .... To fulfill this land — a new land — with people in self-control."

Frost's plain words, used to capture the vision behind Madison's complex system of government, could not have been better chosen. Self-control, by the individual citizen and by the majority, is the essence of Madison's dream of republican self-government. Like Madison, Frost understood that in the end, after all has been done to institute a system of institutional checks and safeguards, to establish formal laws protecting this or preventing that, the destiny of the American Republic would be decided by the people's willingness and ability to cherish their own rights as well as respect the rights of others. The "new and more noble course" of freedom, Madison taught, is a road worthy of our choosing. Its path is marked out and lit for us by our very humanity and the eternal challenge of self-government.

Robert Frost had the acuteness to hear Madison's gentle plea. He has reminded us that the Father of the Constitution, in his soft and quiet voice, speaks to each of us across the ages: "*You* are the tender at the sacred hearth of liberty, and of the noble aspirations that are the American dream."

—COLLEEN SHEEHAN

A LIST of the
BEST QUOTATIONS
FROM THE
AMERICAN FOUNDERS,
OF GOOD USE in ESSAYS,
SPEECHES, and DAILY
CONVERSATION

❦ Quotation Categories

Advice

Early to bed, early to rise makes a man healthy, wealthy, and wise.

Benjamin Franklin, Poor Richard's Almanack, 1735

Labor to keep alive in your breast that little spark of celestial fire called conscience.

George Washington, The Rules of Civility, circa 1748

Wish not so much to live long as to live well.

Benjamin Franklin, Poor Richard's Almanack, 1746

Moderation in temper is always a virtue, but moderation in principle is always a vice.

Thomas Paine, Letter Addressed to the Addressers on the Late Proclamation, 1792

In planning, forming, and arranging laws, deliberation is always becoming, and always useful.

James Wilson, Lectures on Law, 1791

Strive to be the greatest man in your country, and you may be disappointed. Strive to be the best and you may succeed.

Benjamin Franklin, Poor Richard's Almanack, 1747

A spoonful of honey will catch more flies than a gallon of vinegar.

Benjamin Franklin, Poor Richard's Almanack, 1748

Adore God. Reverence and cherish your parents. Love your neighbor as yourself, and your country more than yourself. Be just. Be true. Murmur not at the ways of Providence. So shall the life into which you have entered be the portal to one of eternal and ineffable bliss.

Thomas Jefferson, letter to Thomas Jefferson Smith, February 21, 1825

The cunning of the fox is as murderous as the violence of the wolf.

Thomas Paine, *The American Crisis* No. 1, Dec. 19, 1776

Resolve to perform what you ought. Perform without fail
what you resolve.

Benjamin Franklin, *Autobiography*, 1771

It is of great importance to set a resolution, not to be shaken,
never to tell an untruth. There is no vice so mean, so pitiful, so
contemptible; and he who permits himself to tell a lie once, finds
it much easier to do it a second and a third time, till at length it
becomes habitual; he tells lies without attending to it, and truths
without the world's believing him. This falsehood of the tongue
leads to that of the heart, and in time depraves all its good
disposition.

Thomas Jefferson, letter to Peter Carr, August 19, 1785

❧ America

I am not a Virginian, but an American.

Patrick Henry, speech delivered at the First Continental
Congress, September 6, 1774

The cause of America is in a great measure the cause of all
mankind.

Thomas Paine, *Common Sense*, 1776

It is a part of the American character to consider nothing as des-
perate; to surmount every difficulty by resolution and contrivance.

Thomas Jefferson, letter to Martha Jefferson, March 28, 1787

This country and this people seem to have been made
for each other.

John Jay, Federalist No. 2, October 31, 1787

The name of American, which belongs to you, in your national
capacity, must always exalt the just pride of Patriotism, more than
any appellation derived from local discriminations.

George Washington, Farewell Address, September 19, 1796

Is it not the glory of the people of America, that, whilst they have paid a decent regard to the opinions of former times and other nations, they have not suffered a blind veneration for antiquity, for custom, or for names, to overrule the suggestions of their own good sense, the knowledge of their own situation, and the lessons of their own experience?

James Madison, Federalist No. 14, November 30, 1787

The Citizens of America, placed in the most enviable condition, as the sole Lords and Proprietors of a vast Tract of Continent, comprehending all the various soils and climates of the World, and abounding with all the necessaries and conveniencies of life, are now by the late satisfactory pacification, acknowledged to be possessed of absolute freedom and Independency; They are, from this period, to be considered as the Actors on a most conspicuous Theatre, which seems to be peculiarly designated by Providence for the display of human greatness and felicity; Here, they are not only surrounded with every thing which can contribute to the completion of private and domestic enjoyment, but Heaven has crowned all its other blessings, by giving a fairer opportunity for political happiness, than any other Nation has ever been favored with. Nothing can illustrate these observations more forcibly, than a recollection of the happy conjuncture of times and circumstances, under which our Republic assumed its rank among the Nations.

George Washington, Circular to the States, June 8, 1783

The American Revolution

What a glorious morning this is!

Samuel Adams's comment to John Hancock at the Battle of Lexington, Massachusetts, April 19, 1775

The Sun never shined on a cause of greater worth.

Thomas Paine, *Common Sense*, 1776

Don't fire unless fired upon. But if they want a war let it begin here.

> Captain John Parker, commander of the militiamen
> at Lexington, Massachusetts, on sighting British troops, April 19, 1775

Objects of the most stupendous magnitude, and measure in which the lives and liberties of millions yet unborn are intimately interested, are now before us. We are in the very midst of a revolution the most complete, unexpected and remarkable of any in the history of nations.

> John Adams, letter to William Cushing, June 9, 1776

We have it in our power to begin the world over again.

> Thomas Paine, *Common Sense*, 1776

We know the Race is not to the swift nor the Battle to the Strong. Do you not think an Angel rides in the Whirlwind and directs this Storm?

> John Page, letter to Thomas Jefferson, July 20, 1776

We fight not to enslave, but to set a country free, and to make room upon the earth for honest men to live in.

> Thomas Paine, *The American Crisis* No. 4, September 11, 1777

Under all those disadvantages no men ever show more spirit or prudence than ours. In my opinion nothing but virtue has kept our army together through this campaign.

> Colonel John Brooks, letter written from Valley Forge, January 5, 1778

Our cause is noble; it is the cause of mankind!

> George Washington, letter to James Warren, March 31, 1779

It is yet to be decided, whether the Revolution must ultimately be considered as a blessing or a curse: a blessing or a curse, not to the present age alone, for with our fate will the destiny on unborn millions be involved.

> George Washington, Circular to the States, June 8, 1783

Mr. Adams Tells Mr. Jefferson to Write a Declaration of Independence

"You ask why so young a man as Mr. Jefferson was placed at the head of the Committee for preparing a Declaration of Independence? . . . Mr. Jefferson came into Congress, in June, 1775, and brought with him a reputation for literature, science, and a happy talent of composition. Writings of his were handed about, remarkable for the peculiar felicity of expression. Though a silent member in Congress, he was so prompt, frank, explicit, and decisive upon committees and in conversation, not even Samuel Adams was more so, that he soon seized upon my heart; and upon this occasion I gave him my vote, and did all in my power to procure the votes of others. I think he had one more vote than any other, and that placed him at the head of the committee. I had the next highest number, and that placed me the second. The committee met, discussed the subject, and then appointed Mr. Jefferson and me to make the draught, I suppose because we were the two first on the list.

The sub-committee met. Jefferson proposed to me to make the draught. I said, 'I will not.' 'You should do it.' 'Oh! No.' 'Why will you not? You ought to do it.' 'I will not.' 'Why?' 'Reasons enough.' 'What can be your reasons?' 'Reason first — You are a Virginian, and a Virginian ought to appear at the head of this business. Reason second — I am obnoxious, suspected, and unpopular. You are very much otherwise. Reason third — You can write ten times better than I can.' 'Very well.' 'When you have it drawn up, we will have a meeting.' "

John Adams, letter to Timothy Pickering, August 6, 1822

They accomplished a revolution which has no parallel in the annals of human society. They reared the fabrics of governments which have no model on the face of the globe. They formed the design of a great Confederacy, which it is incumbent on their successors to improve and perpetuate.

James Madison, Federalist No. 14, November 30, 1787

It seems to have been reserved to the people of this country, by their conduct and example, to decide the important question, whether societies of men are really capable or not of establishing good government from reflection and choice, or whether they are forever destined to depend for their political constitutions on accident and force.

Alexander Hamilton, Federalist No. 1, October 27, 1787

But what do we mean by the American Revolution? Do we mean the American war? The Revolution was effected before the war commenced. The Revolution was in the minds and hearts of the people; a change in their religious sentiments, of their duties and obligations....This radical change in the principles, opinions, sentiments, and affections of the people was the real American Revolution.

John Adams, letter to H. Niles, February 13, 1818

The foundation of our Empire was not laid in the gloomy age of Ignorance and Superstition, but at an Epocha when the rights of mankind were better understood and more clearly defined, than at any former period, the researches of the human mind, after social happiness, have been carried to a great extent, the Treasures of knowledge, acquired by the labours of Philosophers, Sages and Legislatures, through a long succession of years, are laid open for our use, and their collected wisdom may be happily applied in the Establishment of our forms of Government; the free cultivation of Letters, the unbounded extension of Commerce, the progressive refinement of Manners, the growing liberality of sentiment, and above all, the pure and benign light of Revelation, have had a meliorating influence on mankind and increased the blessings of Society. At this auspicious period, the United States came into existence as a Nation, and if their Citizens should not be completely free and happy, the fault will be entirely their own.

George Washington, Circular to the States, June 8, 1783

Arms

No freeman shall ever be debarred the use of arms.

Thomas Jefferson, Draft Constitution for Virginia, June 1776

Before a standing army can rule, the people must be disarmed; as they are in almost every kingdom of Europe. The supreme power in America cannot enforce unjust laws by the sword; because the whole body of the people are armed, and constitute a force superior to any band of regular troops that can be, on any pretence, raised in the United States.

Noah Webster, An Examination of the
Leading Principles of the Federal Constitution, October 10, 1787

To suppose arms in the hands of citizens, to be used at individual discretion, except in private self-defense, or by partial orders of towns, counties or districts of a state, is to demolish every constitution, and lay the laws prostrate, so that liberty can be enjoyed by no man; it is a dissolution of the government. The fundamental law of the militia is, that it be created, directed and commanded by the laws, and ever for the support of the laws.

John Adams, *A Defense of the Constitutions of Government
of the United States of America*, 1787-1788

Who are the militia? Are they not ourselves? It is feared, then, that we shall turn our arms each man against his own bosom. Congress have no power to disarm the militia. Their swords, and every other terrible implement of the soldier, are the birthright of an American...[T]he unlimited power of the sword is not in the hands of either the federal or state governments, but, where I trust in God it will ever remain, in the hands of the people.

A Pennsylvanian, *The Pennsylvania Gazette*, February 20, 1788

🍃 Budget

A penny saved is twopence clear.

Benjamin Franklin, Poor Richard's Almanack, 1737

He that goes a borrowing goes a sorrowing.

Benjamin Franklin, Poor Richard's Almanack, 1758

The principle of spending money to be paid by posterity, under the name of funding, is but swindling futurity on a large scale.

Thomas Jefferson, letter to John Taylor, May 28, 1816

The most productive system of finance will always be the least burdensome.

James Madison, Federalist No. 39, January 16, 1788

The same prudence which in private life would forbid our paying our own money for unexplained projects, forbids it in the dispensation of the public moneys.

Thomas Jefferson, letter to Shelton Gilliam, June 19, 1808

There is not a more important and fundamental principle in legislation, than that the ways and means ought always to face the public engagements; that our appropriations should ever go hand in hand with our promises.

James Madison, speech delivered in the House of Representatives, April 22, 1790

The multiplication of public offices, increase of expense beyond income, growth and entailment of a public debt, are indications soliciting the employment of the pruning knife.

Thomas Jefferson, letter to Spencer Roane, March 9, 1821

As on the one hand, the necessity for borrowing in particular emergencies cannot be doubted, so on the other, it is equally evident that to be able to borrow upon good terms, it is essential that the credit of a nation should be well established.

Alexander Hamilton, Report on Public Credit, January 9, 1790

 Bureaucracy

He has erected a multitude of New Offices, and sent hither swarms of Officers to harass our people, and eat out their substance.

The Declaration of Independence, July 4, 1776

I think we have more machinery of government than is necessary, too many parasites living on the labor of the industrious.

Thomas Jefferson, letter to William Ludlow, September 6, 1824

There are more instances of the abridgment of the freedom of the people by gradual and silent encroachments of those in power than by violent and sudden usurpations.

James Madison, speech to the Virginia Ratifying Convention, June 16, 1788

If we can prevent the government from wasting the labors of the people, under the pretence of taking care of them, they must become happy.

Thomas Jefferson, letter to Thomas Cooper, November 29, 1802

It will be of little avail to the people that the laws are made by men of their own choice, if the laws be so voluminous that they cannot be read, or so incoherent that they cannot be understood; if they be repealed or revised before they are promulgated, or undergo such incessant changes that no man who knows what the law is today can guess what it will be to-morrow.

James Madison, Federalist No. 62, February 27, 1788

Character

(*See also Religion and Morality, Virtue*)

The first transactions of a nation, like those of an individual upon his first entrance into life make the deepest impression, and are to form the leading traits in its character.

George Washington, letter to John Armstrong, April 25, 1788

Neither the wisest constitution nor the wisest laws will secure the liberty and happiness of a people whose manners are universally corrupt.

Samuel Adams, from an essay in *The Public Advertiser*, circa 1749

It is the manners and spirit of a people which preserve a republic in vigor. A degeneracy in these is a canker which soon eats to the heart of its laws and constitution.

Thomas Jefferson, *Notes on the State of Virginia*, Query XIX, 1787

Nothing is more essential to the establishment of manners in a State than that all persons employed in places of power and trust must be men of unexceptionable characters. The public cannot be too curious concerning the characters of public men.

Samuel Adams, letter to James Warren, November 4, 1775

In selecting men for office, let principle be your guide. Regard not the particular sect or denomination of the candidate — look to his character.

Noah Webster, Letters to a Young Gentleman Commencing His Education, 1789

Your love of liberty — your respect for the laws — your habits of industry — and your practice of the moral and religious obliga-tions, are the strongest claims to national and individual happiness.

George Washington, letter to the Residents of Boston, October 27, 1789

Nothing is more certain than that a general profligacy and corrup-tion of manners make a people ripe for destruction. A good form of government may hold the rotten materials together for some time, but beyond a certain pitch, even the best constitution will be ineffectual, and slavery must ensue.

John Witherspoon, The Dominion of Providence Over the Passions of Men, 1776

A good moral character is the first essential in a man, and that the habits contracted at your age are generally indelible, and your con-duct here may stamp your character though life. It is therefore highly important that you should endeavor not only to be learned but virtuous.

George Washington, letter to George Steptoe Washington, December 5, 1790

Charity

(See also Poverty)

Let your heart feel for the afflictions and distresses of everyone, and let your hand give in proportion to your purse, remembering … that it is not everyone who asketh that deserveth charity.

George Washington, letter to Bushrod Washington, January 15, 1783

I deem it the duty of every man to devote a certain proportion of his income for charitable purposes…. However disposed the mind may feel to unlimited good, our means having limits, we are necessarily circumscribed by them.

Thomas Jefferson, letter to Drs. Rogers and Slaughter, March 2, 1806

The government of the United States is a definite government, confined to specified objects. It is not like the state governments, whose powers are more general. Charity is no part of the legislative duty of the government.

James Madison, speech delivered in the House of Representatives, January 10, 1794

It is a duty certainly to give our sparings to those who want; but to see also that they are faithfully distributed, and duly apportioned to the respective wants of those receivers. And why give through agents whom we know not, to persons whom we know not, and in countries from which we get no account, where we can do it at short hand, to objects under our eye, through agents we know, and to supply wants we see?

Thomas Jefferson, letter to Michael Megear, May 29, 1823

Citizenship

Citizens by birth or choice of a common country, that country has a right to concentrate your affections.

George Washington, Farewell Address, September 19, 1796

When we assumed the Soldier, we did not lay aside the Citizen; and we shall most sincerely rejoice with you in the happy hour when the establishment of American Liberty, upon the most firm and solid foundations shall enable us to return to our Private Stations in the bosom of a free, peacefully and happy Country.

George Washington, address to the New York Legislature, June 26, 1775

Let each citizen remember at the moment he is offering his vote that he is not making a present or a compliment to please an individual — or at least that he ought not so to do; but that he is executing one of the most solemn trusts in human society for which he is accountable to God and his country.

Samuel Adams, in the *Boston Gazette*, April 16, 1781

All possess alike liberty of conscience, and immunities of citizenship. It is now no more that toleration is spoken of, as if it was by the indulgence of one class of people, that another enjoyed the exercise of their inherent natural rights, for, happily, the Government of the United States, which gives to bigotry no sanction, to persecution no assistance, requires only that they who live under its protection should demean themselves as good citizens in giving it on all occasions their effectual support.

George Washington, letter to the Hebrew Congregation of Newport, Rhode Island, September 9, 1790

❦ Commerce

No nation was ever ruined by trade, even seemingly the most disadvantageous.

Benjamin Franklin, *Principles of Trade*, 1774

I think all the world would gain by setting commerce at perfect liberty.

Thomas Jefferson, letter to John Adams, July 7, 1785

A people ... who are possessed of the spirit of commerce, who see and who will pursue their advantages may achieve almost anything.

George Washington, letter to Benjamin Harrison, October 10, 1784

Industry is increased, commodities are multiplied, agriculture and manufacturers flourish: and herein consists the true wealth and prosperity of a state.

Alexander Hamilton, *Report on a National Bank,* December 13, 1790

War is not the best engine for us to resort to; nature has given us one in our commerce, which if properly managed, will be a better instrument for obliging the interested nations of Europe to treat us with justice.

Thomas Jefferson, letter to Thomas Pickney, May 29, 1797

Measures which serve to abridge the free competition of foreign Articles, have a tendency to occasion an enhancement of prices.

Alexander Hamilton, *Report on Manufactures,* December 5, 1791

It should be our endeavor to cultivate the peace and friendship of every nation.... Our interest will be to throw open the doors of commerce, and to knock off all its shackles, giving perfect freedom to all persons for the vent to whatever they may choose to bring into our ports, and asking the same in theirs.

Thomas Jefferson, *Notes on the State of Virginia,* Query XXII, 1787

I own myself the friend to a very free system of commerce, and hold it as a truth, that commercial shackles are generally unjust, oppressive and impolitic — it is also a truth, that if industry and labour are left to take their own course, they will generally be directed to those objects which are the most productive, and this in a more certain and direct manner than the wisdom of the most enlightened legislature could point out.

James Madison, speech to the Congress, April 9, 1789

Harmony, liberal intercourse with all Nations, are recommended by policy, humanity and interest. But even our Commercial policy should hold an equal and impartial hand: neither seeking nor granting exclusive favours or preferences; consulting the natural course of things; diffusing and diversifying by gentle means the streams of Commerce, but forcing nothing; establishing with Powers so disposed; in order to give trade a stable course.

George Washington, Farewell Address, September 19, 1796

Congress/Legislature

(See also House of Representatives, Senate)

One hundred and seventy-three despots would surely be as oppressive as one.

James Madison, Federalist No. 48, February 1, 1788

Had every Athenian citizen been a Socrates, every Athenian assembly would still have been a mob.

James Madison, Federalist No. 55, February 15, 1788

The legislative department is everywhere extending the sphere of its activity and drawing all power into its impetuous vortex.

James Madison, Federalist No. 48, February 1, 1788

It would reduce the whole instrument to a single phrase, that of instituting a Congress with power to do whatever would be for the good of the United States; and, as they would be the sole judges of the good or evil, it would be also a power to do whatever evil they please.

Thomas Jefferson, Opinion on the Constitutionality of a National Bank, February 15, 1791

If Congress can do whatever in their discretion can be done by money, and will promote the General Welfare, the Government is no longer a limited one, possessing enumerated powers, but an indefinite one, subject to particular exceptions.

James Madison, letter to Edmund Pendleton, January 21, 1792

The members of the legislative department ... are numerous. They are distributed and dwell among the people at large. Their connections of blood, of friendship, and of acquaintance embrace a great proportion of the most influential part of the society ... they are more immediately the confidential guardians of their rights and liberties.

James Madison, Federalist No. 50, February 5, 1788

Constitution

The Constitution is the guide which I never will abandon.

George Washington, letter to the Boston Selectmen, July 28, 1795

It is impossible for the man of pious reflection not to perceive in it [the Constitution] a finger of that Almighty hand which has been so frequently and signally extended to our relief in the critical stages of the revolution.

James Madison, Federalist No. 37, January 11, 1788

In questions of power, then, let no more be heard of confidence in man, but bind him down from mischief by the chains of the Constitution.

Thomas Jefferson, fair copy of the drafts of the Kentucky Resolutions of 1798

In the formation of our constitution the wisdom of all ages is collected — the legislators of antiquity are consulted, as well as the opinions and interests of the millions who are concerned. It short, it is an empire of reason.

Noah Webster, An Examination into the Leading Principles of the Federal Constitution, 1787

The basis of our political systems is the right of the people to make and to alter their Constitutions of Government. But the Constitution which at any time exists, 'till changed by an explicit and authentic act of the whole People is sacredly obligatory upon all.

George Washington, Farewell Address, September 19, 1796

If it be asked, What is the most sacred duty and the greatest source of our security in a Republic? The answer would be, An inviolable respect for the Constitution and Laws — the first growing out of the last.... A sacred respect for the constitutional law is the vital principle, the sustaining energy of a free government.

Alexander Hamilton, essay in *The American Daily Advertiser*, August 28, 1794

The Case of the Lost Papers

"When the Convention first opened at Philadelphia, there were a number of propositions brought forward as great leading principles for the new Government to be established for the United States. A copy of these propositions was given to each Member with the injunction to keep everything a profound secret. One morning, by accident, one of the Members dropt his copy of the propositions, which being luckily picked up by General Mifflin was presented to General Washington, our President, who put it in his pocket. After the debates of the Day were over, and the question for adjournment was called for, the General arose from his seat, and previous to his putting the question addressed the Convention in the following manner:

> Gentlemen —
> I am sorry to find that some one Member of this Body, has been so neglectful of the secrets of the Convention as to drop in the State House a copy of their proceedings, which by accident was picked up and delivered to me this Morning. I must entreat Gentlemen to be more careful, least our transactions get into the News Papers, and disturb the public repose by premature speculations. I know not whose Paper it is, but there it is (throwing it down on the table), let him who owns it take it.

At the same time he bowed, picked up his Hat, and quitted the room with a dignity so severe that every Person seemed alarmed; for my part I was extremely so, for putting my hand in my pocket I missed my copy of the same Paper, but advancing up to the Table my fears soon dissipated; I found it to be the hand writing of another Person. When I went to my lodgings at the Indian Queen, I found my copy in a coat pocket which I had pulled off that Morning. It is something remarkable that no Person ever owned the Paper. "

William Pierce, Constitutional Convention delegate from Georgia, anecdote recorded in *Farrand's Records of the Federal Convention of 1787*

A constitution founded on these principles introduces knowledge among the people, and inspires them with a conscious dignity becoming freemen; a general emulation takes place, which causes good humor, sociability, good manners, and good morals to be general. That elevation of sentiment inspired by such a government, makes the common people brave and enterprising. That ambition which is inspired by it makes them sober, industrious, and frugal.

John Adams, Thoughts on Government, 1776

I join cordially in admiring and revering the Constitution of the United States, the result of the collected wisdom of our country. That wisdom has committed to us the important task of proving by example that a government, if organized in all its parts on the Representative principle unadulterated by the infusion of spurious elements, if founded, not in the fears & follies of man, but on his reason, on his sense of right, on the predominance of the social over his dissocial passions, may be so free as to restrain him in no moral right, and so firm as to protect him from every moral wrong.

Thomas Jefferson, letter to Amos Marsh, November 20, 1801

The blessed Religion revealed in the word of God will remain an eternal and awful monument to prove that the best Institution may be abused by human depravity; and that they may even, in some instances be made subservient to the vilest purposes. Should, hereafter, those incited by the lust of power and prompted by the Supineness or venality of their Constituents, overleap the known barriers of this Constitution and violate the unalienable rights of humanity: it will only serve to shew, that no compact among men (however provident in its construction and sacred in its ratification) can be pronounced everlasting an inviolable, and if I may so express myself, that no Wall of words, that no mound of parchm[en]t can be so formed as to stand against the sweeping torrent of boundless ambition on the one side, aided by the sapping current of corrupted morals on the other.

George Washington, fragments of the Draft First Inaugural Address, April 1789

❦ Constitutional Convention

It appears to me, then, little short of a miracle, that the Delegates from so many different States ... should unite in forming a system of national Government, so little liable to well founded objections.

George Washington, letter to Marquis de Lafayette, February 7, 1788

There never was an assembly of men, charged with a great and arduous trust, who were more pure in their motives, or more exclusively or anxiously devoted to the object committed to them.

James Madison, in a "sketch never finished," circa 1835

I have lived, Sir, a long time; and the longer I live, the more convincing proofs I see of this Truth, that God governs in the Affairs of Men. And if a Sparrow cannot fall to the Ground without his Notice, is it probable that an Empire can rise without his Aid?

Benjamin Franklin, motion for Prayers in the Constitutional Convention, June 28, 1787

You give me a credit to which I have no claim in calling me "the writer of the Constitution of the United States." This was not, like the fabled Goddess of Wisdom, the offspring of a single brain. It ought to be regarded as the work of many heads and many hands.

James Madison, letter to William Cogswell, March 10, 1834

The deliberate union of so great and various a people in such a place, is without all partiality or prejudice, if not the greatest exertion of human understanding, the greatest single effort of national deliberation that the world has ever seen.

John Adams quoted in a letter from Rufus King to Theophilus Parsons, February 20, 1788

The example of changing a constitution by assembling the wise men of the state, instead of assembling armies, will be worth as much to the world as the former examples we had given them. The constitution, too, which was the result of our deliberation, is unquestionably the wisest ever yet presented to men.

Thomas Jefferson, letter to David Humphreys, March 18, 1789

It is too probable that no plan we propose will be adopted. Perhaps another dreadful conflict is to be sustained. If, to please the people, we offer what we ourselves disprove, how can we afterwards defend our work? Let us raise a standard to which the wise and the honest can repair. The event is in the hand of God.

George Washington, as quoted by Gouverneur Morris, recorded in
Farrand's Records of the Federal Convention of 1787, March 25, 1787

Whilst the last members were signing it Doctr. Franklin looking towards the Presidents Chair, at the back of which a rising sun happened to be painted, observed to a few members near him, that Painters had found it difficult to distinguish in their art a rising from a setting sun. "I have," said he, "often and often in the course of the Session, and the vicissitudes of my hopes and fears as to its issue, looked at that behind the President without being able to tell whether it was rising or setting: But now at length I have the happiness to know that it is a rising and not a setting Sun."

James Madison, *Farrand's Records of the
Federal Convention of 1787*, September 17, 1787

'Tis done. We have become a nation.

Benjamin Rush on the ratification of the Constitution,
letter to Boudinot, July 9, 1788

❧ Constitutional Interpretation

Our peculiar security is in the possession of a written Constitution. Let us not make it a blank paper by construction.

Thomas Jefferson, letter to Wilson Nicholas, September 7, 1803

The first and governing maxim in the interpretation of a statute is to discover the meaning of those who made it.

James Wilson, Of the Study of Law in the United States, circa 1790

The Constitution ought to be the standard of construction for the laws, and that wherever there is an evident opposition, the laws ought to give place to the Constitution. But this doctrine is not deducible from any circumstance peculiar to the plan of convention, but from the general theory of a limited Constitution.

Alexander Hamilton, Federalist No. 81, May 28, 1788

On every question of construction carry ourselves back to the time when the Constitution was adopted, recollect the spirit manifested in the debates and instead of trying what meaning may be squeezed out of the text, or invented against it, conform to the probable one in which it was passed.

Thomas Jefferson, letter to William Johnson, June 12, 1823

I entirely concur in the propriety of resorting to the sense in which the Constitution was accepted and ratified by the nation. . . . If the meaning of the text be sought in the changeable meaning of the words composing it, it is evident that the shape and attributes of the Government must partake of the changes to which the words and phrases of all living languages are constantly subject. What a metamorphosis would be produced in the code of law if all its ancient phraseology were to be taken in its modern sense.

James Madison, letter to Henry Lee, June 25, 1824

It is an established rule of construction, where a phrase will bear either of two meanings to give it that which will allow some meaning to the other parts of the instrument, and not that which will render all the others useless. Certainly no such universal power was meant to be given to them. [The Constitution] was intended to lace them up straightly within the enumerated powers, and those without which, as means, these powers could not be carried into effect.

Thomas Jefferson, Opinion on the Constitutionality of a National Bank, February 15, 1791

 Courage

I have not yet begun to fight!

Captain John Paul Jones's response to the enemies' demand to surrender, September 23, 1779

The battle, sir, is not to the strong alone; it is to the vigilant, the active, the brave.

Patrick Henry, speech to the Virginia Convention, March 23, 1775

These are the times that try men's souls. The summer soldier and the sunshine patriot will, in this crisis, shrink from the service of his country; but he that stands it now, deserves the love and thanks of man and woman.

Thomas Paine, The American Crisis No. 1, December 19, 1776

I have no notion of being hanged for half treason. When a subject draws his sword against his prince, he must cut his way through, if he means afterward to sit down in safety.

Colonel Joseph Reed to Mr. Pettit, September 29, 1775
(Reed was an aide-de-camp to General Washington)

Is life so dear or peace so sweet as to be purchased at the price of chains and slavery? Forbid it, Almighty God. I know not what course others may take, but as for me, give me liberty or give me death!

Patrick Henry, speech to the Virginia Convention, March 23, 1775

There is a time for all things, a time to preach and a time to pray, but those times have passed away. There is a time to fight, and that time has now come.

Rev. Peter Muhlenberg, sermon delivered at Woodstock, VA, January, 1776

'Tis the business of little minds to shrink; but he whose heart is firm, and whose conscience approves his conduct, will pursue his principles unto death.

Thomas Paine, The American Crisis No. 1, December 19, 1776

We have therefore to resolve to conquer or die: Our Country's own Honor, all call upon us for vigorous and manly exertion, and if we now shamefully fail, we shall become infamous to the whole world. Let us therefore rely upon the goodness of the Cause, and the aid of the supreme Being, in whose hands Victory is, to animate and encourage us to great and noble Actions.

George Washington, General Orders, July 2, 1776

Declaration of Independence

Everything that is right or reasonable pleads for separation. The blood of the slain, the weeping voice of nature cries, 'tis time to part.

Thomas Paine, Common Sense, January 9, 1776

We are confirmed in the opinion, that the present age would be deficient in their duty to God, their posterity and themselves, if they do not establish an American republic. This is the only form of government we wish to see established; for we can never be willingly subject to any other King than He who, being possessed of infinite wisdom, goodness and rectitude, is alone fit to possess unlimited power.

Instructions of Malden, Massachusetts, for a declaration of
independence, May 27, 1776

Resolved: That these colonies are, and of right ought to be, free and independent states, that they are absolved of all allegiance to the British Crown, and that all political connection between them and the state of Great Britain is, and ought to be, totally dissolved. That it is expedient forthwith to take the most effectual measures for forming foreign Alliances. That a plan of confederation be prepared and transmitted to the respective colonies for their consideration and approbation.

Richard Henry Lee, Resolution in Congress, June 7, 1776

In my judgement it is not only ripe for the measure, but in danger of becoming rotten for the want of it.

John Witherspoon, debate in Congress on the Declaration, July, 1776

It ought to be commemorated, as the Day of Deliverance by solemn Acts of Devotion to God Almighty. It ought to be solemnized with Pomp and Parade, with Shews, Games, Sports, guns, Bells, Bonfires and Illuminations from one End of this Continent to the other from this Time forward forever more. You will think me transported with Enthusiasm but I am not. I am well aware of the Toil and Blood and Treasure, that it will cost Us to maintain this Declaration, and support and defend these States. Yet through all the Gloom I can see the Rays of ravishing Light and Glory. I can see that the End is more than worth all the Means. And that Posterity will tryumph in that Days Transaction, even altho We should rue it, which I trust in God We shall not.

John Adams, letter to Abigail Adams, July 3, 1776

There! His Majesty can now read my name without glasses. And he can double the reward on my head!

John Hancock (attributed), upon signing the Declaration of Independence, July 4, 1776

We must all hang together, or assuredly we shall all hang separately.

Benjamin Franklin (attributed) at the signing of the Declaration of Independence, July 4, 1776

My hand trembles, but my heart does not.

Rhode Island Delegate Stephen Hopkins (attributed), at the signing of the Declaration of Independence, July 4, 1776

The Declaration of Independence ... [is the] declaratory charter of our rights, and the rights of man.

Thomas Jefferson, letter to Samuel Adams Wells, May 12, 1819

The flames kindled on the 4th of July 1776, have spread over too much of the globe to be extinguished by the feeble engines of despotism; on the contrary, they will consume these engines and all who work them.

Thomas Jefferson, letter to John Adams, September 12, 1821

On the distinctive principles of the Government of our own state, and that of the U. States, the best guides are to be found in ... The Declaration of Independence, as the fundamental Act of Union of these States.

James Madison, letter to Thomas Jefferson, February 8, 1825

This was the object of the Declaration of Independence. Not to find out new principles, or new arguments, never before thought of, not merely to say things which had never been said before; but to place before mankind the common sense of the subject, in terms so plain and firm as to command their assent, and to justify our-selves in the independent stand we are compelled to take. Neither aiming at originality of principle or sentiment, nor yet copied from any particular and previous writing, it was intended to be an expression of the American mind, and to give to that expression the proper tone and spirit called for by the occasion.

Thomas Jefferson, letter to Henry Lee, May 8, 1825

Independence forever.

John Adams's toast for the celebration of the fiftieth anniversary
of the Declaration of Independence, July 4, 1826

❦ Democracy

(See also Republican Government)

The known propensity of a democracy is to licentiousness which the ambitious call, and ignorant believe to be liberty.

Fisher Ames, speech at the Massachusetts Ratifying Convention, January 15, 1788

Remember democracy never lasts long. It soon wastes, exhausts, and murders itself. There never was a democracy yet that did not commit suicide.

John Adams, letter to John Taylor, April 15, 1814

Democracies have ever been spectacles of turbulence and con-tention; have ever been found incompatible with personal security, or the rights of property; and have, in general, been as short in their lives as they have been violent in their deaths.

James Madison, Federalist No. 10, November 23, 1787

Democracy will soon degenerate into an anarchy, such an anarchy that every man will do what is right in his own eyes and no man's life or property or reputation or liberty will be secure, and every one of these will soon mould itself into a system of subordination of all the moral virtues and intellectual abilities, all the powers of wealth, beauty, wit and science, to the wanton pleasures, the capri-cious will, and the execrable cruelty of one or a very few.

John Adams, An Essay on Man's Lust for Power, August 29, 1763

Education

Knowledge is power.

> Thomas Jefferson, letter to Joseph C. Cabel, January 22, 1820

Knowledge is, in every country, the surest basis of public happiness.

> George Washington, First Annual Message, January 8, 1790

A fine genius in his own country is like gold in the mine.

> Benjamin Franklin, *Poor Richard's Almanack*, 1733

Children should be educated and instructed in the principles of freedom.

> John Adams, A Defense of the Constitutions of Government of
> the United States of America, 1787

If a nation expects to be ignorant — and free — in a state of civilization, it expects what never was and never will be.

> Thomas Jefferson, letter to Colonel Charles Yancey, January 6, 1816

What spectacle can be more edifying or more seasonable, than that of Liberty and Learning, each leaning on the other for their mutual & surest support?

> James Madison, letter to W.T. Barry, August 4, 1822

Enlighten the people, generally, and tyranny and oppressions of body and mind will vanish like spirits at the dawn of day.

> Thomas Jefferson, letter to Dupont de Nemours, April 24, 1816

Law and liberty cannot rationally become the objects of our love, unless they first become the objects of our knowledge.

> James Wilson, Of the Study of the Law in the United States, circa 1790

The best service that can be rendered to a Country, next to that of giving it liberty, is in diffusing the mental improvement equally essential to the preservation, and the enjoyment of the blessing.

> James Madison, letter to Littleton Dennis Teackle, March 29, 1826

The best means of forming a manly, virtuous, and happy people will be found in the right education of youth. Without this foundation, every other means, in my opinion, must fail.

George Washington, letter to George Chapman, December 15, 1784

Religion, morality and knowledge being necessary to good government and the happiness of mankind, schools and the means of education shall forever be encouraged.

The Northwest Ordinance, July 23, 1787

No one more sincerely wishes the spread of information among mankind than I do, and none has greater confidence in its effect towards supporting free and good government.

Thomas Jefferson, letter to Trustees for the Lottery of East Tennessee College, May 6, 1810

No people will tamely surrender their Liberties, nor can any be easily subdued, when knowledge is diffusd and Virtue is preservd. On the Contrary, when People are universally ignorant, and debauchd in their Manners, they will sink under their own weight without the Aid of foreign Invaders.

Samuel Adams, letter to James Warren, November 4, 1775

Promote then as an object of primary importance, Institutions for the general diffusion of knowledge. In proportion as the structure of a government gives force to public opinion, it is essential that public opinion should be enlightened.

George Washington, Farewell Address, September 19, 1796

A popular Government, without popular information, or the means of acquiring it, is but a Prologue to a Farce or a Tragedy; or, perhaps both. Knowledge will forever govern ignorance: And a people who mean to be their own Governors, must arm themselves with the power which knowledge gives.

James Madison, letter to W.T. Barry, August 4, 1822

It is an object of vast magnitude that systems of education should be adopted and pursued which may not only diffuse a knowledge of the sciences but may implant in the minds of the American youth the principles of virtue and of liberty and inspire them with just and liberal ideas of government and with an inviolable attachment to their own country.

Noah Webster, On the Education of Youth in America, 1790

It should be your care, therefore, and mine, to elevate the minds of our children and exalt their courage; to accelerate and animate their industry and activity; to excite in them an habitual contempt of meanness, abhorrence of injustice and inhumanity, and an ambition to excel in every capacity, faculty, and virtue. If we suffer their minds to grovel and creep in infancy, they will grovel all their lives.

John Adams, *Dissertation on the Canon and Feudal Law*, 1765

❧ Equality

We hold these truths to be self-evident, that all men are created equal....

The Declaration of Independence, July 4, 1776

Equal laws protecting equal rights [are] the best guarantee of loyalty and love of country.

James Madison, letter to Jacob de la Motta, August 1820

The foundation on which all [constitutions] are built is the natural equality of man, the denial of every preeminence but that annexed to legal office, and particularly the denial of a preeminence by birth.

Thomas Jefferson, letter to George Washington, April 16, 1784

The dons, the bashaws, the grandees, the patricians, the sachems, the nabobs, call them by what names you please, sigh and groan and fret, and sometimes stamp and foam and curse, but all in vain. The decree is gone forth, and it cannot be recalled, that a more equal liberty than has prevailed in other parts of the earth must be established in America.

John Adams, letter to Patrick Henry, June 3, 1776

I rejoice in a belief that intellectual light will spring up in the dark corners of the earth; that freedom of enquiry will produce liberality of conduct; that mankind will reverse the absurd position that the many were made for the few; and that they will not continue slaves in one part of the globe, when they can become freemen in another.

George Washington, Fragments of the Draft First Inaugural
Address, April 1789

Family

(See also Marriage)

The happiest moments of my life have been the few which I have past at home in the bosom of my family.

Thomas Jefferson, letter to Francis Willis Jr., April 18, 1790

I hope some future day will bring me the happiness of seeing my family again collected under our own roof, happy in ourselves and blessed in each other.

Abigail Adams, letter to John Adams, March 15, 1784

Religion in a Family is at once its brightest Ornament & its best Security.

Samuel Adams, letter to Thomas Wells, November 22, 1780

The foundation of national morality must be laid in private families. . . . How is it possible that Children can have any just Sense of the sacred Obligations of Morality or Religion if, from their earliest Infancy, they learn their Mothers live in habitual Infidelity to their fathers, and their fathers in as constant Infidelity to their Mothers?

John Adams, diary, June 2, 1778

The importance of piety and religion; of industry and frugality; of prudence, economy, regularity and an even government; all . . . are essential to the well-being of a family.

Samuel Adams, letter to Thomas Wells, November 22, 1780

What is it that affectionate parents require of their Children; for all their care, anxiety, and toil on their accounts? Only that they would be wise and virtuous, Benevolent and kind.

Abigail Adams, letter to John Quincy Adams, November 20, 1783

It is the duty of parents to maintain their children decently, and according to their circumstances; to protect them according to the dictates of prudence; and to educate them according to the suggestions of a judicious and zealous regard for their usefulness, their respectability and happiness.

James Wilson, Lectures on Law, 1791

As long as Property exists, it will accumulate in Individuals and Families. As long as Marriage exists, Knowledge, Property and Influence will accumulate in Families.

John Adams, letter to Thomas Jefferson, July 16, 1814

The Federal Government

Were we directed from Washington when to sow, and when to reap, we should soon want bread.

Thomas Jefferson, *Autobiography*, 1821

The general government is not to be charged with the whole power of making and administering laws: its jurisdiction is limited to certain enumerated objects, which concern all the members of the republic, but which are not to be attained by the separate provisions of any.

James Madison, Federalist No. 14, November 30, 1787

When all government, domestic and foreign, in little as in great things, shall be drawn to Washington as the center of all power, it will render powerless the checks provided of one government on another.

Thomas Jefferson, letter to Charles Hammond, August 18, 1821

The great leading objects of the federal government, in which revenue is concerned, are to maintain domestic peace, and provide for the common defense. In these are comprehended the regulation of commerce that is, the whole system of foreign intercourse; the support of armies and navies, and of the civil administration.

Alexander Hamilton, remark made at the New York
Ratifying Convention, June 27, 1788

 # Federalism

The powers delegated by the proposed Constitution to the federal government are few and defined. Those which are to remain in the State governments are numerous and indefinite.

James Madison, Federalist No. 45, January 26, 1788

The State governments possess inherent advantages, which will ever give them an influence and ascendancy over the National Government, and will for ever preclude the possibility of federal encroachments. That their liberties, indeed, can be subverted by the federal head, is repugnant to every rule of political calculation.

Alexander Hamilton, speech delivered at the New York
Ratifying Convention, June 20, 1788

The States can best govern our home concerns and the general government our foreign ones. I wish, therefore ... never to see all offices transferred to Washington, where, further withdrawn from the eyes of the people, they may more secretly be bought and sold at market.

Thomas Jefferson, letter to Judge William Johnson, June 12, 1823

While the constitution continues to be read, and its principles known, the states must, by every rational man, be considered as essential component parts of the union; and therefore the idea of sacrificing the former to the latter is totally inadmissible.

Alexander Hamilton, speech at the New York Ratifying Convention, June 24, 1788

I consider the foundation of the Constitution as laid on this ground that 'all powers not delegated to the United States, by the Constitution, nor prohibited by it to the states, are reserved to the states or to the people.' To take a single step beyond the boundaries thus specially drawn around the powers of Congress, is to take possession of a boundless field of power, not longer susceptible of any definition.

Thomas Jefferson, Opinion on the Constitutionality of a
National Bank, February 15, 1791

This balance between the National and State governments ought to be dwelt on with peculiar attention, as it is of the utmost importance. It forms a double security to the people. If one encroaches on their rights they will find a powerful protection in the other. Indeed, they will both be prevented from overpassing their constitutional limits by a certain rivalship, which will ever subsist between them.

Alexander Hamilton, speech at the New York Ratifying Convention, June 21, 1788

God

God alone is the judge of the hearts of men.

George Washington, letter to Benedict Arnold, September 14, 1775

It is the duty of all Nations to acknowledge the providence of Almighty God, to obey his will, to be grateful for his benefits, and humbly to implore his protection and favors.

George Washington, Thanksgiving Proclamation, October 3, 1789

A State, I cheerfully admit, is the noblest work of Man: But Man, himself, free and honest, is, I speak as to this world, the noblest work of God....

James Wilson, *Chisholm v. Georgia*, February 18, 1793

May the father of all mercies scatter light, and not darkness, upon our paths, and make us in all our several vocations useful here, and in His own due time and way everlastingly happy.

George Washington, letter to the Hebrew Congregation of
Newport, Rhode Island, August 17, 1790

The belief in a God All Powerful wise and good, is so essential to the moral order of the world and to the happiness of man, that arguments which enforce it cannot be drawn from too many sources nor adapted with too much solicitude to the different characters and capacities impressed with it.

James Madison, letter to Frederick Beasley, November 20, 1825

And can the liberties of a nation be thought secure when we have removed their only firm basis, a conviction in the minds of the people that these liberties are the gift of God? That they are not to be violated but with his wrath? Indeed I tremble for my country when I reflect that God is just: that his justice cannot sleep for ever.

Thomas Jefferson, *Notes on the State of Virginia*, Query XVIII, 1781

It is the duty of every man to render to the Creator such homage, and such only, as he believes to be acceptable to him. This duty is precedent both in order of time and degree of obligation, to the claims of Civil Society. Before any man can be considered as a member of Civil Society, he must be considered as a subject of the Governor of the Universe.

James Madison, A Memorial and Remonstrance, circa June 20, 1785

I now make it my earnest prayer, that God would have you, and the State over which you preside, in his holy protection, that he would incline the hearts of the Citizens to cultivate a spirit of subordination and obedience to Government, to entertain a brotherly affection and love for one another, for their fellow Citizens of the United States at large, and particularly for their brethren who have served in the Field, and finally, that he would most graciously be pleased to dispose us all, to do Justice, to love mercy, and to demean ourselves with that Charity, humility and pacific temper of mind, which were the Characteristicks of the Divine Author of our blessed Religion, and without an humble imitation of whose example in these things, we can never hope to be a happy Nation.

George Washington, Circular to the States, June 8, 1783

Government

The natural progress of things is for liberty to yield and government to gain ground.

> Thomas Jefferson, letter to E. Carrington, May 27, 1788

To form a new Government, requires infinite care, and unbounded attention; for if the foundation is badly laid the superstructure must be bad.

> George Washington, letter to John Augustine Washington, May 31, 1776

The care of human life and happiness, and not their destruction, is the first and only legitimate object of good government.

> Thomas Jefferson, letter to the Republican Citizens of Washington County, Maryland, March 31, 1809

The diversity in the faculties of men from which the rights of property originate, is not less an insuperable obstacle to a uniformity of interests. The protection of these faculties is the first object of government.

> James Madison, Federalist No. 10, November 23, 1787

If mankind were to resolve to agree in no institution of government, until every part of it had been adjusted to the most exact standard of perfection, society would soon become a general scene of anarchy, and the world a desert.

> Alexander Hamilton, Federalist No. 65, March 7, 1788

A wise and frugal government ... shall restrain men from injuring one another, shall leave them otherwise free to regulate their own pursuits of industry and improvement, and shall not take from the mouth of labor the bread it has earned. This is the sum of good government.

> Thomas Jefferson, First Inaugural Address, March 4, 1801

It has been said that all Government is an evil. It would be more proper to say that the necessity of any Government is a misfortune. This necessity however exists; and the problem to be solved is, not what form of Government is perfect, but which of the forms is least imperfect.

James Madison, letter to an unidentified correspondent, 1833

The spirit of resistance to government is so valuable on certain occasions, that I wish it to be always kept alive. It will often be exercised when wrong, but better so than not to be exercised at all. I like a little rebellion now and then. It is like a storm in the atmosphere.

Thomas Jefferson, letter to Abigail Adams, February 22, 1787

How prone all human institutions have been to decay; how subject the best-formed and most wisely organized governments have been to lose their check and totally dissolve; how difficult it has been for mankind, in all ages and countries, to preserve their dearest rights and best privileges, impelled as it were by an irresistible fate of despotism.

James Monroe, speech at the Virginia Ratifying Convention, June 10, 1788

If men were angels, no government would be necessary. If angels were to govern men, neither external nor internal controls on government would be necessary. In framing a government which is to be administered by men over men, the great difficulty lies in this: you must first enable the government to control the governed; and in the next place, oblige it to control itself.

James Madison, Federalist No. 51, February 8, 1788

Society in every state is a blessing, but government, even in its best state, is but a necessary evil; in its worst state an intolerable one; for when we suffer or are exposed to the same miseries by a government, which we might expect in a country without government, our calamity is heightened by reflecting that we furnish the means by which we suffer.

Thomas Paine, *Common Sense*, 1776

Energy in government is essential to that security against external and internal danger and to that prompt and salutary execution of the laws which enter into the very definition of good government. Stability in government is essential to national character and to the advantages annexed to it, as well as to that repose and confidence in the minds of the people, which are among the chief blessings of civil society.

James Madison, Federalist No. 37, January 11, 1788

History

A morsel of genuine history is a thing so rare as to be always valuable.

Thomas Jefferson, letter to John Adams, September 8, 1817

It is the duty of every good citizen to use all the opportunities which occur to him, for preserving documents relating to the history our country.

Thomas Jefferson, letter to Hugh P. Taylor, October 4, 1823

Every child in America should be acquainted with his own country. He should read books that furnish him with ideas that will be useful to him in life and practice. As soon as he opens his lips, he should rehearse the history of his own country.

Noah Webster, On the Education of Youth in America, 1788

History by apprising [citizens] of the past will enable them to judge of the future; it will avail them of the experience of other times and other nations; it will qualify them as judges of the actions and designs of men; it will enable them to know ambition under every disguise it may assume; and knowing it, to defeat its views.

Thomas Jefferson, Notes on the State of Virginia, Query XIV, 1787

Without wishing to damp the ardor of curiosity or influence the freedom of inquiry, I will hazard a prediction that, after the most industrious and impartial researchers, the longest liver of you all will find no principles, institutions or systems of education more fit in general to be transmitted to your posterity than those you have received from your ancestors.

John Adams, letter to the young men of Philadelphia, May 7, 1798

❦ House of Representatives

(See also Congress/Legislature, Senate)

We are not to consider ourselves, while here, as at church or school, to listen to the harangues of speculative piety; we are here to talk of the political interests committed to our charge.

Fisher Ames, speech before the House of Representatives, April 8, 1789

Such will be the relation between the House of Representatives and their constituents. Duty, gratitude, interest, ambition itself, are the cords by which they will be bound to fidelity and sympathy with the great mass of the people.

James Madison, Federalist No. 57, February 19, 1788

If the present Congress errs in too much talking, how can it be otherwise in a body to which the people send 150 lawyers, whose trade it is to question everything, yield nothing, & talk by the hour? That 150 lawyers should do business together ought not to be expected.

Thomas Jefferson, *Autobiography*, 1821

If it be asked what is to restrain the House of Representatives from making legal discriminations in favor of themselves and a particular class of the society? I answer, the genius of the whole system, the nature of just and constitutional laws, and above all the vigilant and manly spirit which actuates the people of America, a spirit which nourishes freedom, and in return is nourished by it.

James Madison, Federalist No. 57, February 19, 1788

The house of representatives ... can make no law which will not have its full operation on themselves and their friends, as well as the great mass of society. This has always been deemed one of the strongest bonds by which human policy can connect the rulers and the people together. It creates between them that communion of interest, and sympathy of sentiments, of which few governments have furnished examples; but without which every government degenerates into tyranny.

James Madison, Federalist No. 57, February 19, 1788

❦ Human Nature

The latent causes of faction are thus sown in the nature of man.

James Madison, Federalist No. 10, November 23, 1787

We must take human nature as we find it, perfection falls not to the share of mortals.

George Washington, letter to John Jay, August 15, 1786

There is a certain enthusiasm in liberty, that makes human nature rise above itself, in acts of bravery and heroism.

Alexander Hamilton, *The Farmer Refuted*, February 23, 1775

There is perhaps no one of our natural Passions so hard to subdue as Pride. Disguise it, struggle with it, beat it down, stifle it, mortify it as much as one pleases, it is still alive, and will now and then peek out and show itself....

Benjamin Franklin, *Autobiography*, 1771

As there is a degree of depravity in mankind which requires a certain degree of circumspection and distrust: So there are other qualities in human nature, which justify a certain portion of esteem and confidence. Republican government presupposes the existence of these qualities in a higher degree than any other form.

James Madison, Federalist No. 55, February 15, 1788

And you will, by the dignity of your Conduct, afford occasion for Posterity to say, when speaking of the glorious example you have exhibited to Mankind, had this day been wanting, the World had never seen the last stage of perfection to which human nature is capable of attaining.

George Washington, The Newburgh Address, March 15, 1783

Ambition must be made to counteract ambition. The interest of the man must be connected with the constitutional rights of the place. It may be a reflection on human nature that such devices should be necessary to control the abuses of government. What is government itself but the greatest of all reflections on human nature?

James Madison, Federalist No. 51, February 8, 1788

Human nature itself is evermore an advocate for liberty. There is also in human nature a resentment of injury and indignation against wrong; a love of truth and a veneration of virtue. These amiable passions are the "latent spark" ... If the people are capable of understanding, seeing and feeling the differences between true and false, right and wrong, virtue and vice, to what better principle can the friends of mankind apply than to the sense of this difference?

John Adams, *Novanglus* No. 1, January 23, 1775

❧ Immigration

Let the poor, the needy and oppressed of the Earth, and those who want Land, resort to the fertile plains of our western country, the second land of Promise, and there dwell in peace, fulfilling the first and great commandment.

George Washington, letter to David Humphreys, July 25, 1785

This new world hath been the asylum for the persecuted lovers of civil and religious liberty from every part of Europe. Hither have they fled, not from the tender embraces of the mother, but from the cruelty of the monster.

Thomas Paine, *Common Sense*, 1776

I had always hoped that this land might become a safe and agreeable asylum to the virtuous and persecuted part of mankind, to whatever nation they might belong.

George Washington, letter to Francis Van der Kamp, May 28, 1788

The bosom of America is open to receive not only the Opulent and respectable Stranger, but the oppressed and persecuted of all Nations and Religions; whom we shall welcome to a participation of all our rights and privileges, if by decency and propriety of conduct they appear to merit the enjoyment.

George Washington, Address to the Members of the Volunteer Association of Ireland, December 2, 1783

Born in other countries, yet believing you could be happy in this, our laws acknowledge, as they should do, your right to join us in society, conforming, as I doubt not you will do, to our established rules. That these rules shall be as equal as prudential considerations will admit, will certainly be the aim of our legislatures, general and particular.

Thomas Jefferson, letter to Hugh White, May 2, 1801

International Relations

(See also National Defense, War)

Observe good faith and justice towards all Nations. Cultivate peace and harmony with all.

George Washington, Farewell Address, September 19 1796

Foreign influence is truly the Grecian horse to a republic. We cannot be too careful to exclude its influence.

Alexander Hamilton, *Pacificus* No. 6, July 17, 1793

'Tis our true policy to steer clear of permanent Alliances, with any portion of the foreign world.

George Washington, Farewell Address, September 19 1796

Peace, commerce, and honest friendship with all nations, entangling alliances with none.

Thomas Jefferson, First Inaugural Address, March 4, 1801

Honesty will be found on every experiment, to be the best and only true policy; let us then as a Nation be just.

George Washington, Circular Letter to the States, June 8, 1783

States, like individuals, who observe their engagements, are respected and trusted: while the reverse is the fate of those who pursue an opposite conduct.

Alexander Hamilton, *Report on Public Credit*, January 9, 1790

My anxious recollections, my sympathetic feelings, and my best wishes are irresistibly excited whensoever, in any country, I see an oppressed nation unfurl the banners of freedom.

George Washington, letter to Pierre Auguste Adet, January 1, 1796

We are firmly convinced, and we act on that conviction, that with nations as with individuals our interests soundly calculated will ever be found inseparable from our moral duties.

Thomas Jefferson, Second Inaugural Address, March 4, 1805

There can be no greater error than to expect, or calculate upon real favours from Nation to Nation. 'Tis an illusion which experience must cure, which a just pride ought to discard.

George Washington, Farewell Address, September 19, 1796

If we are to be told by a foreign Power ... what we shall do, and what we shall not do, we have Independence yet to seek, and have contended hitherto for very little.

George Washington, letter to Alexander Hamilton, May 8, 1796

The nation which indulges towards another an habitual hatred, or an habitual fondness, is in some degree a slave. It is a slave to its animosity or to its affection, either of which is sufficient to lead it astray from its duty and its interest.

George Washington, Farewell Address, September 19, 1796

Against the insidious wiles of foreign influence, (I conjure you to believe me fellow citizens) the jealousy of a free people ought to be constantly awake; since history and experience prove that foreign influence is one of the most baneful foes of Republican Government.

George Washington, Farewell Address, September 19, 1796

My ardent desire is, and my aim has been ... to comply strictly with all our engagements. foreign and domestic; but to keep the U States free from political connections with every other Country. To see that they may be independent of all, and under the influence of none. In a word, I want an American character, that the powers of

Europe may be convinced we act for ourselves and not for others; this, in my judgment, is the only way to be respected abroad and happy at home.

George Washington, letter to Patrick Henry, October 9, 1775

Judges and the Judiciary

One single object ... [will merit] the endless gratitude of the society: that of restraining the judges from usurping legislation.

Thomas Jefferson, letter to Edward Livingston, March 25, 1825

Refusing or not refusing to execute a law to stamp it with its final character ... makes the Judiciary department paramount in fact to the Legislature, which was never intended and can never be proper.

James Madison, letter to John Brown, October 1788

There is not a syllable in the plan under consideration which directly empowers the national courts to construe the laws according to the spirit of the Constitution.

Alexander Hamilton, Federalist No. 81, May 28, 1788

A judiciary independent of a king or executive alone, is a good thing; but independence of the will of the nation is a solecism, at least in a republican government.

Thomas Jefferson, letter to Thomas Ritchie, December 25, 1820

Judges, therefore, should be always men of learning and experience in the laws, of exemplary morals, great patience, calmness, coolness, and attention. Their minds should not be distracted with jarring interests; they should not be dependent upon any man, or body of men.

John Adams, *Thoughts on Government*, 1776

The opinion which gives to the judges the right to decide what laws are constitutional and what not, not only for themselves, in their own sphere of action, but for the Legislature and Executive also in their spheres, would make the Judiciary a despotic branch.

Thomas Jefferson, letter to Abigail Adams, September 11, 1804

The Judiciary … has no influence over either the sword or the purse; no direction either of the strength or of the wealth of the society, and can take no active resolution whatever. It may truly be said to have neither force nor will.

Alexander Hamilton, Federalist No. 78, May 28, 1788

The judiciary of the United States is the subtle corps of sappers and miners constantly working under ground to undermine the foundations of our confederated fabric. They are construing our constitution from a co-ordination of a general and special government to a general and supreme one alone.

Thomas Jefferson, letter to Thomas Ritchie, December 25, 1820

The germ of dissolution of our federal government is in the constitution of the federal Judiciary working like gravity by night and by day, gaining a little today and a little tomorrow, and advancing its noiseless step like a thief, over the field of jurisdiction, until all shall be usurped.

Thomas Jefferson, letter to Charles Hammond, August 18, 1821

The dignity and stability of government in all its branches, the morals of the people, and every blessing of society depend so much upon an upright and skillful administration of justice, that the judicial power ought to be distinct from both the legislative and executive, and independent upon both, that so it may be a check upon both, and both should be checks upon that.

John Adams, *Thoughts on Government*, 1776

I acknowledge in the ordinary course of government, that the exposition of the laws and constitution devolves upon the judicial. But I beg to know, upon what principle it can he contended, that any one department draws from the constitution greater powers than another, in marking out the limits of the powers of the several departments.

James Madison, speech before the House of Representatives, June 17, 1789

At the establishment of our constitutions, the judiciary bodies were supposed to be the most helpless and harmless members of the government. Experience, however, soon showed in what way they were to become the most dangerous; that the insufficiency of the means provided for their removal gave them a freehold and irresponsibility in office; that their decisions, seeming to concern individual suitors only, pass silent and unheeded by the public at large; that these decisions, nevertheless, become law by precedent, sapping, by little and little, the foundations of the constitution, and working its change by construction, before any one has perceived that that invisible and helpless worm has been busily employed in consuming its substance.

> Thomas Jefferson, letter to Monsieur A. Coray, October 31, 1823

Justice

Let justice be done though the heavens should fall.

> John Adams, letter to Elbridge Gerry, December 5, 1777

The best and only safe road to honor, glory, and true dignity is justice.

> George Washington, letter to Marquis de Lafayette, September 30, 1779

Equal and exact justice to all men, of whatever persuasion, religious or political.

> Thomas Jefferson, First Inaugural Address, March 4, 1801

Justice is the end of government. It is the end of civil society. It ever has been and ever will be pursued until it be obtained, or until liberty be lost in the pursuit.

> James Madison, Federalist No. 51, February 8, 1788

It will be worthy of a free, enlightened, and, at no distant period, a great Nation, to give to mankind the magnanimous and too novel example of a People always guided by an exalted justice and benevolence.

> George Washington, Farewell Address, September 19, 1796

If individuals be not influenced by moral principles, it is in vain to look for public virtue; it is therefore, the duty of legislators to enforce, both by precept and example, the utility, as well as the necessity, of a strict adherence to the rules of distributive justice.

Message of the Senate to George Washington, May 18, 1789

Last Words

'Tis well.

George Washington, December 14, 1799

Is it the Fourth?

Thomas Jefferson, evening of July 3, 1826; Jefferson died the following morning, July 4, 1826

A dying man can do nothing easy.

Benjamin Franklin, after his daughter asked him to move, April 17, 1790

Remember, my Eliza, you are a Christian.

Alexander Hamilton, speaking to his grieving wife, July 12, 1804

I only regret that I have but one life to lose for my country.

Nathan Hale, before being hanged by the British, September 22, 1776

Thomas Jefferson still lives.

John Adams, upon waking momentarily on the afternoon of July 4, 1826

Nothing more than a change of mind, my dear.

James Madison, responding to his niece, June 28, 1836

Law

A government of laws, and not of men.

John Adams, *Novanglus* No. 7, March 6, 1775

Good government is an empire of laws.

John Adams, *Thoughts on Government*, 1776

But where says some is the King of America? I'll tell you Friend, he reigns above, and doth not make havoc of mankind like the

Royal Brute of Britain ... let it be brought forth placed on the divine law, the word of God; let a crown be placed thereon, by which the world may know, that so far as we approve of monarchy, that in America THE LAW IS KING.

Thomas Paine, Common Sense, 1776

We lay it down as a fundamental, that laws, to be just, must give a reciprocation of right; that, without this, they are mere arbitrary rules of conduct, founded in force, and not in conscience.

Thomas Jefferson, Notes on the State of Virginia, 1782

Wise politicians will be cautious about fettering the government with restrictions that cannot be observed, because they know that every break of the fundamental laws, though dictated by necessity, impairs that sacred reverence which ought to be maintained in the breast of rulers towards the constitution of a country.

Alexander Hamilton, Federalist No. 25, December 21, 1787

Where there is no law, there is no liberty; and nothing deserves the name of law but that which is certain and universal in its operation upon all the members of the community.

Benjamin Rush, letter to David Ramsay, circa April 1788

Without liberty, law loses its nature and its name, and becomes oppression. Without law, liberty also loses its nature and its name, and becomes licentiousness.

James Wilson, Of the Study of the Law in the United States, circa 1790

Laws are made for men of ordinary understanding and should, therefore, be construed by the ordinary rules of common sense. Their meaning is not to be sought for in metaphysical subtleties which may make anything mean everything or nothing at pleasure.

Thomas Jefferson, letter to William Johnson, June 12, 1823

❦ Laws of Nature

The propitious smiles of Heaven can never be expected on a nation that disregards the eternal rules of order and right, which Heaven itself has ordained.

George Washington, First Inaugural Address, April 30, 1789

In the supposed state of nature, all men are equally bound by the laws of nature, or to speak more properly, the laws of the Creator.

Samuel Adams, letter to the Legislature of Massachusetts, January 17, 1794

The law of nature and the law of revelation are both Divine: they flow, though in different channels, from the same adorable source. It is indeed preposterous to separate them from each other.

James Wilson, Of the Law of Nature, 1804

When in the Course of human events, it becomes necessary for one people to dissolve the political bands which have connected them with another, and to assume among the Powers of the earth, the separate and equal station to which the Law of Nature and Nature's God entitle them, a decent respect to the opinions of mankind requires that they should declare the causes which impel them to the separation.

The Declaration of Independence, July 4, 1776

We have duties, for the discharge of which we are accountable to our Creator and benefactor, which no human power can cancel. What those duties are, is determinable by right reason, which may be, and is called, a well informed conscience. What this conscience dictates as our duty, is so; and that power which assumes a control over it, is an usurper; for no power can be pleaded to justify the control, as any consent in this case is void.

The Essex Result, May 12, 1778

To grant that there is a supreme intelligence who rules the world and has established laws to regulate the actions of his creatures; and still to assert that man, in a state of nature, may be considered as perfectly free from all restraints of law and government, appears to a common understanding altogether irreconcilable. Good and wise men, in all ages, have embraced a very dissimilar theory. They have supposed that the deity, from the relations we stand in to himself and to each other, has constituted an eternal and immutable law, which is indispensably obligatory upon all mankind, prior to any human institution whatever. This is what is called the law of nature....Upon this law depend the natural rights of mankind.

Alexander Hamilton, The Farmer Refuted, 1775

Liberty

Where liberty dwells, there is my country.

Benjamin Franklin (attributed), letter to Benjamin Vaughn, March 14, 1783

Liberty, once lost, is lost forever.

John Adams, letter to Abigail Adams, July 17, 1775

Liberty, when it begins to take root, is a plant of rapid growth.

George Washington, letter to James Madison, March 2, 1788

The boisterous sea of liberty is never without a wave.

Thomas Jefferson, letter to Richard Rush, October 20, 1820

Proclaim liberty throughout the land unto all the inhabitants thereof.

Leviticus 25:10 (Inscription on the Liberty Bell)

Our attachment to no nation upon earth should supplant our attachment to liberty.

Thomas Jefferson, Declaration of the Causes and Necessities of Taking Up Arms, July 6, 1775

They that can give up essential liberty to purchase a little temporary safety, deserve neither liberty nor safety.

Benjamin Franklin, Historical Review of Pennsylvania, 1759

The God who gave us life, gave us liberty at the same time; the hand of force may destroy, but cannot disjoin them.

Thomas Jefferson, A Summary View of the Rights of British America, August 1774

Liberty is not to be enjoyed, indeed it cannot exist, without the habits of just subordination; it consists, not so much in removing all restraint from the orderly, as in imposing it on the violent.

Fisher Ames, Essay on Equality, December 15, 1801

Interwoven as is the love of liberty with every ligament of your hearts, no recommendation of mine is necessary to fortify or confirm the attachment.

George Washington, Farewell Address, September 19, 1796

He that would make his own liberty secure, must guard even his enemy from oppression; for if he violates this duty, he establishes a precedent that will reach to himself.

Thomas Paine, *Dissertation on First-Principles of Government*, December 23, 1791

Honor, justice, and humanity, forbid us tamely to surrender that freedom which we received from our gallant ancestors, and which our innocent posterity have a right to receive from us.

Thomas Jefferson, Declaration of the Causes and Necessities of Taking Up Arms, July 6, 1775

Liberty must at all hazards be supported. We have a right to it, derived from our Maker. But if we had not, our fathers have earned and bought it for us, at the expense of their ease, their estates, their pleasure, and their blood.

John Adams, *A Dissertation on the Canon and Feudal Law*, 1765

The establishment of Civil and Religious Liberty was the Motive which induced me to the Field — the object is attained — and it now remains to be my earnest wish & prayer, that the Citizens of the United States could make a wise and virtuous use of the blessings placed before them.

George Washington, letter to the Reformed German Congregation of New York City, November 27, 1783

Liberty is a word which, according as it is used, comprehends the most good and the most evil of any in the world. Justly understood it is sacred next to those which we appropriate in divine adoration; but in the mouths of some it means anything.

Oliver Ellsworth, A Landholder No. III, November 19, 1787

In Europe, charters of liberty have been granted by power. America has set the example . . . of charters of power granted by liberty. This revolution in the practice of the world, may, with an honest praise, be pronounced the most triumphant epoch of its history, and the most consoling presage of its happiness.

James Madison, essay in The National Gazette, January 18, 1792

Marriage

(See also Family)

Harmony in the married state is the very first object to be aimed at.

Thomas Jefferson, letter to Mary Jefferson Eppes, January 7, 1798

I have always considered marriage as the most interesting event of one's life, the foundation of happiness or misery.

George Washington, letter to Burwell Bassett, May 23, 1785

Keep your eyes wide open before marriage, half shut afterwards.

Benjamin Franklin, Poor Richard's Almanack, 1738

More permanent and genuine happiness is to be found in the sequestered walks of connubial life than in the giddy rounds of promiscuous pleasure.

George Washington, letter to the Marquis de la Rourie, August 10, 1786

When divorces can be summoned to the aid of levity, of vanity, or of avarice, a state of marriage frequently becomes a state of war or strategem.

James Wilson, Lectures on Law, 1791

The happy State of Matrimony is, undoubtedly, the surest and most lasting Foundation of Comfort and Love; the Source of all that endearing Tenderness and Affection which arises from Relation and Affinity; the grand Point of Property; the Cause of all good Order in the World, and what alone preserves it from the utmost Confusion; and, to sum up all, the Appointment of infinite Wisdom for these great and good Purposes.

Benjamin Franklin, Rules and Maxims for Promoting Matrimonial Happiness, October 8, 1730

It is not necessary to enumerate the many advantages, that arise from this custom of early marriages. They comprehend all the society can receive from this source; from the preservation, and increase of the human race. Every thing useful and beneficial to man, seems to be connected with obedience to the laws of his nature, the inclinations, the duties, and the happiness of individuals, resolve themselves into customs and habits, favourable, in the highest degree, to society. In no case is this more apparent, than in the customs of nations respecting marriage.

Samuel Williams, The Natural and Civil History of Vermont, 1794

 # National Defense

(See also International Relations, War)

National defense is one of the cardinal duties of a statesman.

John Adams, letter to James Lloyd, January 1815

Millions for defense, but not one cent for tribute.

Representative Robert Goodloe Harper, Address, June 18, 1798
(Harper was the Chairman of the Committee on Ways and Means)

Those who expect to reap the blessings of freedom, must, like men, undergo the fatigues of supporting it.

Thomas Paine, *The American Crisis* No. 4, September 11, 1777

America united with a handful of troops, or without a single soldier, exhibits a more forbidding posture to foreign ambition than

America disunited, with a hundred thousand veterans ready for combat.

James Madison, Federalist No. 14, November 30, 1787

The circumstances that endanger the safety of nations are infinite, and for this reason no constitutional shackles can wisely be imposed on the power to which the care of it is committed.

Alexander Hamilton, Federalist No. 23, December 17, 1787

A universal peace, it is to be feared, is in the catalogue of events, which will never exist but in the imaginations of visionary philosophers, or in the breasts of benevolent enthusiasts.

James Madison, essay in *The National Gazette,* February 2, 1792

There is a rank due to the United States among nations which will be withheld, if not absolutely lost, by the reputation of weakness.

George Washington, Fifth Annual Address to Congress, December 3, 1793

Opinion

Public opinion sets bounds to every government, and is the real sovereign in every free one.

James Madison, Public Opinion, December 19, 1791

The good opinion of mankind, like the lever of Archimedes, with the given fulcrum, moves the world.

Thomas Jefferson, letter to M. Correa, December 27, 1814

A little matter will move a party, but it must be something great that moves a nation.

Thomas Paine, *Rights of Man,* 1792

Nothing is so contagious as opinion, especially on questions which, being susceptible of very different glosses, beget in the mind a distrust of itself.

James Madison, letter to Benjamin Rush, March 7, 1790

It is on great occasions only, and after time has been given for cool and deliberate reflection, that the real voice of the people can be known.

George Washington, letter to Edward Carrington, May 1, 1796

Every difference of opinion is not a difference of principle. We have called by different names brethren of the same principle.

Thomas Jefferson, First Inaugural Address, March 4, 1801

In proportion as the structure of a government gives force to public opinion, it is essential that public opinion should be enlightened.

George Washington, Farewell Address, September 19, 1796

There is no maxim in my opinion which is more liable to be misapplied, and which therefore needs elucidation than the current one that the interest of the majority is the political standard of right and wrong.... In fact it is only reestablishing under another name and a more specious form, force as the measure of right....

James Madison, letter to James Monroe, October 5, 1786

Experience having long taught me the reasonableness of mutual sacrifices of opinion among those who are to act together for any common object, and the expediency of doing what good we can; when we cannot do all we would wish.

Thomas Jefferson, letter to John Randolph, December 1, 1803

As long as the reason of man continues fallible, and he is at liberty to exercise it, different opinions will be formed. As long as the connection subsists between his reason and his self-love, his opinions and his passions will have a reciprocal influence on each other.

James Madison, Federalist No. 10, November 23, 1787

 Patriotism

Guard against the impostures of pretended patriotism.

George Washington, Farewell Address, September 19, 1796

Our obligations to our country never cease but with our lives.

John Adams, letter to Benjamin Rush, April 18, 1808

Love your neighbor as yourself and your country more than yourself.

Thomas Jefferson, letter to Thomas Jefferson Smith, February 21, 1825

Patriotism is as much a virtue as justice, and is as necessary for the support of societies as natural affection is for the support of families.

Benjamin Rush, letter to His Fellow Countrymen: On Patriotism, October 20, 1773

Our own Country's Honor, all call upon us for a vigorous and manly exertion, and if we now shamefully fail, we shall become infamous to the whole world. Let us therefore rely upon the goodness of the Cause, and the aid of the supreme Being, in whose hands Victory is, to animate and encourage us to great and noble Actions.

George Washington, General Orders, July 2, 1776

The hour is fast approaching, on which the Honor and Success of this army, and the safety of our bleeding Country depend. Remember officers and Soldiers, that you are Freemen, fighting for the blessings of Liberty - that slavery will be your portion, and that of your posterity, if you do not acquit yourselves like men.

George Washington, General Orders, August 23, 1776

Our country is in danger, but not to be despaired of. Our enemies are numerous and powerful; but we have many friends, determining to be free, and heaven and earth will aid the resolution. On you depend the fortunes of America. You are to decide the important question, on which rest the happiness and liberty of millions yet unborn. Act worthy of yourselves.

Dr. Joseph Warren, Boston Massacre Oration, March 6, 1775

It should be the highest ambition of every American to extend his views beyond himself, and to bear in mind that his conduct will not only affect himself, his country, and his immediate posterity;

but that its influence may be co-extensive with the world, and stamp political happiness or misery on ages yet unborn.

George Washington, letter to the Legislature of Pennsylvania, September 5, 1789

 # The People

Here, sir, the people govern.

Alexander Hamilton, speech at the New York Ratifying Convention, June 17, 1778

Governments are instituted among men, deriving their just powers from the consent of the governed.

The Declaration of Independence, July 4, 1776

Every government degenerates when trusted to the rulers of the people alone. The people themselves, therefore, are its only safe depositories.

Thomas Jefferson, *Notes on the State of Virginia,* Query XIV, 1781

The fabric of American empire ought to rest on the solid basis of THE CONSENT OF THE PEOPLE. The streams of national power ought to flow from that pure, original fountain of all legitimate authority.

Alexander Hamilton, Federalist No. 22, December 14, 1787

Democratical States must always feel before they can see: it is this that makes their Governments slow, but the people will be right at last.

George Washington, letter to Marquis de Lafayette, July 25, 1785

But the mild voice of reason, pleading the cause of an enlarged and permanent interest, is but too often drowned, before public bodies as well as individuals, by the clamors of an impatient avidity for immediate and immoderate gain.

James Madison, Federalist No. 42, January 22, 1788

No people can be bound to acknowledge and adore the invisible hand, which conducts the Affairs of men more than the People of the United States. Every step, by which they have advanced to the

Don't Bet Against Washington

' When the Convention to form a Constitution was sitting in Philadelphia in 1787, of which General Washington was president, he had stated evenings to receive the calls of his friends. At an interview between Hamilton, the Morrises, and others, the former remarked that Washington was reserved and aristocratic even to his intimate friends, and allowed no one to be familiar with him. Gouverneur Morris said that was a mere fancy, and he could be as familiar with Washington as with any of his other friends. Hamilton replied, 'If you will, at the next reception evenings, gently slap him on the shoulder and say, "My dear General, how happy I am to see you look so well!" a supper and wine shall be provided for you and a dozen of your friends.' The challenge was accepted. On the evening appointed, a large number attended; and at an early hour Gouverneur Morris entered, bowed, shook hands, laid his left hand on Washington's shoulder, and said, 'My dear General, I am very happy to see you look so well!' Washington withdrew his hand, stepped suddenly back, fixed his eye on Morris for several minutes with an angry frown, until the latter retreated abashed, and sought refuge in the crowd. The company looked on in silence. At the supper, which has provided by Hamilton, Morris said, 'I have won the bet, but paid dearly for it, and nothing could induce me to repeat it.' **"**

George Read, Constitutional Convention delegate from Delaware, anecdote recorded in *Farrand's Records of the Federal Convention of 1787* character of an independent nation, seems to have been distinguished by some token of providential agency.

George Washington, First Inaugural Address, April 30, 1789

I know no safe depository of the ultimate powers of the society but the people themselves; and if we think them not enlightened enough to exercise their control with a wholesome discretion, the remedy is not to take it from them, but to inform their discretion by education. This is the true corrective of abuses of constitutional power.

Thomas Jefferson, letter to William Charles Jarvis, September 28, 1820

Political Leaders

Enlightened statesmen will not always be at the helm.

James Madison, Federalist No. 10, November 23, 1787

Nothing so strongly impels a man to regard the interest of his constituents, as the certainty of returning to the general mass of the people, from whence he was taken, where he must participate in their burdens.

George Mason, speech to the Virginia Ratifying Convention, June 17, 1788

The great principles of right and wrong are legible to every reader; to pursue them requires not the aid of many counselors. The whole art of government consists in the art of being honest. Only aim to do your duty, and mankind will give you credit where you fail.

Thomas Jefferson, A Summary View of the Rights of British America, 1775

I leave to others the sublime delights of riding in the storm, better pleased with sound sleep & a warmer berth below it encircled, with the society of neighbors, friends & fellow laborers of the earth rather than with spies & sycophants ... I have no ambition to govern men. It is a painful and thankless office.

Thomas Jefferson, letter to John Adams, December 28, 1796

When occasions present themselves, in which the interests of the people are at variance with their inclinations, it is the duty of the persons whom they have appointed to be the guardians of those interests, to withstand the temporary delusion, in order to give them time and opportunity for more cool and sedate reflection.

Alexander Hamilton, The Federalist No. 71, March 18, 1788

I suppose, indeed, that in public life, a man whose political principles have any decided character and who has energy enough to give them effect must always expect to encounter political hostility from those of adverse principles.

Thomas Jefferson, letter to Richard M. Johnson, March 10, 1808

The aim of every political constitution is, or ought to be, first to obtain for rulers men who possess most wisdom to discern, and most virtue to pursue, the common good of the society; and in the next place, to take the most effectual precautions for keeping them virtuous whilst they continue to hold their public trust.

James Madison, Federalist No. 57, February 19, 1788

An honest man can feel no pleasure in the exercise of power over his fellow citizens....There has never been a moment of my life in which I should have relinquished for it the enjoyments of my family, my farm, my friends & books.

Thomas Jefferson, letter to John Melish, January 13, 1813

If men of wisdom and knowledge, of moderation and temperance, of patience, fortitude and perseverance, of sobriety and true republican simplicity of manners, of zeal for the honour of the Supreme Being and the welfare of the commonwealth; if men possessed of these other excellent qualities are chosen to fill the seats of government, we may expect that our affairs will rest on a solid and permanent foundation.

Samuel Adams, letter to Elbridge Gerry, November 27, 1780

❦ Politics and Parties

The greatest good we can do our country is to heal its party divisions and make them one people.

> Thomas Jefferson, letter to John Dickinson, July 23, 1801

Public affairs go on pretty much as usual: perpetual chicanery and rather more personal abuse than there used to be.

> John Adams, letter to Thomas Jefferson, April 17, 1826

In politics, as in religion, it is equally absurd to aim at making proselytes by fire and sword. Heresies in either can rarely be cured by persecution.

> Alexander Hamilton, Federalist No. 1, October 27, 1797

I have accepted a seat in the [Massachusetts] House of Representatives, and thereby have consented to my own ruin, to your ruin, and the ruin of our children. I give you this warning, that you may prepare your mind for your fate.

> John Adams, letter to Abigail Adams, May 1770

We should be unfaithful to ourselves if we should ever lose sight of the danger to our liberties if anything partial or extraneous should infect the purity of our free, fair, virtuous, and independent elections.

> John Adams, Inaugural Address, March 4, 1797

It is too early for politicians to presume on our forgetting that the public good, the real welfare of the great body of the people, is the supreme object to be pursued; and that no form of government whatever has any other value than as it may be fitted for the attainment of this object.

> James Madison, Federalist No. 45, January 26, 1788

Let me now take a more comprehensive view, and warn you in the most solemn manner against the baneful effects of the Spirit of Party. . . . A fire not to be quenched; it demands a uniform vigilance to prevent its bursting into a flame, lest instead of warming, it should consume.

George Washington, Farewell Address, September 19, 1796

I must study politics and war that my sons may have liberty to study mathematics and philosophy. My sons ought to study mathematics and philosophy, geography, natural history and naval architecture, navigation, commerce and agriculture, in order to give their children a right to study painting, poetry, music, architecture, statuary, tapestry, and porcelain.

John Adams, letter to Abigail Adams, circa 1780

During the contest of opinion through which we have passed the animation of discussions and of exertions has sometimes worn an aspect which might impose on strangers unused to think freely and to speak and to write what they think; but this being now decided by the voice of the nation, announced according to the rules of the Constitution, all will, of course, arrange themselves under the will of the law, and unite in common efforts for the common good. . . . Let us, then, fellow-citizens, unite with one heart and one mind. Let us restore to social intercourse that harmony and affection without which liberty and even life itself are but dreary things. And let us reflect that, having banished from our land that religious intolerance under which mankind so long bled and suffered, we have yet gained little if we countenance a political intolerance as despotic, as wicked, and capable of as bitter and bloody persecutions.

Thomas Jefferson, First Inaugural Address, March 4, 1801

 # Poverty

(See also Charity)

Having been poor is no shame, but being ashamed of it, is.

Benjamin Franklin, *Poor Richard's Almanack*, 1749

I am for doing good to the poor, but I differ in opinion of the means. I think the best way of doing good to the poor, is not making them easy in poverty, but leading or driving them out of it.

Benjamin Franklin, On the Price of Corn and
Management of the Poor, November 1766

Dependence begets subservience and venality, suffocates the germ of virtue, and prepares fit tools for the designs of ambition.

Thomas Jefferson, *Notes on the State of Virginia*, Query XIX, 1787

Repeal that [welfare] law, and you will soon see a change in their manners. . . . Industry will increase, and with it plenty among the lower people; their circumstances will mend, and more will be done for their happiness by inuring them to provide for themselves, than could be done by dividing all your estates among them.

Benjamin Franklin, letter to Collinson, May 9, 1753

 # Power

Arbitrary power is most easily established on the ruins of liberty abused to licentiousness.

George Washington, Circular to the States, June 8, 1783

All men having power ought to be distrusted to a certain degree.

James Madison, speech at the Constitutional Convention, July 11, 1787

A fondness for power is implanted, in most men, and it is natural to abuse it, when acquired.

Alexander Hamilton, *The Farmer Refuted*, February 23, 1775

Wherever the real power in a Government lies, there is the danger of oppression.

James Madison, letter to Thomas Jefferson, October 17, 1788

Governments are instituted among Men, deriving their just powers from the consent of the governed.

The Declaration of Independence, July 4, 1776

The essence of Government is power; and power, lodged as it must be in human hands, will ever be liable to abuse.

James Madison, speech at the Virginia Constitutional Convention December 2, 1829

Where an excess of power prevails, property of no sort is duly respected. No man is safe in his opinions, his person, his faculties, or his possessions.

James Madison, essay in the *National Gazette*, March 27, 1792

The spirit of encroachment tends to consolidate the powers of all the departments in one, and thus to create whatever the form of government, a real despotism. A just estimate of that love of power, and proneness to abuse it, which predominates in the human heart is sufficient to satisfy us of the truth of this position.

George Washington, Farewell Address, September 19, 1796

It will not be denied that power is of an encroaching nature and that it ought to be effectually restrained from passing the limits assigned to it. After discriminating, therefore, in theory, the several classes of power, as they may in their nature be legislative, executive, or judiciary, the next and most difficult task is to provide some practical security for each, against the invasion of the others.

James Madison, Federalist No. 48, February 1, 1788

 # The Presidency

The second office of this government is honorable & easy, the first is but a splendid misery.

Thomas Jefferson, letter to Elbridge Gerry, May 13, 1797

In times of peace the people look most to their representatives; but in war, to the executive solely.

Thomas Jefferson, letter to Caeser Rodney, February 10, 1810

The executive branch of this government never has, nor will suffer, while I preside, any improper conduct of its officers to escape with impunity.

George Washington, letter to Gouverneur Morris, December 22, 1795

I Pray Heaven to Bestow The Best of Blessing on this house, and on all that shall hereafter Inhabit it. May none but Honest and Wise Men ever rule under This Roof!

> John Adams, letter to Abigail Adams, November 2, 1800
> (engraved over the fireplace in the State Dining Room of the White House)

All see, and most admire, the glare which hovers round the external trappings of elevated office. To me there is nothing in it, beyond the lustre which may be reflected from its connection with a power of promoting human felicity.

> George Washington, letter to Catherine Macaulay Graham, January 9, 1790

I am free to acknowledge that his powers are full great, and greater than I was disposed to make them. Nor, entre nous, do I believe they would have been so great had not many of the members cast their eyes towards General Washington as President; and shaped their Ideas of the Powers to be given to a President, by their opinions of his Virtue.

> Pierce Butler (Constitutional Convention delegate from South Carolina), letter to Weedon Butler, May 5, 1778

[The President] is the dignified, but accountable magistrate of a free and great people. The tenure of his office, it is true, is not hereditary; nor is it for life: but still it is a tenure of the noblest kind: by being the man of the people, he is invested; by continuing to be the man of the people, his investiture will be voluntarily, and cheerfully, and honourably renewed.

> James Wilson, Lectures on Law, 1791

Energy in the executive is a leading character in the definition of good government. It is essential to the protection of the community against foreign attacks; it is not less essential to the steady administration of the laws; to the protection of property against those irregular and high-handed combinations which sometimes interrupt the ordinary course of justice; to the security of liberty against the enterprises and assaults of ambition, of faction, and of anarchy.

> Alexander Hamilton, Federalist No. 69, March 14, 1788

❦ The Press

Where the press is free and every man able to read, all is safe.

Thomas Jefferson, letter to Charles Yancey, January 6, 1816

Newspapers ... serve as chimnies to carry off noxious vapors and smoke.

Thomas Jefferson, letter to Thaddeus Kosciusko, April 2, 1802

No government ought to be without censors: & where the press is free, no one ever will.

Thomas Jefferson, letter to George Washington, September 9, 1792

We are, heart and soul, friends to the freedom of the press.... It is a precious pest, and a necessary mischief, and there would be no liberty without it.

Fisher Ames, Review of the Pamphlet on the State of the British Constitution, 1807

The right of freely examining public characters and measures, and of free communication among the people thereon . . . has ever been justly deemed the only effectual guardian of every other right.

James Madison, Virginia Resolutions, December 21, 1798

If by the liberty of the press were understood merely the liberty of discussing the propriety of public measures and political opinions, let us have as much of it as you please: But if it means the liberty of affronting, calumniating and defaming one another, I, for my part, own myself willing to part with my share of it.

Benjamin Franklin, An Account of the Supremest Court of Judicature in Pennsylvania, viz. The Court of the Press, September 12, 1789

Property

One of the most essential branches of English liberty is the freedom of one's house. A man's house is his castle.

James Otis, On the Writs of Assistance, 1761

He who is permitted by law to have no property of his own, can with difficulty conceive that property is founded in anything but force.

Thomas Jefferson, letter to Bancroft, January 26, 1788

Government is instituted to protect property of every sort; as well that which lies in the various rights of individuals, as that which the term particularly expresses. This being the end of government, that alone is a just government which impartially secures to every man whatever is his own.

James Madison, Essay on Property, March 29, 1792

The moment the idea is admitted into society that property is not as sacred as the laws of God, and that there is not a force of law and public justice to protect it, anarchy and tyranny commence. If 'Thou shalt not covet' and 'Thou shalt not steal' were not commandments of Heaven, they must be made inviolable precepts in every society before it can be civilized or made free.

John Adams, *A Defense of the Constitutions of Government of the United States of America*, 1787

Public Service

Every post is honorable in which a man can serve his country.

George Washington, letter to Benedict Arnold, September 14, 1775

I was summoned by my country, whose voice I can never hear but with veneration and love.

George Washington, First Inaugural Address, April 30, 1789

I am not influenced by the expectation of promotion or pecuniary reward. I wish to be useful, and every kind of service necessary for the public good, become honorable by being necessary.

> Captain Nathan Hale, remark to Captain William Hull, who had
> attempted to dissuade him from volunteering for a spy mission
> for General Washington, September 1776

The consciousness of having discharged that duty which we owe to our country is superior to all other considerations.

> George Washington, letter to James Madison, March 2, 1788

Public Speaking

Here comes the orator! With his flood of words, and his drop of reason.

> Benjamin Franklin, *Poor Richard's Almanack*, 1735

Speak seldom, but to important subjects, except such as particularly relate to your constituents, and, in the former case, make yourself perfectly master of the subject.

> George Washington, letter to Bushrod Washington, November 10, 1787

I should consider the speeches of Livy, Sallust, and Tacitus, as pre-eminent specimens of logic, taste and that sententious brevity which, using not a word to spare, leaves not a moment for inattention to the hearer. Amplification is the vice of modern oratory.

> Thomas Jefferson, letter to David Harding, April 20, 1824

Religion and Morality

O! 'tis easier to keep Holidays than Commandments.

> Benjamin Franklin, *Poor Richard's Almanack*, 1743

If men are so wicked with religion, what would they be if without it.

> Benjamin Franklin, letter to Thomas Paine (date unknown)

Religion and good morals are the only solid foundation of public liberty and happiness.

Samuel Adams, letter to John Trumbull, October 16, 1778

Without religion, I believe that learning does real mischief to the morals and principles of mankind.

Benjamin Rush, letter to John Armstrong, March 19, 1783

Religion is the only solid Base of morals and Morals are the only possible Support of free governments.

Gouverneur Morris, letter to George Gordon, June 28, 1792

Without religion morals are the effects of causes as purely physical as pleasant breezes and fruitful seasons.

Benjamin Rush, letter to John Adams, August 20, 1811

Statesmen, my dear Sir, may plan and speculate for Liberty, but it is Religion and Morality alone, which can establish the Principles upon which Freedom can securely stand.

John Adams, letter to Zabdiel Adams, June 21, 1776

The Hand of providence has been so conspicuous in all this, that he must be worse than an infidel that lacks faith, and more than wicked, that has not gratitude enough to acknowledge his obligations.

George Washington, letter to Thomas Nelson, August 20, 1778

Reading, reflection and time have convinced me that the interests of society require the observation of those moral precepts ... in which all religions agree.

Thomas Jefferson, Westmoreland County petition, November 2, 1785

Religion is the only solid basis of good morals; therefore education should teach the precepts of religion and the duties of man towards God.

Gouverneur Morris, Notes on the Form of a Constitution for France, circa 1791

Religion and virtue are the only foundations, not of republicanism and of all free government, but of social felicity under all government and in all the combinations of human society.

John Adams, letter to Benjamin Rush, August 28, 1811

The foundations of our national policy will be laid in the pure and immutable principles of private morality, and the preeminence of free government be exemplified by all the attributes which can win the affections of its citizens, and command the respect of the world.

George Washington, First Inaugural Address, April 30, 1789

The only foundation for a useful education in a republic is to be laid in religion. Without this there can be no virtue, and without virtue there can be no liberty, and liberty is the object and life of all republican governments.

Benjamin Rush, On the Mode of Education Proper in a Republic, 1806

We have no government armed with power capable of contending with human passions unbridled by morality and religion. Avarice, ambition, revenge, or gallantry, would break the strongest cords of our Constitution as a whale goes through a net. Our Constitution was made only for a moral and religious people. It is wholly inadequate to the government of any other.

John Adams, Address to the Military, October 11, 1798

Of all the dispositions and habits which least to political prosperity, Religion and morality are indispensable supports. In vain would that man claim the tribute of Patriotism who should labor to subvert these great Pillars of human happiness — these firmest props of the duties of Men and citizens. The mere Politician, equally with the pious man ought to respect and to cherish them. A volume could not trace all their connections with private and public felicity. Let it simply be asked where is the security for property, for reputation, for life, if the sense of religious obligation desert the oaths, which are the instruments of investigation in Courts of Justice? And let us with caution indulge the supposition, that morality can be maintained without religion. Whatever may be conceded to the influence of refined education on minds of peculiar structure, reason and experience both forbid us to expect that National morality can prevail in exclusion of religious principle.

George Washington, Farewell Address, September 19, 1796

❦ Religious Liberty

We are teaching the world the great truth that Governments do better without Kings & Nobles than with them. The merit will be doubled by the other lesson that Religion flourishes in greater purity, without than with the aid of Government.

James Madison, letter to Edward Livingston, July 10, 1822

Conscience is the most sacred of all property.

James Madison, Essay on Property, March 29, 1792

The liberty enjoyed by the people of these states of worshiping Almighty God agreeably to their conscience, is not only among the choicest of their blessings, but also of their rights.

George Washington, Letter to the Annual Meeting of Quakers, September 1789

Let the pulpit resound with the doctrine and sentiments of religious liberty. Let us hear of the dignity of man's nature, and the noble rank he holds among the works of God.

John Adams, *Dissertation on the Canon and Feudal Law*, 1765

Religious bondage shackles and debilitates the mind and unfits it for every noble enterprise, every expanded prospect.

James Madison, letter to William Bradford, April 1, 1774

There is not a single instance in history in which civil liberty was lost, and religious liberty preserved entire. If therefore we yield up our temporal property, we at the same time deliver the conscience into bondage.

John Witherspoon, The Dominion of Providence Over the Passions of Men, 1776

The legitimate powers of government extend to such acts only as are injurious to others. But it does me no injury for my neighbour

to say there are twenty gods, or no god. It neither picks my pocket
nor breaks my leg.

Thomas Jefferson, Notes on the State of Virginia, Query XVII, 1787

It is the duty of every man to render to the Creator such homage
and such only as he believes to be acceptable to him. This duty is
precedent, both in order of time and in degree of obligation, to the
claims of Civil Society.

James Madison, Memorial and Remonstrance
Against Religious Assessments, circa June 20, 1785

Religion, or the duty which we owe to our creator, and the manner
of discharging it, can be directed only by reason and conviction,
not by force or violence; and therefore all men are equally entitled
to the free exercise of religion, according to the dictates of conscience; and this is the mutual duty of all to practice Christian
forbearance, love, and charity towards each other.

Virginia Bill of Rights, Article 16, June 12, 1776

It is the right as well as the duty of all men in society, publicly
and at stated seasons, to worship the Supreme Being, the great
Creator and Preserver of the universe. And no subject shall be
hurt, molested, or restrained in his person, liberty, or estate, for
worshipping God in the manner and season most agreeable to the
dictates of his own conscience; or for his religion profession of
sentiments; provided he doth not disturb the public peace, or
obstruct others in their religious worship....

Massachusetts Bill of Rights, Part the First, 1780

It is now no more that toleration is spoken of as if it were the
indulgence of one class of people that another enjoyed the exercise
of their inherent natural rights, for happily, the Government of the
United States, which gives to bigotry no sanction, to persecution
no assistance, requires only that they who live under its protection
should demean themselves as good citizens in giving it on all
occasions their effectual support.

George Washington, letter to the
Hebrew Congregation of Newport, Rhode Island, August 17, 1790

❧ Republican Government

(See also Democracy)

The republican is the only form of government which is not eternally at open or secret war with the rights of mankind.

Thomas Jefferson, letter to William Hunter, March 11, 1790

A republic, by which I mean a government in which the scheme of representation takes place, opens a different prospect and promises the cure for which we are seeking.

James Madison, Federalist No. 10, November 23, 1787

Although a republican government is slow to move, yet when once in motion, its momentum becomes irresistible.

Thomas Jefferson, letter to Francis C. Gray, March 4, 1815

A lady asked Dr. Franklin, "Well, Doctor, what have we got a republic or a monarchy?" — "A republic," replied the Doctor, "if you can keep it."

Convention delegate James McHenry, anecdote from Farrand's Records of the Federal Convention of 1787

The preservation of the sacred fire of liberty, and the destiny of the republican model of government, are justly considered deeply, perhaps as finally, staked on the experiment entrusted to the hands of the American people.

George Washington, First Inaugural Address, April 30, 1789

Sometimes it is said that man can not be trusted with government of himself. Can he, then, be trusted with the government of others? Or have we found angels in the forms of kings to govern him? Let history answer this question.

Thomas Jefferson, First Inaugural Address, March 4, 1801

There is no good government but what is republican. That the only valuable part of the British constitution is so; because the true idea of a republic is "an empire of laws, and not of men." That, as a republic is the best of governments, so that particular arrangement of the powers of society, or, in other words, that form of government which is best contrived to secure an impartial and exact execution of the law, is the best of republics.

John Adams, *Thoughts on Government*, 1776

If we resort for a criterion to the different principles on which different forms of government are established, we may define a republic to be, or at least may bestow that name on, a government which derives all its powers directly or indirectly from the great body of the people, and is administered by persons holding their offices during pleasure for a limited period, or during good behavior.

James Madison, Federalist No. 39, January 16, 1788

The republican principle demands that the deliberate sense of the community should govern the conduct of those to whom they intrust the management of their affairs; but it does not require an unqualified complaisance to every sudden breeze of passion or to every transient impulse which the people may receive from the arts of men, who flatter their prejudices to betray their interests.

Alexander Hamilton, Federalist No. 71, March 18, 1788

Rights

In a word, as a man is said to have a right to his property, he may be equally said to have a property in his rights.

James Madison, Essay on Property, March 29, 1792

The sacred rights of mankind are not to be rummaged for, among old parchments, or musty records. They are written, as with a sun beam, in the whole volume of human nature, by the hand of the divinity itself; and can never be erased or obscured by mortal power.

Alexander Hamilton, *The Farmer Refuted*, February 23, 1775

We hold these truths to be self-evident, that all men are created equal, that they are endowed by their Creator with certain unalienable Rights, that among these are Life, Liberty and pursuit of

Happiness, that to secure these rights, governments are instituted among men, deriving their just powers from the consent of the governed.

The Declaration of Independence, July 4, 1776

Government, in my humble opinion, should be formed to secure and to enlarge the exercise of the natural rights of its members; and every government, which has not this in view, as its principal object, is not a government of the legitimate kind.

James Wilson, Lectures on Law, 1791

All, too, will bear in mind this sacred principle, that though the will of the majority is in all cases to prevail, that will to be rightful must be reasonable; that the minority possess their equal rights, which equal law must protect, and to violate would be oppression.

Thomas Jefferson, First Inaugural Address, March 4, 1801

It is sufficiently obvious, that persons and property are the two great subjects on which Governments are to act; and that the rights of persons, and the rights of property, are the objects, for the protection of which Government was instituted. These rights cannot well be separated.

James Madison, speech at the Virginia Convention, December 2, 1829

All eyes are opened, or opening, to the rights of man. The general spread of the light of science has already laid open to every view the palpable truth, that the mass of mankind has not been born with saddles on their backs, nor a favored few booted and spurred, ready to ride legitimately, by the grace of God.

Thomas Jefferson, letter to Roger C. Weightman, June 24, 1826

If men through fear, fraud or mistake, should in terms renounce and give up any essential natural right, the eternal law of reason and the great end of society, would absolutely vacate such renunciation; the right to freedom being the gift of God Almighty, it is not in the power of Man to alienate this gift, and voluntarily become a slave.

John Adams, Rights of the Colonists, 1772

The fundamental source of all your errors, sophisms and false reasonings is a total ignorance of the natural rights of mankind. Were you once to become acquainted with these, you could never entertain a thought, that all men are not, by nature, entitled to a parity of privileges. You would be convinced, that natural liberty is a gift of the beneficent Creator to the whole human race, and that civil liberty is founded in that; and cannot be wrested from any people, without the most manifest violation of justice.

Alexander Hamilton, The Farmer Refuted, February 23, 1775

 # Senate

(See also Congress, House of Representatives)

Such an institution may be sometimes necessary as a defense to the people against their own temporary errors and delusions.

James Madison, Federalist No. 63, March 1, 1788

In forming the Senate, the great anchor of the Government, the questions as they came within the first object turned mostly on the mode of appointment, and the duration of it.

James Madison, letter to Thomas Jefferson, October 24, 1787

Those gentlemen, who will be elected senators, will fix themselves in the federal town, and become citizens of that town more than of your state.

George Mason, speech to the Virginia Ratifying Convention, June 14, 1788

There is a tradition that, on his return from France, Jefferson called Washington to account at the breakfast-table for having agreed to a second chamber. "Why," asked Washington, "did you pour that coffee into your saucer?" "To cool it," quoth Jefferson. "Even so," said Washington, "we pour legislation into the senatorial saucer to cool it."

anecdote from Farrand's Records of the Federal Convention of 1787

The rich, the well-born, and the able, acquire and influence among the people that will soon be too much for simple honesty and plain sense, in a house of representatives. The most illustrious of them must, therefore, be separated from the mass, and placed by themselves in a senate; this is, to all honest and useful intents, an ostracism.

John Adams, *A Defense of the Constitutions of Government of the United States of America,* 1787

As our president bears no resemblance to a king so we shall see the Senate has no similitude to nobles. First, not being hereditary, their collective knowledge, wisdom, and virtue are not precarious. For by these qualities alone are they to obtain their offices, and they will have none of the peculiar qualities and vices of those men who possess power merely because their father held it before them.

Tench Coxe, *An American Citizen* No. 2, September 28, 1787

Separation of Powers

The accumulation of all powers, legislative, executive, and judiciary, in the same hands, whether of one, a few, or many, and whether hereditary, self-appointed, or elective, may justly be pronounced the very definition of tyranny.

James Madison, Federalist No. 48, February 1, 1788

A dependence on the people is, no doubt, the primary control on the government; but experience has taught mankind the necessity of auxiliary precautions.

James Madison, Federalist No. 51, February 6, 1788

The principle of the Constitution is that of a separation of legislative, Executive and Judiciary functions, except in cases specified. If this principle be not expressed in direct terms, it is clearly the spirit of the Constitution, and it ought to be so commented and acted on by every friend of free government.

Thomas Jefferson, letter to James Madison, January 1797

Nothing has yet been offered to invalidate the doctrine that the meaning of the Constitution may as well be ascertained by the Legislative as by the Judicial authority.

James Madison, speech before the House of Representatives, June 18, 1789

An elective despotism was not the government we fought for; but one in which the powers of government should be so divided and balanced among the several bodies of magistracy as that no one could transcend their legal limits without being effectually checked and restrained by the others.

James Madison, Federalist No. 58, February 20, 1788

My construction of the constitution is . . . that each department is truly independent of the others, and has an equal right to decide for itself what is the meaning of the constitution in the cases submitted to its action; and especially, where it is to act ultimately and without appeal.

Thomas Jefferson, letter to Samuel Adams Wells, May 12, 1819

The great security against a gradual concentration of the several powers in the same department consists in giving to those who administer each department the necessary constitutional means and personal motives to resist encroachment of the others.

James Madison, Federalist No. 10, November 23,1787

To preserve the republican form and principles of our Constitution and cleave to the salutary distribution of powers which that [the Constitution] has established ... are the two sheet anchors of our Union. If driven from either, we shall be in danger of foundering.

Thomas Jefferson, letter to Judge William Johnson, June 12, 1823

I acknowledge, in the ordinary course of government, that the exposition of the laws and Constitution devolves upon the Judiciary. But I beg to know upon what principle it can be contended that any one department draws from the Constitution greater powers than another in marking out the limits of the powers of the several departments.

James Madison, speech before the House of Representatives, June 17, 1789

Good constitutions are formed upon a comparison of the liberty of the individual with the strength of government: If the tone of either be too high, the other will be weakened too much. It is the happiest possible mode of conciliating these objects, to institute one branch peculiarly endowed with sensibility, another with knowledge and firmness. Through the opposition and mutual control of these bodies, the government will reach, in its regular operations, the perfect balance between liberty and power.

Alexander Hamilton, speech at the New York Ratifying Convention, June 25, 1788

What is to be the consequence, in case the Congress shall misconstrue this part [the necessary and proper clause] of the Constitution and exercise powers not warranted by its true meaning, I answer the same as if they should misconstrue or enlarge any other power vested in them...the success of the usurpation will depend on the executive and judiciary departments, which are to expound and give effect to the legislative acts; and in a last resort a remedy must be obtained from the people, who can by the elections of more faithful representatives, annul the acts of the usurpers.

James Madison, Federalist No. 44, January 25, 1788

Slavery

I believe a time will come when an opportunity will be offered to abolish this lamentable evil.

Patrick Henry, letter to Robert Pleasants, January 18, 1773

Nothing is more certainly written in the book of fate than that these people are to be free.

Thomas Jefferson, *Autobiography*, 1821

[The Convention] thought it wrong to admit in the Constitution the idea that there could be property in men.

James Madison, Records of the Convention, August 25, 1787

There is not a man living who wishes more sincerely than I do, to see a plan adopted for the abolition of it.

George Washington, letter to Robert Morris, April 12, 1786

We have seen the mere distinction of color made in the most enlightened period of time, a ground of the most oppressive dominion ever exercised by man over man.

James Madison, speech at the Constitutional Convention, June 6, 1787

Slavery is such an atrocious debasement of human nature, that its very extirpation, if not performed with solicitous care, may sometimes open a source of serious evils.

Benjamin Franklin, An Address to the Public, November, 1789

The love of justice and the love of country plead equally the cause of these people, and it is a moral reproach to us that they should have pleaded it so long in vain.

Thomas Jefferson, letter to Edward Coles, August 25, 1814

Every measure of prudence, therefore, ought to be assumed for the eventual total extirpation of slavery from the United States .... I have, throughout my whole life, held the practice of slavery in ...abhorrence.

John Adams, letter to Robert J. Evans, June 8, 1819

We have the wolf by the ears, and we can neither hold him, nor safely let him go. Justice is in one scale, and self-preservation in the other.

Thomas Jefferson, letter to John Holmes, April 22, 1820

He has waged cruel war against human nature itself, violating its most sacred right of life and liberty in the persons of a distant people who never offended him, captivating & carrying them into slavery in another hemisphere, or to incur miserable death in their transportation thither.

Thomas Jefferson, deleted portion from a draft of the Declaration of Independence, June 1776

It is much to be wished that slavery may be abolished. The honour of the States, as well as justice and humanity, in my opinion, loudly call upon them to emancipate these unhappy people. To contend for our own liberty, and to deny that blessing to others, involves an inconsistency not to be excused.

John Jay, letter to R. Lushington, March 15, 1786

It is due to justice; due to humanity; due to truth; to the sympathies of our nature; in fine, to our character as a people, both abroad and at home, that they should be considered, as much as possible, in the light of human beings, and not as mere property. As such, they are acted upon by our laws, and have an interest in our laws.

James Madison, speech to the Virginia Ratifying Convention, December 2, 1829

❦ Taxation

No Taxation without Representation!

Anonymous, slogan in response to British Tax Policy, circa 1765

No taxes can be devised which are not more or less inconvenient and unpleasant.

George Washington, Farewell Address, September 19, 1796

Our new Constitution is now established, and has an appearance that promises permanency; but in this world nothing can be said to be certain, except death and taxes.

Benjamin Franklin, letter to Jean-Baptiste Leroy, November 13, 1789

Excessive taxation ... will carry reason & reflection to every man's door, and particularly in the hour of election.

Thomas Jefferson, letter to John Taylor, November 26, 1798

It is a singular advantage of taxes on articles of consumption that they contain in their own nature a security against excess. They prescribe their own limit, which cannot be exceeded without defeating the end purposed — that is, an extension of the revenue.

Alexander Hamilton, Federalist No. 21, December 12, 1787

Taxes should be continued by annual or biennial reeactments, because a constant hold, by the nation, of the strings of the public purse is a salutary restraint from which an honest government ought not wish, nor a corrupt one to be permitted, to be free.

Thomas Jefferson, letter to John Wayles Eppes, June 24, 1813

The apportionment of taxes on the various descriptions of property is an act which seems to require the most exact impartiality; yet there is, perhaps, no legislative act in which greater opportunity and temptation are given to a predominant party to trample on the rules of justice. Every shilling which they overburden the inferior number is a shilling saved to their own pockets.

James Madison, Federalist No. 10, November 23, 1787

If, from the more wretched parts of the old world, we look at those which are in an advanced stage of improvement, we still find the greedy hand of government thrusting itself into every corner and crevice of industry, and grasping the spoil of the multitude. Invention is continually exercised, to furnish new pretenses for revenues and taxation. It watches prosperity as its prey and permits none to escape without tribute.

Thomas Paine, *Rights of Man*, 1791

To take from one, because it is thought his own industry and that of his fathers has acquired too much, in order to spare to others, who, or whose fathers, have not exercised equal industry and skill, is to violate arbitrarily the first principle of association, the guarantee to everyone the free exercise of his industry and the fruits acquired by it.

Thomas Jefferson, letter to Joseph Milligan, April 6, 1816

Truth

There is but one straight course, and that is to seek truth and pursue it steadily.

George Washington, letter to Edmund Randolph, July 31, 1795

Experience is the oracle of truth; and where its responses are unequivocal, they ought to be conclusive and sacred.

James Madison and Alexander Hamilton, Federalist No. 20, December 11, 1787

In disquisitions of every kind there are certain primary truths, or first principles, upon which all subsequent reasoning must depend. These contain an internal evidence which, antecedent to all reflection or combination, commands the assent of the mind.

Alexander Hamilton, Federalist No. 31, January 1, 1788

It is error alone which needs the support of government. Truth can stand by itself. Subject opinion to coercion: whom will you make your inquisitors?

Thomas Jefferson, *Notes on the State of Virginia,* Query 17, 1781

Facts are stubborn things; and whatever may be our wishes, our inclination, or the dictates of our passions, they cannot alter the state of facts and evidence.

John Adams, in defense of the British soldiers on trial for the Boston Massacre, December 4, 1770

Freedom had been hunted round the globe; reason was considered as rebellion; and the slavery of fear had made men afraid to think. But such is the irresistible nature of truth, that all it asks, and all it wants, is the liberty of appearing.

Thomas Paine, *Rights of Man,* 1791

Man, once surrendering his reason, has no remaining guard against absurdities the most monstrous, and like a ship without rudder, is the spot of every wind. With such persons, gullability, which they call faith, takes the helm from the hand of reason and the mind becomes a wreck.

Thomas Jefferson, letter to James Smith, December 8, 1822

It is natural to man to indulge in the illusions of hope. We are apt to shut our eyes against a painful truth — and listen to the song of that syren, till she transforms us into beasts. Is this the part of wise men, engaged in a great and arduous struggle for liberty? Are we disposed to be of the number of those, who having eyes, see not, and having ears, hear not, the things which so nearly concern their temporal salvation? For my part, whatever anguish of spirit it might cost, I am willing to know the whole truth; to know the worst, and to provide for it.

Patrick Henry, speech to the Virginia Convention, March 23, 1775

Tyranny

I have sworn upon the altar of God, eternal hostility against every form of tyranny over the mind of men.

Thomas Jefferson, letter to Benjamin Rush, September 23, 1800

There is a natural and necessary progression from the extreme of anarchy to the extreme of tyranny.

George Washington, Circular to the States, June 8, 1783

Tyranny, like hell, is not easily conquered; yet we have this consolation with us, that the harder the conflict, the more glorious the triumph.

Thomas Paine, *American Crisis* No. 1, December 19, 1776

Of those men who have overturned the liberties of republics, the greatest number have begun their career by paying an obsequious court to the people, commencing demagogues and ending tyrants.

Alexander Hamilton, Federalist No. 1, October 27, 1797

Union

Union, the last anchor of our hope, and that alone which is to prevent this heavenly country from becoming an arena of gladiators.

Thomas Jefferson, letter to Elbridge Gerry, May 13, 1797

Whenever the dissolution of the Union arrives, America will have reason to exclaim, in the words of the poet: "FAREWELL! A LONG FAREWELL TO ALL MY GREATNESS."

John Jay, Federalist No. 2, October 31, 1787

We are either a United people, or we are not. If the former, let us, in all matters of general concern act as a nation, which have national objects to promote, and a national character to support. If we are not, let us no longer act a farce by pretending to it.

George Washington, letter to James Madison, November 30, 1785

If there be any among us who would wish to dissolve this Union or to change its republican form, let them stand undisturbed as monuments of the safety with which error of opinion may be tolerated where reason is left free to combat it.

Thomas Jefferson, First Inaugural Address, March 4, 1801

Every man who loves peace, every man who loves his country, every man who loves liberty ought to have it ever before his eyes that he may cherish in his heart a due attachment to the Union of America and be able to set a due value on the means of preserving it.

James Madison, Federalist No. 41, January 19, 1788

 # Virtue

Be in general virtuous, and you will be happy.

Benjamin Franklin, letter to John Alleyne, August 9, 1768

Few men have virtue to withstand the highest bidder.

George Washington, letter to Robert Howe, August 17, 1779

When we are planning for posterity, we ought to remember that virtue is not hereditary.

Thomas Paine, *Common Sense*, 1776

A popular government cannot flourish without virtue in the people.

Richard Henry Lee, letter to Colonel Martin Pickett, March 5, 1786

I pronounce it as certain that there was never yet a truly great man that was not at the same time truly virtuous.

Benjamin Franklin, *The Busy-Body* No. III, February 18, 1728

'Tis substantially true, that virtue or morality is a necessary spring of popular government. The rule indeed extends with more or less force to every species of free Government.

George Washington, Farewell Address, September 19, 1796

To suppose that any form of government will secure liberty or happiness without any virtue in the people, is a chimerical idea.

James Madison, speech to the Virginia Ratifying Convention, June 20, 1788

Those who labour in the earth are the chosen people of God, if ever he had a chosen people, whose breasts he has made his peculiar deposit for substantial and genuine virtue.

Thomas Jefferson, *Notes on the State of Virginia*, Query XIX, 1787

The virtues of men are of more consequence to society than their abilities; and for this reason, the heart should be cultivated with more assiduity than the head.

Noah Webster, On the Education of Youth in America, 1788

There is no truth more thoroughly established than that there exists in the economy and course of nature an indissoluble union between virtue and happiness; between duty and advantage; between the genuine maxims of an honest and magnanimous policy, and the solid rewards of public prosperity and felicity.

George Washington, First Inaugural Address, April 30, 1789

A general dissolution of principles and manners will more surely overthrow the liberties of America than the whole force of the common enemy. While the people are virtuous they cannot be subdued; but when once they lose their virtue then will be ready to surrender their liberties to the first external or internal invader.

Samuel Adams, letter to James Warren, February 12, 1779

Public virtue cannot exist in a nation without private, and public virtue is the only foundation of republics. There must be a positive passion for the public good, the public interest, honour, power and glory, established in the minds of the people, or there can be no republican government, nor any real liberty: and this public passion must be superiour to all private passions.

John Adams, letter to Mercy Warren, April 16, 1776

Illustrious examples are displayed to our view that we may imitate as well as admire. Before we can be distinguished by the same honors, we must be distinguished by the same virtues. What are those virtues? They are chiefly the same virtues, which we have already seen to be descriptive of the American character — the love of liberty, and the love of law.

James Wilson, Of the Study of the Law in the United States, circa 1790

We ought to consider what is the end of government before we determine which is the best form. Upon this point all speculative politicians will agree that the happiness of society is the end of government, as all divines and moral philosophers will agree that the happiness of the individual is the end of man.... All sober inquirers after truth, ancient and modern, pagan and Christian, have declared that the happiness of man, as well as his dignity, consists in virtue.

John Adams, *Thoughts on Government*, 1776

Is there no virtue among us? If there be not, we are in a wretched situation. No theoretical checks — no form of government can render us secure. To suppose that any form of government will secure liberty or happiness without any virtue in the people, is a chimerical idea, if there be sufficient virtue and intelligence in the community, it will be exercised in the selection of these men. So that we do not depend on their virtue, or put confidence in our rulers, but in the people who are to choose them.

James Madison, speech to the Virginia Ratifying Convention, June 20, 1788

 War

(See also International Relations, National Defense)

To be prepared for war, is one of the most effectual means of preserving peace.

George Washington, First Annual Message, January 8, 1790

It is a principle incorporated into the settled policy of America, that as peace is better than war, war is better than tribute.

James Madison, letter to the Dey of Algiers, August 1816

If we desire to insult, we must be able to repel it; if we desire to secure peace, one of the most powerful instruments of our rising prosperity, it must be known, that we are at all times ready for War.

George Washington, Fifth Annual Address to Congress, December 13, 1793

To judge from the history of mankind, we shall be compelled to conclude that the fiery and destructive passions of war reign in the human breast with much more powerful sway than the mild and beneficent sentiments of peace; and that to model our political systems upon speculations of lasting tranquillity would be to calculate on the weaker springs of human character.

Alexander Hamilton, Federalist No. 34, January 4, 1788

 # Work

Have you something to do to-morrow; do it to-day.

Benjamin Franklin, *Poor Richard's Almanack*, 1742

Work as if you were to live 100 Years, Pray as if you were to die To-morrow.

Benjamin Franklin, *Poor Richard's Almanack*, 1757

When men are employ'd, they are best content'd.

Benjamin Franklin, *Autobiography*, 1771

A mind always employed is always happy. This is the true secret, the grand recipe, for felicity. The idle are the only wretched.

Thomas Jefferson, letter to Martha Jefferson, May 21, 1787

To cherish and stimulate the activity of the human mind, by multiplying the objects of enterprise, is not among the least considerable of the expedients, by which the wealth of a nation may be promoted.

Alexander Hamilton, *Report on Manufactures*, December 1791

In our private pursuits it is a great advantage that every honest employment is deemed honorable. I am myself a nail-maker.

Thomas Jefferson, letter to Jean Nicolas Démeunier, April 29, 1795

GREAT DOCUMENTS
of the AMERICAN
FOUNDING,
INTRODUCED AND
EXPLAINED

About the Declaration there is a finality that is exceedingly restful. It is often asserted that the world has made a great deal of progress since 1776, that we have had new thoughts and new experiences which have given us a great advance over the people of that day, and that we may therefore very well discard their conclusions for something more modern. But that reasoning can not be applied to this great charter. If all men are created equal, that is final. If they are endowed with inalienable rights, that is final. If governments derive their just powers from the consent of the governed, that is final. No advance, no progress can be made beyond these propositions. If anyone wishes to deny their truth or their soundness, the only direction in which he can proceed historically is not forward, but backward toward the time when there was no equality, no rights of the individual, no rule of the people.

Calvin Coolidge, *The Inspiration of the Declaration,*
July 5, 1926, celebrating the 150th anniversary of the Declaration
of Independence

INTRODUCTION TO
THE DECLARATION OF
INDEPENDENCE

⟾◈⟽

'Nothing of importance this day," George III wrote in his diary on July 4, 1776. Even after having received a rather ominous communication from his American colonies with that date, he never quite realized how wrong he had been.

As a practical matter, the Declaration of Independence publicly announced to the world the unanimous decision of the American colonies to declare themselves free and independent states, absolved from any allegiance to Great Britain. England had been waging war against the Americans for fourteen months, since the shot heard 'round the world at Concord, and General Washington was already moving a Continental army toward New York when the colonists decided to effect the final break. The Declaration of Independence formally recognized this immediate situation. But its real significance — then as well as now — was as a statement of the conditions of legitimate political authority and the proper ends of government, and as a proclamation of a new basis of political rule in the sovereignty of the people. James Madison, the Father of the Constitution, called it "the fundamental Act of Union of these States."

On June 7, 1776, Richard Henry Lee, a delegate to the Second Continental Congress from Virginia, proposed resolutions to declare that "these United Colonies are, and of right ought to be, free and independent states," to establish a confederation and to seek foreign alliances. Each of these matters was referred to a select committee. On June 28, the committee to draft a statement embodying the first resolution submitted "A Declaration by the Representatives of the United States of America, in General Congress Assembled." Congress passed Lee's resolution in favor of independence on July 2, and then took three days to debate and amend the committee's draft before approving it on July 4. The separation of Lee's resolution and the committee's draft suggests that more was required than a simple statement of withdrawal from the British empire; a "decent respect for the opinions of mankind" demanded a broader statement of principle.

Although Congress had appointed a distinguished committee — including John Adams, Benjamin Franklin, Roger Sherman, and Robert Livingston — the Declaration of Independence is chiefly the work of Thomas Jefferson. By his own account, Jefferson was neither aiming at originality nor taking from any particular writings but was expressing the "harmonizing sentiments of the day," as expressed in conversation, letters, essays, or "the elementary books of public right, as Aristotle, Cicero, Locke, Sidney, etc." In this he was correct: the basic theory of the document reflected English Whig theory as it had evolved in the preceding century and a half. George Mason, for instance, had anticipated much of its substance in his draft of the Virginia Declaration of Rights in June 1776. Certainly the Declaration's language stressing man's natural rights calls to mind the great influence of John Locke. But the idea of government created by the consent of the governed (known as the social compact theory of government) was well established in the colonies. So was the idea that the purpose of government is to secure the people's safety and happiness (the commonwealth theory). Jefferson intended the Declaration to be "an expression of the American mind," and wrote so as to "place before mankind the common sense of the subject, in terms so plain and firm as to command their assent."

The structure of the Declaration of Independence is that of a common-law legal document; the stated purpose is to "declare the causes" which impelled the Americans to separate from the British. The document's famous second paragraph is a powerful synthesis of American constitutional and republican government theories. Its opening words are striking: "We hold these Truths to be self-evident, that all Men are created equal, that they are endowed by their Creator with certain unalienable Rights, that among these are Life, Liberty and the Pursuit of Happiness." All men have a right to liberty only in so far as they are by nature equal, which is to say none are naturally superior, and deserve to rule, or inferior, and deserve to be ruled. Because men are endowed with these rights, the rights are unalienable, which means that they cannot be given up or taken away. And because individuals equally possess these rights, governments derive their just powers from the consent of those governed. The purpose of government is to secure these fundamental rights and, although prudence tells us that governments should not be changed for trivial reasons, the people retain the right to alter or abolish government when it becomes destructive of these ends.

The remainder of the document is a bill of indictment accusing King George III of some thirty offenses, some constitutional, some legal and some matters of policy. (One of the best: "He has erected a multitude of New Offices, and sent hither swarms of Officers to harass our People, and eat out their substance.") The key charge was that the king had conspired with Parliament to subject America to a "jurisdiction foreign to our constitution." At this point in their constitutional development, the Americans argued that a common king with authority over each of the colonies was their only binding legal connection with Great Britain. Parliament was not a party to the various original compacts with the individual colonies, they held, and thus could not regulate their internal affairs; the king was, however, but through his actions leading up to the American Revolution, he had intentionally violated those agreements. By explicitly placing America outside his protection, George III had himself dissolved their obligations of allegiance. The combined charges against the king were intended to demonstrate a history of repeated injuries, all having the object of establishing "an absolute tyranny" over America. And while the colonists were "disposed to suffer, while Evils are sufferable,î the time had come to end the relationship: "But when a long train of abuses and usurpations, pursuing invariably the same Object, evinces a design to reduce them under absolute Despotism, it is their right, it is their duty, to throw off such Government."

The Declaration of Independence and the liberties recognized in it are grounded in a higher law to which all human laws are answerable. This higher law can be understood to derive from reason — the truths of the Declaration are held to be "self-evident" — but also revelation. There are four references to God in the document: to "the laws of nature and nature's God"; to all men being "created equal" and "endowed by their Creator with certain unalienable rights"; to "the Supreme Judge of the world for the rectitude of our intentions"; and to "the protection of divine Providence." The first term suggests a deity that is knowable by human reason, but the others — God as creator, as judge and as providence — are more biblical, and add (and were assuredly intended to add) a theological context to the document. "And can the liberties of a nation be thought secure when we have removed their only firm basis, a conviction in the minds of the people that these liberties are a gift of God?" Jefferson asked in his *Notes on the State of Virginia*, "That they are not to be violated but with his wrath?"

One charge that Jefferson had included, but Congress removed, was that the king had "waged cruel war against human nature" by introducing slavery and allowing the slave trade into the American colonies. The words offended delegates from Georgia and South Carolina, who were unwilling to acknowledge that slavery violated the "most sacred rights of life and liberty," and the passage was dropped for the sake of unanimity. This dispute foreshadowed the central debate of the American Civil War, which Abraham Lincoln saw as a test to determine whether a nation "conceived in liberty and dedicated to the proposition that all men are created equal" could endure. (See Note on Slavery, p. 281)

Nevertheless, the true significance of the Declaration lies in its trans-historical meaning. As far back as Magna Carta, British subjects (such as the Whigs during the Glorious Revolution of 1688) had always petitioned for justice to their long-held rights as Englishmen. Early on, American objections to British misrule — as when they were taxed without their consent — had been based on appeals to the British (unwritten) constitution. But for the Declaration of Independence, and numerous other documents like it at the time of the American Revolution, British law was important but ultimately insufficient. The appeal was not to any conventional law or political contract but to the equal rights possessed by all men — English or Scottish, Protestant or Catholic, white or black — and "the separate and equal station to which the Laws of Nature and nature's God" entitled them as a people.

What is revolutionary about the Declaration of Independence, then, is not that a particular group of Americans declared their independence under particular circumstances but that they did so by appealing to — and promising to base their particular government on — a universal standard of justice. It is in this sense that Abraham Lincoln praised "the man who, in the concrete pressure of a struggle for national independence by a single people, had the coolness, forecast, and capacity to introduce into a merely revolutionary document, an abstract truth, applicable to all men and all times." It was this truth which established in principle that the practice of slavery was fundamentally incompatible with American liberty.

On July 5, copies of the Declaration were sent to various state assemblies, conventions, and committees of safety. It appeared in the *Pennsylvania Evening Post* on July 6, was first publicly proclaimed on July 8 in Philadelphia, and General Washington had it read aloud to his assembled soldiers on July 9.

— MATTHEW SPALDING

THE DECLARATION OF INDEPENDENCE

IN CONGRESS, July 4, 1776.
The unanimous Declaration of the thirteen united States of America,

WHEN IN THE COURSE OF HUMAN EVENTS, it becomes necessary for one people to dissolve the political bands which have connected them with another, and to assume among the powers of the earth, the separate and equal station to which the Laws of Nature and of Nature's God entitle them, a decent respect to the opinions of mankind requires that they should declare the causes which impel them to the separation.

We hold these truths to be self-evident, that all men are created equal, that they are endowed by their Creator with certain unalienable Rights, that among these are Life, Liberty and the pursuit of Happiness. — That to secure these rights, Governments are instituted among Men, deriving their just powers from the consent of the governed, — That whenever any Form of Government becomes destructive of these ends, it is the Right of the People to alter or to abolish it, and to institute new Government, laying its foundation on such principles and organizing its powers in such form, as to them shall seem most likely to effect their Safety and Happiness. Prudence, indeed, will dictate that Governments long established should not be changed for light and transient causes; and accordingly all experience hath shewn, that mankind are more disposed to suffer, while evils are sufferable, than to right themselves by abolishing the forms to which they are accustomed. But when a long train of abuses and usurpations, pursuing invariably the same Object evinces a design to reduce them under absolute Despotism, it is their right, it is their duty, to throw off such

Statement of Rights

Consent of the Governed

Prudence Will Dictate

Government, and to provide new Guards for their future security.—Such has been the patient sufferance of these Colonies; and such is now the necessity which constrains them to alter their former Systems of Government. The history of the present King of Great Britain is a history of repeated injuries and usurpations, all having in direct object the establishment of an absolute Tyranny over these States. To prove this, let Facts be submitted to a candid world.

Charges Against King George III

He has refused his Assent to Laws, the most wholesome and necessary for the public good.

He has forbidden his Governors to pass Laws of immediate and pressing importance, unless suspended in their operation till his Assent should be obtained; and when so suspended, he has utterly neglected to attend to them.

He has refused to pass other Laws for the accommodation of large districts of people, unless those people would relinquish the right of Representation in the Legislature, a right inestimable to them and formidable to tyrants only.

He has called together legislative bodies at places unusual, uncomfortable, and distant from the depository of their public Records, for the sole purpose of fatiguing them into compliance with his measures.

Local Governments

He has dissolved Representative Houses repeatedly, for opposing with manly firmness his invasions on the rights of the people.

He has refused for a long time, after such dissolutions, to cause others to be elected; whereby the Legislative powers, incapable of Annihilation, have returned to the People at large for their exercise; the State remaining in the mean time exposed to all the dangers of invasion from without, and convulsions within.

Immigration

He has endeavoured to prevent the population of these States; for that purpose obstructing the Laws for Naturalization of Foreigners; refusing to pass others to encourage their migrations hither, and raising the conditions of new

Appropriations of Lands.

He has obstructed the Administration of Justice, by refusing his Assent to Laws for establishing Judiciary powers.

Administration of Justice

He has made Judges dependent on his Will alone, for the tenure of their offices, and the amount and payment of their salaries.

He has erected a multitude of New Offices, and sent hither swarms of Officers to harrass our people, and eat out their substance.

He has kept among us, in times of peace, Standing Armies without the Consent of our legislatures.

He has affected to render the Military independent of and superior to the Civil power.

He has combined with others to subject us to a jurisdiction foreign to our constitution, and unacknowledged by our laws; giving his Assent to their Acts of pretended Legislation:

Combined with Parliament

For Quartering large bodies of armed troops among us:

For protecting them, by a mock Trial, from punishment for any Murders which they should commit on the Inhabitants of these States:

For cutting off our Trade with all parts of the world:

For imposing Taxes on us without our Consent:

Taxation Without Consent

For depriving us in many cases, of the benefits of Trial by Jury:

For transporting us beyond Seas to be tried for pretended offences

For abolishing the free System of English Laws in a neighbouring Province, establishing therein an Arbitrary government, and enlarging its Boundaries so as to render it at once an example and fit instrument for introducing the same absolute rule into these Colonies:

For taking away our Charters, abolishing our most valuable Laws, and altering fundamentally the Forms of our Governments:

For suspending our own Legislatures, and declaring them-

selves invested with power to legislate for us in all cases whatsoever.

He has abdicated Government here, by declaring us out of
his Protection and waging War against us.

He has plundered our seas, ravaged our Coasts, burnt our
towns, and destroyed the lives of our people.

He is at this time transporting large Armies of foreign
Mercenaries Mercenaries to compleat the works of death, desolation and
tyranny, already begun with circumstances of Cruelty & perfidy
scarcely paralleled in the most barbarous ages, and totally
unworthy the Head of a civilized nation.

He has constrained our fellow Citizens taken Captive on
the high Seas to bear Arms against their Country, to become
the executioners of their friends and Brethren, or to fall themselves by their Hands.

Domestic He has excited domestic insurrections amongst us, and has
Insurrections endeavoured to bring on the inhabitants of our frontiers, the
merciless Indian Savages, whose known rule of warfare, is an
undistinguished destruction of all ages, sexes and conditions.

In every stage of these Oppressions We have Petitioned for
Redress in the most humble terms: Our repeated Petitions
have been answered only by repeated injury. A Prince whose
character is thus marked by every act which may define a
Tyrant, is unfit to be the ruler of a free people.

Nor have We been wanting in attentions to our Brittish
Previous Appeals brethren. We have warned them from time to time of attempts
by their legislature to extend an unwarrantable jurisdiction over
us. We have reminded them of the circumstances of our emi-
gration and settlement here. We have appealed to their native
justice and magnanimity, and we have conjured them by the
ties of our common kindred to disavow these usurpations,
which, would inevitably interrupt our connections and correspondence. They too have been deaf to the voice of justice and
of consanguinity. We must, therefore, acquiesce in the necessity, which denounces our Separation, and hold them, as we hold

the rest of mankind, Enemies in War, in Peace Friends.

We, therefore, the Representatives of the united States of America, in General Congress, Assembled, appealing to the Supreme Judge of the world for the rectitude of our intentions, do, in the Name, and by Authority of the good People of these Colonies, solemnly publish and declare, That these United Colonies are, and of Right ought to be Free and Independent States; that they are Absolved from all Allegiance to the British Crown, and that all political connection between them and the State of Great Britain, is and ought to be totally dissolved; and that as Free and Independent States, they have full Power to levy War, conclude Peace, contract Alliances, establish Commerce, and to do all other Acts and Things which Independent States may of right do. And for the support of this Declaration, with a firm reliance on the protection of divine Providence, we mutually pledge to each other our Lives, our Fortunes and our sacred Honor.

Supreme Judge

Formal Declaration

Divine Providence

The 56 signatures on the Declaration:

Delaware:
Caesar Rodney
George Read
Thomas McKean

Connecticut:
Roger Sherman
Samuel Huntington
William Williams
Oliver Wolcott

Georgia:
Button Gwinnett
Lyman Hall
George Walton

Maryland:
Samuel Chase
William Paca
Thomas Stone
Charles Carroll of Carrollton

Massachusetts:
Samuel Adams
John Adams
Robert Treat Paine
Elbridge Gerry
John Hancock

New Hampshire:
Josiah Bartlett
Matthew Thornton
William Whipple

New Jersey:
Richard Stockton
John Witherspoon
Francis Hopkinson
John Hart
Abraham Clark

New York:
William Floyd
Philip Livingston
Francis Lewis
Lewis Morris

North Carolina:
William Hooper
Joseph Hewes
John Penn

Pennsylvania:
Robert Morris
Benjamin Rush
Benjamin Franklin
John Morton
George Clymer
James Smith
George Taylor
James Wilson
George Ross

Rhode Island:
Stephen Hopkins
William Ellery

South Carolina:
Edward Rutledge
Thomas Heyward, Jr.
Thomas Lynch, Jr.
Arthur Middleton

Virginia:
George Wythe
Richard Henry Lee
Thomas Jefferson
Benjamin Harrison
Thomas Nelson, Jr.
Francis Lightfoot Lee
Carter Braxton

A Note on
the Signers of the
Declaration of
Independence

━━━▷◆◁━━━

"…we mutually pledge to each other our Lives,
our Fortunes and our sacred Honor."

Declaration of Independence, July 4, 1776

Fifty-six individuals from the original 13 colonies participated in the Second Continental Congress and signed the Declaration of Independence. Pennsylvania sent nine delegates to the Second Congress, followed by Virginia with seven and Massachusetts and New Jersey each with five. Connecticut, Maryland, New York, and South Carolina each sent four delegates. Delaware, Georgia, New Hampshire, and North Carolina each sent three. Rhode Island, the smallest colony, sent only two delegates to Philadelphia.

Nine of the signers were born outside of the colonies, two were brothers, two were cousins, and one was an orphan. The average age of a signer was 45. The oldest delegate was Benjamin Franklin of Pennsylvania, who was 70 when he signed the Declaration. The youngest was Thomas Lynch Jr., of South Carolina, who was 27.

Eighteen of the signers were merchants or businessmen, 14 were farmers, and four were doctors. Forty-two signers had served in their colonial legislatures. Twenty-two were lawyers — although William Hooper of North Carolina was "disbarred" when he spoke out against the Crown — and nine were judges. Stephen Hopkins had been Governor of Rhode Island.

Although two others previously had been members of the clergy, John Witherspoon of New Jersey was the only active clergyman to attend — he wore his pontificals to the sessions. Almost all were Protestant Christians; Charles Carroll of Maryland was the only Roman Catholic signer.

Seven of the signers were educated at Harvard, four each at Yale and William & Mary, and three at the College of New Jersey (now Princeton). John Witherspoon was president of Princeton and George Wythe was a professor at William & Mary, where his students included the author of the Declaration of Independence, Thomas Jefferson.

Seventeen of the signers served in the military during the American Revolution. Thomas Nelson was a colonel in the Second Virginia Regiment and then commanded Virginia military forces at the Battle of Yorktown. William Whipple served with the New Hampshire militia and was one of the commanding officers in the decisive Saratoga campaign. Oliver Wolcott led the Connecticut regiments sent to defend New York, and he commanded a brigade of militia that took part in the defeat of General Burgoyne. Caesar Rodney was a major general in the Delaware militia, and John Hancock was the same in the Massachusetts militia.

Five of the signers were captured by the British during the war. Captains Edward Rutledge, Thomas Heyward, and Arthur Middleton (South Carolina) were all captured at the Battle of Charleston in 1780: Colonel George Walton was wounded and captured at the Battle of Savannah. Richard Stockton of New Jersey, who never recovered from his incarceration at the hands of British Loyalists, died in 1781.

Colonel Thomas McKean of Delaware wrote John Adams that he was "hunted like a fox by the enemy — compelled to remove my family five times in a few months, and at last fixed them in a little log house on the banks of the Susquehanna . . . and they were soon obliged to move again on account of the incursions of the Indians." Abraham Clark of New Jersey had two of his sons captured by the British during the war. John Witherspoon's three sons fought in the war and one, a major in the New Jersey Brigade, was killed at the Battle of Germantown.

Eleven signers had their homes and property destroyed. Francis Lewis's New York home was destroyed and his wife was taken prisoner. John Hart's farm and mills were destroyed when the British invaded New Jersey, and Hart died while fleeing capture. Carter Braxton and Thomas Nelson (both of Virginia) lent large sums of their personal fortunes to support the war effort, but were never repaid.

Fifteen of the signers participated in their states' constitutional conventions, and six — Roger Sherman, Robert Morris, Benjamin Franklin, George Clymer, James Wilson, and George Reed — signed the United States Constitution. Elbridge Gerry of Massachusetts attended the federal convention and, though he later supported the document, refused to sign the Constitution.

After the Revolution, 13 of the signers went on to become governors, and 18 served in their state legislatures. Sixteen became state and federal judges. Seven became members of the United States House of Representatives, and six became United States Senators. James Wilson and Samuel Chase became justices of the United States Supreme Court.

Thomas Jefferson, John Adams, and Elbridge Gerry each became vice president, and John Adams and Thomas Jefferson became president. The sons of signers John Adams and Benjamin Harrison also became president.

Five signers played major roles in the establishment of colleges and universities: Benjamin Franklin and the University of Pennsylvania, Thomas Jefferson and the University of Virginia, Benjamin Rush and Dickinson College, Lewis Morris and New York University, and George Walton and the University of Georgia.

John Adams, Thomas Jefferson, and Charles Carroll were the longest surviving signers. Adams and Jefferson both died on July 4, 1826, the 50th anniversary of the Declaration of Independence. Charles Carroll of Maryland died in 1832, at the age of 95; he was the last of the signers to die.

— MATTHEW SPALDING

Sources: Robert Lincoln, *Lives of the Presidents of the United States, with Biographical Notices of the Signers of the Declaration of Independence* (Brattleboro Typographical Company, 1839); John and Katherine Bakeless, Signers of the Declaration (Boston: Houghton Mifflin, 1969); *Biographical Directory of the United States Congress, 1774-1989* (Washington, D.C.: U.S. Government Printing Office, 1989).

Let the American youth never forget, that they possess a noble inheritance, bought by the toils, and sufferings, and blood on their ancestors; and capable, if wisely improved, and faithfully guarded, of transmitting to their latest posterity all the substantial blessings of life, the peaceful enjoyment of liberty, property, religion, and independence. The structure has been erected by architects of consummate skill and fidelity; its foundations are solid; its compartments are beautiful, as well as useful; its arrangements are full of wisdom and order; and its defences are impregnable from without. It has been reared for immortality, if the work of man may justly aspire to such a title. It may, nevertheless, perish in an hour by the folly, or corruption, or negligence of its only keepers, THE PEOPLE.

Joseph Story, Commentaries on the Constitution
of the United States, 1833

Introduction to the United States Constitution

━━━▷◆◁━━━

I t was 11 years after the Declaration of Independence — and four years after American victory in the Revolutionary War — when a small group of delegates convened in Philadelphia to create a new charter for governing the young nation. The result was the longest lasting, most successful, most enviable, and most imitated constitution man has ever known. The United States Constitution has secured an unprecedented degree of human freedom, upholding the rule of law, securing the blessings of liberty, and providing the framework for the people of America to build a great, prosperous, and just nation unlike any other in the world.

The United States had established an earlier constitution in 1781, called the Articles of Confederation, the result of Richard Henry Lee's 1776 motion in Congress that also led to the Declaration of Independence. Each state governed itself through elected representatives, and the state representatives in turn elected a weak central government. But the national government was so feeble and its powers so limited, that this system proved unworkable. There was no independent executive and Congress could not impose taxes to cover national expenses, which meant the Confederation was ineffectual. And because all 13 colonies had to ratify amendments, one state's refusal prevented any reform. By the end of the war, in 1783, it was increasingly clear that the Confederation was, as

George Washington observed, "a shadow without the substance." Alexander Hamilton argued that it was bringing the country "to the last stage of national humiliation."

Beyond this dilemma, the Americans faced a larger problem. Absolutely committed to the idea of popular government, they were also aware that previous attempts to establish such a government had almost always failed. Popular governments usually led to "majority tyranny," an overbearing many disregarding the rights of a minority. This was the problem in the individual states which, dominated by their popular legislatures, routinely violated rights of property and contract. In the *Federalist Papers*, James Madison famously described this as the problem of faction, the latent causes of which are "sown in the nature of man." (See sidebar, p. 99) The challenge was to create stable institutional arrangements that would secure the rights promised in the Declaration of Independence, while preserving a republican form of government that reflected the consent of the governed and avoided majority tyranny. Previous solutions usually rendered government powerless, and thus susceptible to all the problems with which the Founders were most concerned. The American solution would be to create a strong government of limited powers, all carefully enumerated in a written constitution.

In 1785, representatives from Maryland and Virginia met at Mount Vernon to discuss interstate trade. Then, in 1786, delegates from several states gathered at a conference in Annapolis, Maryland, to discuss commercial matters and issued a report calling for a general convention of all the states "to render the constitution of government adequate to the exigencies of the Union." The next year, from May 25 to September 17, 1787, delegates from 12 states met in what is now Independence Hall at Philadelphia to "form a more perfect Union" and establish a government that would "secure the Blessings of Liberty to ourselves and our posterity."

The Constitutional Convention was one of the most remarkable bodies ever assembled. Not only were there leaders in the fight for independence, such as Roger Sherman and John Dickinson, and leading thinkers just coming into prominence, such as James Madison, Alexander Hamilton and Gouverneur Morris, but also legendary figures, such as Benjamin Franklin and George Washington, who was chosen as president of the Convention. Every state was represented, except for one: Rhode Island, fearful that a strong national government would injure its lucrative trade, opposed revising the Articles of Confederation and sent no delegates. Patrick Henry and Samuel Adams, both of whom opposed the creation of a strong central government, also did not attend the convention. Notably absent were John Jay, who was U.S. secretary of foreign affairs, and John Adams and Thomas Jefferson, who were out of the country on government missions. Nevertheless, John Adams declared the three-and-a-half month convention "the greatest single effort of national deliberation that the world has ever seen." Jefferson described it as "an assembly of demigods."

From the beginning, the convention discarded the Articles of Confederation and focused on a set of resolutions known as the Virginia Plan. Largely the work of James Madison, the Virginia Plan proposed the creation of a supreme national government with separate legislative, executive, and judicial branches. The delegates generally agreed on the powers that should be lodged in a national legislature, but disagreed on how the states and popular opinion should be reflected in it. Under the Virginia Plan, population would determine representation in both houses of Congress. To protect the principle of state equality, small state delegates rallied around William Paterson's alternative New Jersey Plan to amend the Articles of Confederation, which would preserve each state's equal vote in a one-house Congress with slightly augmented powers. Although the delegates rejected the New Jersey Plan, they eventually adopted what is called the Great Compromise, under which the House of Representatives would be apportioned based on population and each state would have two votes in the Senate. As a precaution against having to assume the financial burdens of the smaller states, the larger states exacted an agreement that revenue bills could originate only in the House, where the more populous states would have greater representation.

All of the legislative powers "herein granted" by the new Constitution to Congress are meticulously listed, mostly in Article I, Section 8. The powers do not seem very extensive: apart from some relatively minor matters, the Constitution added to the authority already granted in the Articles only the powers to regulate commerce and to apportion "direct" taxes among the states according to population. But the point is clear: Congress only has the powers delegated to it in the Constitution. If Congress could do whatever it wanted, Madison noted, then the government was "no longer a limited one, possessing enumerated powers, but an indefinite one, subject to particular exceptions."

By contrast, in Article II, the "executive Power [is] vested in a President of the United States of America." The President is the commander in chief of the armed forces and, with the consent of the Senate, appoints judges and other federal officers and makes treaties with other nations. The President plays an important role in legislation through the veto power granted in Article I, Section 7, and is also charged to "take care that the laws be faithfully executed" — a responsibility that is itself restricted by Congress's limited powers. Nevertheless, the implication is that there is an executive power inherent in the office itself. The delegates devoted less attention to the executive branch, largely because of the widespread assumption that General George Washington would be the first to hold — and by his precedents define — the newly created office. They did create the Electoral College system to encourage the election of chief executives with broad, national appeal.

Even less attention was given to the structure of the judiciary in Article III: the judicial power was placed in "one supreme Court and in such inferior courts as the Congress may from time to time ordain and establish." The judiciary's most important function is to decide "cases" and "controversies" — that is, lawsuits. By the Judiciary Act of 1789 Congress approved a Supreme Court with a Chief Justice and five associates, and created 13 district courts, three circuit courts, and the office of the Attorney General.

There have been federal trial courts (United States District Courts) in every state since 1789, and intermediate Courts of Appeal since 1891. Although it is not mentioned in the Constitution, it was generally recognized that the Supreme Court would also exercise a judicial review role — deciding whether state or federal laws at issue were constitutional — in the new government. "The judiciary," Hamilton promised, "is beyond comparison the weakest of the three departments of power."

Article IV provided that every state would give its "Full Faith and Credit" to the laws and decisions of every other state, and that all citizens would enjoy the privileges and immunities of citizenship in every state. It also provided for the admission of new states as *states*, not *colonies*, on an equal footing with the original 13.

The process for amending the Constitution is provided for in Article V, and Article VI makes the United States Constitution the "supreme Law of the Land" and binds federal and state officials by oath to its support. It also contains a significant expression of religious liberty in its ban on religious tests for public office.

Auxiliary Precautions

THREE IMPORTANT INSTITUTIONAL MECHANISMS are at work in the structure of the Constitution: the extended republic, the separation of powers, and federalism. The Founders believed that citizen virtue was crucial for the success of republican government and thought that limited government would allow for and even encourage the flourishing of civil society. Nevertheless, they knew that passion and interest were a permanent part of human nature and could not be controlled by parchment barriers alone. "A dependence on the people is, no doubt, the primary control on the government," Madison explained in the *Federalist Papers*, "but experience has taught mankind the necessity of auxiliary precautions." Rather than hoping for the best, the Founders designed a system that would harness these opposite and rival interests to supply "the defect of better motives."

The effect of representation — of individual citizens being represented in the government rather than ruling through direct participatory democracy — is to refine and moderate public opinion through a deliberative process. Extending the Republic — literally increasing the size of the nation — would take in a greater number and variety of opinions, making it harder for a majority to form on narrow interests contrary to the common good. The majority that did develop would be more settled, and, by necessity, would encompass (and represent) a wider diversity of opinion. This idea that bigger is better reversed the prevailing assumption that republican government could work only in small states.

The Founders also knew, again as Madison explained, that "the accumulation of all powers, legislative, executive, and judiciary, in the same hands, whether of one, a few, or many, and whether hereditary, self-appointed, or elective, may justly be pronounced the very definition of tyranny." In order to distribute power and prevent its accumulation, they created three separate branches of government, each performing its own functions and duties. Each branch also would share a few powers — as when the President shares the legislative power through the veto — so that they would have an incentive to check each other. Jefferson called the "republican form and principles of our Constitution" and "the salutary distribution of powers," which the Constitution established, the "two sheet anchors of our Union." "If driven from either," he predicted, "we shall be in danger of foundering."

And although national powers were clearly enhanced by the Constitution, the federal government was to exercise only delegated powers, the remainder being reserved to the states or to the people. Despite the need for additional national authority, the framers remained distrustful of government in general and of a centralized federal government in particular. "The powers delegated by the proposed Constitution to the federal government are few and defined," Madison wrote in Federalist No. 45, "Those which are to remain in the State governments are numerous and indefinite." And to give the states more leverage against the national government, equal state representation in the Senate was blended into the national legislature (and guaranteed in Article V). "This balance between the National and State governments ought to be dwelt on with peculiar attention, as it is of the utmost importance," Hamilton argued at the New York State ratifying convention. "It forms a double security to the people. If one encroaches on their rights they will find a powerful protection in the other. Indeed, they will both be prevented from overpassing their constitutional limits by a certain rivalship, which will ever subsist between them."

In early August a "Committee of Detail" reworked the resolutions of the expanded Virginia Plan into a draft Constitution. In mid September, the convention concluded the work of writing the Constitution and gave this draft to a "Committee of Style" to polish the language. (The notable literary quality of the Constitution, an unusual feature in documents of state, is due principally to Gouverneur Morris of Pennsylvania.) The delegates continued revising the draft until September 17 — now celebrated as Constitution Day — when 39 delegates representing 12 states signed the Constitution and sent it to the Congress of the Confederation, and the Convention officially adjourned.

Many of the original 55 delegates had returned home over the course of the long Convention and were not present at the end. Of those that were, only three delegates — Edmund Randolph and George Mason of Virginia and Elbridge Gerry of Massachusetts — opposed the Constitution and chose not to sign. Randolph thought the Constitution was not sufficiently republican, and was wary of creating a single executive. Mason and Gerry (who later supported the Constitution and served in the First Congress) were concerned about the lack of a declaration of rights. Despite these objections, George Washington thought that it was "little short of a miracle" that the delegates could agree on the Constitution. Thomas Jefferson, who was also concerned about the lack of a bill of rights, nevertheless wrote that the Constitution "is unquestionably the wisest ever yet presented to men."

On September 28, Congress sent the Constitution to the states, which in turn referred it to ratifying conventions chosen by the people. Delaware was the first state to ratify the Constitution on December 7, 1787; the last of the 13 original colonies was Rhode Island, on May 29, 1790, two-and-a-half years later. In accordance with Article VII of the Constitution, the new government was approved with the ratification of the ninth state — New Hampshire on June 21, 1788.

Amendments to the Constitution

THERE HAD BEEN SOME DISCUSSION among the delegates of the need for a bill of rights, a proposal that was rejected by the Convention. The lack of a bill of rights like that found in most state constitutions, however, became a rallying cry for the Anti-Federalists during the ratification debate. The advocates of the Constitution (led by James Madison) agreed to add one in the first session of Congress. Ratified on December 15, 1791, the first ten amendments — the Bill of Rights — include sweeping restrictions on the federal government and its ability to limit certain fundamental rights and procedural matters. (See sidebar, p. 114) The Ninth and 10th Amendments briefly encapsulate the twofold theory of the Constitution: the purpose of the Constitution is to protect *rights* which stem not from the government but from the people themselves, and the *powers* of the national government are limited to only those delegated to it by the Constitution on behalf of the people.

The monumental exception to the Constitution's securing of fundamental rights, of course, was slavery. Although the words "slave" or "slavery" were kept out of the Constitution (Madison recorded in his notes that the delegates "thought it wrong to admit in the Constitution the idea that there could be property in men"), the framers made three concessions to the institution for the sake of unanimity: apportionment for Representatives and taxation purposes would be determined by the number of free persons and three-fifths "of all other Persons" (Art. I, Sec. 2);

Congress was prohibited until 1808 from blocking the migration and importation "of such Persons as any of the states now existing shall think proper to admit" (Art. I, Sec. 9); and the privileges and immunities clause (Art. IV, Sec. 2) guaranteed the return of any "Person held to service of labour" in one state who had escaped to another state. (See Note on Slavery, p. 281)

In the end, it required a Civil War to reconcile the protections of the Constitution with the principles expressed in the Declaration of Independence. The U. S. Civil War was followed by the enactment of the 13th, 14th, and 15th Amendments (ratified in 1865, 1868, and 1870, respectively) that abolished slavery; conferred citizenship on all persons born or naturalized in the United States and established the principle that a state cannot "deprive any person of life, liberty, or property, without due process of law"; and made clear that the right of citizens to vote cannot be denied or abridged on account of race, color or previous condition of servitude.

In addition to the Bill of Rights and the Civil War amendments, there have been several other amendments to the Constitution. The *Chisholm v. Georgia* case led to the enactment of the 11th Amendment (1795), limiting the jurisdiction of the federal judiciary with regard to suits against states. The dispute over the election of 1800 led to the enactment of the 12th Amendment (1804), changing the method of electing the president and vice president.

There were four amendments during the Progressive Era, at the beginning of the 20th century. The 16th Amendment (1913) gave Congress the power to levy taxes on incomes, from whatever source derived, without apportionment among the several states. The 17th Amendment (1913) provided for the direct election of senators by popular vote. The 18th Amendment (1919), the so-called Prohibition Amendment, prohibited the manufacture, sale, or transportation of intoxicating liquors. (It was repealed by the 21st Amendment in 1933.) And the 19th Amendment (1920) extended to women the right to vote.

The most recent change was the 27th Amendment, which provided that any pay raise Congress votes itself will not take effect until after an intervening congressional election. It was ratified in 1992, 203 years after James Madison wrote and proposed it as part of the original Bill of Rights.

A Momentous Work

WHEN THE CONSTITUTIONAL CONVENTION assembled for the last time on the morning of September 17, 1787, Major William Jackson, the secretary of the Convention, read the completed document aloud to the delegates for one last time. Thereupon Benjamin Franklin, the 81-year-old patriarch of the group, immediately rose to speak. Unable to complete the address, he gave his speech to James Wilson to read, who later gave it to James Madison to record in his notes. Franklin declared that he supported the new Constitution — "with all its faults, if they are such" — because he thought a new government was necessary for the young nation. He continued:

> I doubt too whether any other convention we can obtain may be able to make a better Constitution. For when you assemble a number of men to have the advantage of their joint wisdom, you inevitably assemble with those men, all their prejudices, their passions, their errors of opinion, their local interests, and their selfish views. From such an Assembly can a perfect production be expected? It therefore astonishes me, Sir, to find this system approaching so near to perfection as it does; and I think it will astonish our enemies.... Thus I consent, Sir, to this Constitution because I expect no better, and because I am not sure, that it is not the best. The opinions I have had of its errors, I sacrifice to the public good. I have never whispered a syllable of them abroad. Within these walls they were born, and here they shall die. On the whole, Sir, I cannot help expressing a wish that every member of the Convention who may still have objections to it, would with me, on this occasion doubt a little of his own infallibility, and to make manifest our unanimity, put his name to this instrument.

As the delegates came forward, one at a time, to sign their names to the final document, James Madison recorded Franklin's final comment, just before the Constitutional Convention was dissolved. Franklin had noted the sun painted on the back of President Washington's chair. "I have often, and often in the course of the Session, and the vicissitudes of my hopes and fears as to its issue, looked at that behind the President without being able to tell whether it was rising or setting. But now at length I have the happiness to know that it is a rising and not a setting Sun."

"The business being thus closed," George Washington recorded in his private diary, the delegates proceeded to City Tavern on Second Street near Walnut, "dined together and took a cordial leave of each other."

> After which I returned to my lodgings, did some business with and received the papers from the secretary of the Convention, and retired to meditate on the momentous work which had been executed.

— MATTHEW SPALDING

THE CONSTITUTION OF THE UNITED STATES OF AMERICA

We the People of the United States, in Order to form
a more perfect Union, establish Justice, insure domestic
Tranquility, provide for the common defense, promote the
general Welfare, and secure the Blessings of Liberty to ourselves and our Posterity, do ordain and establish this
Constitution for the United States of America.

Preamble

Article. I.

Section. 1.

All legislative Powers herein granted shall be vested in a
Congress of the United States, which shall consist of a Senate
and House of Representatives.

Legislative Branch

Section. 2.

The House of Representatives shall be composed of Members
chosen every second Year by the People of the several States,
and the Electors in each State shall have the Qualifications
requisite for Electors of the most numerous Branch of the
State Legislature.

House of Representatives

No Person shall be a Representative who shall not have
attained to the Age of twenty five Years, and been seven Years
a Citizen of the United States, and who shall not, when elected, be an Inhabitant of that State in which he shall be chosen.

Requirements of Office

[Representatives and direct Taxes shall be apportioned
among the several States which may be included within this
Union, according to their respective Numbers, which shall be
determined by adding to the whole Number of free Persons,
including those bound to Service for a Term of Years, and
excluding Indians not taxed, three fifths of all other Persons.]

Changed by Section 2 of the Fourteenth mendment

The actual Enumeration shall be made within three Years after the first Meeting of the Congress of the United States, and within every subsequent Term of ten Years, in such Manner as they shall by Law direct. The Number of Representatives shall not exceed one for every thirty Thousand, but each State shall have at Least one Representative; and until such enumeration shall be made, the State of New Hampshire shall be entitled to chuse three, Massachusetts eight, Rhode-Island and Providence Plantations one, Connecticut five, New-York six, New Jersey four, Pennsylvania eight, Delaware one, Maryland six, Virginia ten, North Carolina five, South Carolina five, and Georgia three.

When vacancies happen in the Representation from any State, the Executive Authority thereof shall issue Writs of Election to fill such Vacancies.

Speaker The House of Representatives shall chuse their Speaker and other Officers; and shall have the sole Power of

Impeachment Impeachment.

Section. 3.

Senate The Senate of the United States shall be composed of two Senators from each State, [chosen by the Legislature

Changed by the Seventeenth Amendment thereof] for six Years; and each Senator shall have one Vote. Immediately after they shall be assembled in Consequence of the first Election, they shall be divided as equally as may be into three Classes. The Seats of the Senators of the first Class shall be vacated at the Expiration of the second Year, of the second Class at the Expiration of the fourth Year, and of the third Class at the Expiration of the sixth Year, so that one third may be chosen every second Year; [and if Vacancies happen by Resignation, or otherwise, during the Recess of the Legislature of any State, the Executive thereof may make temporary

Changed by the Seventeenth Amendment Appointments until the next Meeting of the Legislature, which shall then fill such Vacancies.]

Requirements of Office No Person shall be a Senator who shall not have attained to the Age of thirty Years, and been nine Years a Citizen of the United States, and who shall not, when elected, be an Inhabitant of that State for which he shall be chosen.

The Vice President of the United States shall be President of the Senate, but shall have no Vote, unless they be equally divided. *Role of Vice President*

The Senate shall chuse their other Officers, and also a President pro tempore, in the Absence of the Vice President, or when he shall exercise the Office of President of the United States.

The Senate shall have the sole Power to try all Impeachments. When sitting for that Purpose, they shall be on Oath or Affirmation. When the President of the United States is tried, the Chief Justice shall preside: And no Person shall be convicted without the Concurrence of two thirds of the Members present. *Impeachment*

Judgment in Cases of Impeachment shall not extend further than to removal from Office, and disqualification to hold and enjoy any Office of honor, Trust or Profit under the United States: but the Party convicted shall nevertheless be liable and subject to Indictment, Trial, Judgment and Punishment, according to Law.

Section. 4.

The Times, Places and Manner of holding Elections for Senators and Representatives, shall be prescribed in each State by the Legislature thereof; but the Congress may at any time by Law make or alter such Regulations, except as to the Places of chusing Senators. *Elections*

The Congress shall assemble at least once in every Year, and such Meeting shall be [on the first Monday in December,] unless they shall by Law appoint a different Day. *Changed by Section 2 of the Twentieth Amendment*

Section. 5.

Each House shall be the Judge of the Elections, Returns and Qualifications of its own Members, and a Majority of each shall constitute a Quorum to do Business; but a smaller Number may adjourn from day to day, and may be authorized to compel the Attendance of absent Members, in such Manner, and under such Penalties as each House may provide.

Rules of Proceedings   Each House may determine the Rules of its Proceedings, punish its Members for disorderly Behaviour, and, with the Concurrence of two thirds, expel a Member.

Each House shall keep a Journal of its Proceedings, and from time to time publish the same, excepting such Parts as may in their Judgment require Secrecy; and the Yeas and Nays of the Members of either House on any question shall, at the Desire of one fifth of those Present, be entered on the Journal. Neither House, during the Session of Congress, shall, without the Consent of the other, adjourn for more than three days, nor to any other Place than that in which the two Houses shall be sitting.

Section. 6.

The Senators and Representatives shall receive a Compensation for their Services, to be ascertained by Law, and paid out of the Treasury of the United States. They shall in all Cases, except Treason, Felony and Breach of the Peace, be privileged **Privilege from Arrest** from Arrest during their Attendance at the Session of their respective Houses, and in going to and returning from the same; and for any Speech or Debate in either House, they shall not be questioned in any other Place.

No Senator or Representative shall, during the Time for which he was elected, be appointed to any civil Office under the Authority of the United States, which shall have been created, or the Emoluments whereof shall have been encreased during such time; and no Person holding any Office under the United States, shall be a Member of either House during his Continuance in Office.

Section. 7.

All Bills for raising Revenue shall originate in the House of Representatives; but the Senate may propose or concur with Amendments as on other Bills.

Every Bill which shall have passed the House of Representatives and the Senate, shall, before it become a Law, be presented to the President of the United States: If he approve he shall sign it, but if not he shall return it, with his Objections to that House in which it shall have originated, who shall enter the Objections at large on their Journal, and proceed to reconsider it. If after such Reconsideration two thirds of that House shall agree to pass the Bill, it shall be sent, together with the Objections, to the other House, by which it shall likewise be reconsidered, and if approved by two thirds of that House, it shall become a Law. But in all such Cases the Votes of both Houses shall be determined by yeas and Nays, and the Names of the Persons voting for and against the Bill shall be entered on the Journal of each House respectively. If any Bill shall not be returned by the President within ten Days (Sundays excepted) after it shall have been presented to him, the Same shall be a Law, in like Manner as if he had signed it, unless the Congress by their Adjournment prevent its Return, in which Case it shall not be a Law.

Every Order, Resolution, or Vote to which the Concurrence of the Senate and House of Representatives may be necessary (except on a question of Adjournment) shall be presented to the President of the United States; and before the Same shall take Effect, shall be approved by him, or being disapproved by him, shall be repassed by two thirds of the Senate and House of Representatives, according to the Rules and Limitations prescribed in the Case of a Bill.

Section. 8.

The Congress shall have Power To lay and collect Taxes, Duties, Imposts and Excises, to pay the Debts and provide for

Marginal notes: Revenue Bills — How a Bill Becomes a Law — Veto — Enumerated Powers of Congress

General Welfare the common Defence and general Welfare of the United
States; but all Duties, Imposts and Excises shall be uniform
throughout the United States;

To borrow Money on the credit of the United States;

Commerce To regulate Commerce with foreign Nations, and among
the several States, and with the Indian Tribes;

To establish an uniform Rule of Naturalization, and uniform Laws on the subject of Bankruptcies throughout the
United States;

To coin Money, regulate the Value thereof, and of foreign
Coin, and fix the Standard of Weights and Measures;

To provide for the Punishment of counterfeiting the
Securities and current Coin of the United States;

To establish Post Offices and post Roads;

To promote the Progress of Science and useful Arts, by
securing for limited Times to Authors and Inventors the exclusive Right to their respective Writings and Discoveries;

Courts To constitute Tribunals inferior to the supreme Court;

To define and punish Piracies and Felonies committed on
the high Seas, and Offences against the Law of Nations;

War Power To declare War, grant Letters of Marque and Reprisal, and
make Rules concerning Captures on Land and Water;

To raise and support Armies, but no Appropriation of
Money to that Use shall be for a longer Term than two Years;

To provide and maintain a Navy;

To make Rules for the Government and Regulation of the
land and naval Forces;

To provide for calling forth the Militia to execute the Laws
of the Union, suppress Insurrections and repel Invasions;

To provide for organizing, arming, and disciplining, the
Militia, and for governing such Part of them as may be
employed in the Service of the United States, reserving to the
States respectively, the Appointment of the Officers, and the
Authority of training the Militia according to the discipline
prescribed by Congress;

To exercise exclusive Legislation in all Cases whatsoever, over such District (not exceeding ten Miles square) as may, by Cession of particular States, and the Acceptance of Congress, become the Seat of the Government of the United States, and to exercise like Authority over all Places purchased by the Consent of the Legislature of the State in which the Same shall be, for the Erection of Forts, Magazines, Arsenals, dock-Yards, and other needful Buildings; — And

District of Columbia

To make all Laws which shall be necessary and proper for carrying into Execution the foregoing Powers, and all other Powers vested by this Constitution in the Government of the United States, or in any Department or Officer thereof.

Necessary and Proper Clause

Section. 9.

The Migration or Importation of such Persons as any of the States now existing shall think proper to admit, shall not be prohibited by the Congress prior to the Year one thousand eight hundred and eight, but a Tax or duty may be imposed on such Importation, not exceeding ten dollars for each Person.

The Privilege of the Writ of Habeas Corpus shall not be suspended, unless when in Cases of Rebellion or Invasion the public Safety may require it.

Habeus Corpus

No Bill of Attainder or ex post facto Law shall be passed.

Ex Post Facto Laws

[No Capitation, or other direct, Tax shall be laid, unless in Proportion to the Census or enumeration herein before directed to be taken.]

Changed by the Sixteenth Amendment

No Tax or Duty shall be laid on Articles exported from any State.

No Preference shall be given by any Regulation of Commerce or Revenue to the Ports of one State over those of another; nor shall Vessels bound to, or from, one State, be obliged to enter, clear, or pay Duties in another.

No Money shall be drawn from the Treasury, but in Consequence of Appropriations made by Law; and a regular Statement and Account of the Receipts and Expenditures of

Appropriations

all public Money shall be published from time to time.

No Titles of Nobility

No Title of Nobility shall be granted by the United States: And no Person holding any Office of Profit or Trust under them, shall, without the Consent of the Congress, accept of any present, Emolument, Office, or Title, of any kind whatever, from any King, Prince, or foreign State.

Section. 10.

Restrictions on States

No State shall enter into any Treaty, Alliance, or Confederation; grant Letters of Marque and Reprisal; coin Money; emit Bills of Credit; make any Thing but gold and silver Coin a Tender in Payment of Debts; pass any Bill of Attainder, ex post facto Law, or Law impairing the Obligation of Contracts, or grant any Title of Nobility.

No State shall, without the Consent of the Congress, lay any Imposts or Duties on Imports or Exports, except what may be absolutely necessary for executing it's inspection Laws: and the net Produce of all Duties and Imposts, laid by any State on Imports or Exports, shall be for the Use of the Treasury of the United States; and all such Laws shall be subject to the Revision and Controul of the Congress.

No State shall, without the Consent of Congress, lay any Duty of Tonnage, keep Troops, or Ships of War in time of Peace, enter into any Agreement or Compact with another State, or with a foreign Power, or engage in War, unless actually invaded, or in such imminent Danger as will not admit of delay.

Article. II.

Section. 1.

Executive Branch

The executive Power shall be vested in a President of the United States of America. He shall hold his Office during the Term of four Years, and, together with the Vice President, chosen for the same Term, be elected, as follows:

Each State shall appoint, in such Manner as the Legislature thereof may direct, a Number of Electors, equal to the whole Number of Senators and Representatives to which the State may be entitled in the Congress: but no Senator or Representative, or Person holding an Office of Trust or Profit under the United States, shall be appointed an Elector.

The Electoral College

[The Electors shall meet in their respective States, and vote by Ballot for two Persons, of whom one at least shall not be an Inhabitant of the same State with themselves. And they shall make a List of all the Persons voted for, and of the Number of Votes for each; which List they shall sign and certify, and transmit sealed to the Seat of the Government of the United States, directed to the President of the Senate. The President of the Senate shall, in the Presence of the Senate and House of Representatives, open all the Certificates, and the Votes shall then be counted. The Person having the greatest Number of Votes shall be the President, if such Number be a Majority of the whole Number of Electors appointed; and if there be more than one who have such Majority, and have an equal Number of Votes, then the House of Representatives shall immediately chuse by Ballot one of them for President; and if no Person have a Majority, then from the five highest on the List the said House shall in like Manner chuse the President. But in chusing the President, the Votes shall be taken by States, the Representation from each State having one Vote; A quorum for this purpose shall consist of a Member or Members from two thirds of the States, and a Majority of all the States shall be necessary to a Choice. In every Case, after the Choice of the President, the Person having the greatest Number of Votes of the Electors shall be the Vice President. But if there should remain two or more who have equal Votes, the Senate shall chuse from them by Ballot the Vice President.]

The Congress may determine the Time of chusing the Electors, and the Day on which they shall give their Votes; which Day shall be the same throughout the United States.

Changed by the Twelfth Amendment

Requirements of Office   No Person except a natural born Citizen, or a Citizen of the United States, at the time of the Adoption of this Constitution, shall be eligible to the Office of President; neither shall any Person be eligible to that Office who shall not have attained to the Age of thirty five Years, and been fourteen Years a Resident within the United States.

[In Case of the Removal of the President from Office, or of his Death, Resignation, or Inability to discharge the Powers and Duties of the said Office, the Same shall devolve on the Vice President, and the Congress may by Law provide for the Case of Removal, Death, Resignation or Inability, both of the President and Vice President, declaring what Officer shall then act as President, and such Officer shall act accordingly, until

Changed by the Twenty-fifth Amendment   the Disability be removed, or a President shall be elected.]

The President shall, at stated Times, receive for his Services, a Compensation, which shall neither be increased nor diminished during the Period for which he shall have been elected, and he shall not receive within that Period any other Emolument from the United States, or any of them.

Oath of Office   Before he enter on the Execution of his Office, he shall take the following Oath or Affirmation: — "I do solemnly swear (or affirm) that I will faithfully execute the Office of President of the United States, and will to the best of my Ability, preserve, protect and defend the Constitution of the United States."

Section. 2.

Commander in Chief   The President shall be Commander in Chief of the Army and Navy of the United States, and of the Militia of the several States, when called into the actual Service of the United States; he may require the Opinion, in writing, of the principal Officer in each of the executive Departments, upon any Subject relating to the Duties of their respective Offices, and he shall have

Reprieves and Pardons   Power to grant Reprieves and Pardons for Offences against the United States, except in Cases of Impeachment.

He shall have Power, by and with the Advice and Consent of the Senate, to make Treaties, provided two thirds of the Senators present concur; and he shall nominate, and by and with the Advice and Consent of the Senate, shall appoint Ambassadors, other public Ministers and Consuls, Judges of the supreme Court, and all other Officers of the United States, whose Appointments are not herein otherwise provided for, and which shall be established by Law: but the Congress may by Law vest the Appointment of such inferior Officers, as they think proper, in the President alone, in the Courts of Law, or in the Heads of Departments. *Treaty Power* *Nominations and Appointments*

The President shall have Power to fill up all Vacancies that may happen during the Recess of the Senate, by granting Commissions which shall expire at the End of their next Session. *Recess Appointments*

Section. 3.

He shall from time to time give to the Congress Information of the State of the Union, and recommend to their Consideration such Measures as he shall judge necessary and expedient; he may, on extraordinary Occasions, convene both Houses, or either of them, and in Case of Disagreement between them, with Respect to the Time of Adjournment, he may adjourn them to such Time as he shall think proper; he shall receive Ambassadors and other public Ministers; he shall take Care that the Laws be faithfully executed, and shall Commission all the Officers of the United States. *State of the Union* *Take Care Clause*

Section. 4.

The President, Vice President and all civil Officers of the United States, shall be removed from Office on Impeachment for, and Conviction of, Treason, Bribery, or other high Crimes and Misdemeanors. *Impeachment*

Article III.

Section. 1.

Judicial Branch
The judicial Power of the United States shall be vested in one supreme Court, and in such inferior Courts as the Congress may from time to time ordain and establish. The Judges, both

Tenure
of the supreme and inferior Courts, shall hold their Offices during good Behaviour, and shall, at stated Times, receive for their Services a Compensation, which shall not be diminished during their Continuance in Office.

Section. 2.

Jurisdiction, Cases and Controversies
The judicial Power shall extend to all Cases, in Law and Equity, arising under this Constitution, the Laws of the United States, and Treaties made, or which shall be made, under their Authority; — to all Cases affecting Ambassadors, other public Ministers and Consuls; — to all Cases of admiralty and maritime Jurisdiction; — to Controversies to which the United States shall be a Party; — to Controversies between two or

Changed by the Eleventh Amendment
more States; — [between a State and Citizens of another State; —] between Citizens of different States; — between Citizens of the same State claiming Lands under Grants of

Changed by the Eleventh Amendment
different States, [and between a State, or the Citizens thereof, and foreign States, Citizens or Subjects.]

Original Jurisdiction
In all Cases affecting Ambassadors, other public Ministers and Consuls, and those in which a State shall be Party, the supreme Court shall have original Jurisdiction. In all the other Cases before mentioned, the supreme Court shall have

Appellate Jurisdiction
appellate Jurisdiction, both as to Law and Fact, with such Exceptions, and under such Regulations as the Congress shall make.

Trial by Jury
The Trial of all Crimes, except in Cases of Impeachment, shall be by Jury; and such Trial shall be held in the State where the said Crimes shall have been committed; but when not committed within any State, the Trial shall be at such Place or Places as the Congress may by Law have directed.

Section. 3.

Treason against the United States, shall consist only in levying War against them, or in adhering to their Enemies, giving them Aid and Comfort. No Person shall be convicted of Treason unless on the Testimony of two Witnesses to the same overt Act, or on Confession in open Court.

Treason

The Congress shall have Power to declare the Punishment of Treason, but no Attainder of Treason shall work Corruption of Blood, or Forfeiture except during the Life of the Person attainted.

Article. IV.

Section. 1.

Full Faith and Credit shall be given in each State to the public Acts, Records, and judicial Proceedings of every other State. And the Congress may by general Laws prescribe the Manner in which such Acts, Records and Proceedings shall be proved, and the Effect thereof.

Relations Among the States

Section. 2.

The Citizens of each State shall be entitled to all Privileges and Immunities of Citizens in the several States.

Privileges and Immunities

A Person charged in any State with Treason, Felony, or other Crime, who shall flee from Justice, and be found in another State, shall on Demand of the executive Authority of the State from which he fled, be delivered up, to be removed to the State having Jurisdiction of the Crime.

Extradition

[No Person held to Service or Labour in one State, under the Laws thereof, escaping into another, shall, in Consequence of any Law or Regulation therein, be discharged from such Service or Labour, but shall be delivered up on Claim of the Party to whom such Service or Labour may be due.]

Changed by the Thirteenth Amendment

Section. 3.

New States may be admitted by the Congress into this Union;

Admission of New States

but no new State shall be formed or erected within the Jurisdiction of any other State; nor any State be formed by the Junction of two or more States, or Parts of States, without the Consent of the Legislatures of the States concerned as well as of the Congress.

Territories

The Congress shall have Power to dispose of and make all needful Rules and Regulations respecting the Territory or other Property belonging to the United States; and nothing in this Constitution shall be so construed as to Prejudice any Claims of the United States, or of any particular State.

Section. 4.

Republican Form of Government

The United States shall guarantee to every State in this Union a Republican Form of Government, and shall protect each of them against Invasion; and on Application of the Legislature, or of the Executive (when the Legislature cannot be convened), against domestic Violence.

Article. V.

Procedures for amending the Constitution

The Congress, whenever two thirds of both Houses shall deem it necessary, shall propose Amendments to this Constitution, or, on the Application of the Legislatures of two thirds of the several States, shall call a Convention for proposing Amendments, which, in either Case, shall be valid to all Intents and Purposes, as Part of this Constitution, when ratified by the Legislatures of three fourths of the several States, or by Conventions in three fourths thereof, as the one or the other Mode of Ratification may be proposed by the Congress; Provided that no Amendment which may be made prior to the Year One thousand eight hundred and eight shall in any Manner affect the first and fourth Clauses in the Ninth Section of the first Article; and that no State, without its Consent, shall be deprived of its equal Suffrage in the Senate.

Article. VI.

All Debts contracted and Engagements entered into, before the Adoption of this Constitution, shall be as valid against the United States under this Constitution, as under the Confederation.

This Constitution, and the Laws of the United States which shall be made in Pursuance thereof; and all Treaties made, or which shall be made, under the Authority of the United States, shall be the supreme Law of the Land; and the Judges in every State shall be bound thereby, any Thing in the Constitution or Laws of any State to the Contrary notwithstanding.

Supreme Law of the Land

The Senators and Representatives before mentioned, and the Members of the several State Legislatures, and all executive and judicial Officers, both of the United States and of the several States, shall be bound by Oath or Affirmation, to support this Constitution; but no religious Test shall ever be required as a Qualification to any Office or public Trust under the United States.

Oath to support Constitution and religious test

No religious tests

Article. VII.

The Ratification of the Conventions of nine States, shall be sufficient for the Establishment of this Constitution between the States so ratifying the Same.

Ratification

Done in Convention by the Unanimous Consent of the States present the Seventeenth Day of September in the Year of our Lord one thousand seven hundred and Eighty seven and of the Independence of the United States of America the Twelfth In witness whereof We have hereunto subscribed our Names,

Attest William Jackson, Secretary

G°. Washington – Presidt and deputy from Virginia

Delaware
Geo: Read
Gunning Bedford jun
John Dickinson
Richard Bassett
Jaco: Broom
Maryland
James McHenry
Dan of St Thos. Jenifer
Danl. Carroll
Virginia
John Blair
James Madison Jr.
North Carolina
Wm. Blount
Richd. Dobbs Spaight
Hu Williamson
South Carolina
J. Rutledge
Charles Cotesworth Pinckney
Charles Pinckney
Pierce Butler
Georgia
William Few
Abr Baldwin

New Hampshire
John Langdon
Nicholas Gilman
Massachusetts
Nathaniel Gorham
Rufus King
Connecticut
Wm. Saml. Johnson
Roger Sherman
New York
Alexander Hamilton
New Jersey
Wil: Livingston
David Brearley
Wm. Paterson
Jona: Dayton
Pennsylvania
B Franklin
Thomas Mifflin
Robt. Morris
Geo. Clymer
Thos. FitzSimons
Jared Ingersoll
James Wilson
Gouv Morris

Amendment I

Congress shall make no law respecting an establishment of religion, or prohibiting the free exercise thereof; or abridging the freedom of speech, or of the press; or the right of the people peaceably to assemble, and to petition the Government for a redress of grievances.

The first ten Amendments — the Bill of Rights — were ratified effective December 15, 1791

Religion, Speech, Press, Assembly and Petition

Amendment II

A well regulated Militia, being necessary to the security of a free State, the right of the people to keep and bear Arms, shall not be infringed.

Right to Bear Arms

Amendment III

No Soldier shall, in time of peace be quartered in any house, without the consent of the Owner, nor in time of war, but in a manner to be prescribed by law.

Quartering of Troops

Amendment IV

The right of the people to be secure in their persons, houses, papers, and effects, against unreasonable searches and seizures, shall not be violated, and no Warrants shall issue, but upon probable cause, supported by Oath or affirmation, and particularly describing the place to be searched, and the persons or things to be seized.

Searches and Seizures

Amendment V

No person shall be held to answer for a capital, or otherwise infamous crime, unless on a presentment or indictment of a Grand Jury, except in cases arising in the land or naval forces, or in the Militia, when in actual service in time of War or public danger; nor shall any person be subject for the same offence to be twice put in jeopardy of life or limb; nor shall be compelled in any criminal case to be a witness against himself, nor be deprived of life, liberty, or property, without due process of

Grand Juries, Double Jeopardy, Self-Incrimination, Due Process

Taking of Property

law; nor shall private property be taken for public use, without just compensation.

Amendment VI

Criminal Court
Procedures

In all criminal prosecutions, the accused shall enjoy the right to a speedy and public trial, by an impartial jury of the State and district wherein the crime shall have been committed, which district shall have been previously ascertained by law, and to be informed of the nature and cause of the accusation; to be confronted with the witnesses against him; to have compulsory process for obtaining witnesses in his favor, and to have the Assistance of Counsel for his defence.

Amendment VII

Trial by Jury
in Civil Cases

In suits at common law, where the value in controversy shall exceed twenty dollars, the right of trial by jury shall be preserved, and no fact tried by a jury, shall be otherwise reexamined in any Court of the United States, than according to the rules of the common law.

Amendment VIII

Bail, Cruel
and Unusual
Punishments

Excessive bail shall not be required, nor excessive fines imposed, nor cruel and unusual punishments inflicted.

Amendment IX

Other Rights
of the People

The enumeration in the Constitution, of certain rights, shall not be construed to deny or disparage others retained by the people.

Amendment X

Powers Reserved
to the States, or
the People

The powers not delegated to the United States by the Constitution, nor prohibited by it to the States, are reserved to the States respectively, or to the people.

Amendment XI

(Ratified February 7, 1795)

The Judicial power of the United States shall not be construed to extend to any suit in law or equity, commenced or prosecuted against one of the United States by Citizens of another State, or by Citizens or Subjects of any Foreign State.

Suits Against States

Amendment XII

(Ratified June 15, 1804)

The Electors shall meet in their respective states and vote by ballot for President and Vice-President, one of whom, at least, shall not be an inhabitant of the same state with themselves; they shall name in their ballots the person voted for as President, and in distinct ballots the person voted for as Vice-President, and they shall make distinct lists of all persons voted for as President, and of all persons voted for as Vice-President, and of the number of votes for each, which lists they shall sign and certify, and transmit sealed to the seat of the government of the United States, directed to the President of the Senate; — the President of the Senate shall, in the presence of the Senate and House of Representatives, open all the certificates and the votes shall then be counted; — The person having the greatest number of votes for President, shall be the President, if such number be a majority of the whole number of Electors appointed; and if no person have such majority, then from the persons having the highest numbers not exceeding three on the list of those voted for as President, the House of Representatives shall choose immediately, by ballot, the President. But in choosing the President, the votes shall be taken by states, the representation from each state having one vote; a quorum for this purpose shall consist of a member or members from two-thirds of the states, and a majority of all the states shall be necessary to a choice. [And if the House of

Election of the President

Representatives shall not choose a President whenever the right of choice shall devolve upon them, before the fourth day of March next following, then the Vice-President shall act as President, as in case of the death or other constitutional dis-

Superseded by Section 3 of the Twentieth Amendment

ability of the President. —] The person having the greatest number of votes as Vice-President, shall be the Vice-President, if such number be a majority of the whole number of Electors appointed, and if no person have a majority, then from the two highest numbers on the list, the Senate shall choose the Vice-President; a quorum for the purpose shall consist of two-thirds of the whole number of Senators, and a majority of the whole number shall be necessary to a choice. But no person constitutionally ineligible to the office of President shall be eligible to that of Vice-President of the United States.

(Ratified December 6, 1865)

Amendment XIII

Section 1.

Prohibition of Slavery

Neither slavery nor involuntary servitude, except as a punishment for crime whereof the party shall have been duly convicted, shall exist within the United States, or any place subject to their jurisdiction.

Section 2.

Congress shall have power to enforce this article by appropriate legislation.

(Ratified July 9, 1868)

Amendment XIV

Section 1.

Citizenship

All persons born or naturalized in the United States, and subject to the jurisdiction thereof, are citizens of the United States and of the State wherein they reside. No State shall

Privileges and Immunities

make or enforce any law which shall abridge the privileges or immunities of citizens of the United States; nor shall any State deprive any person of life, liberty, or property, without due process of law; nor deny to any person within its jurisdiction the equal protection of the laws.

Due Process

Equal Protection

Section 2.

Representatives shall be apportioned among the several States according to their respective numbers, counting the whole number of persons in each State, excluding Indians not taxed. But when the right to vote at any election for the choice of electors for President and Vice-President of the United States, Representatives in Congress, the Executive and Judicial officers of a State, or the members of the Legislature thereof, is denied to any of the male inhabitants of such State, [being twenty-one years of age,] and citizens of the United States, or in any way abridged, except for participation in rebellion, or other crime, the basis of representation therein shall be reduced in the proportion which the number of such male citizens shall bear to the whole number of male citizens twenty-one years of age in such State.

Apportionment

Superseded by Section 1 of the Twenty-sixth Amendment

Section 3.

No person shall be a Senator or Representative in Congress, or elector of President and Vice-President, or hold any office, civil or military, under the United States, or under any State, who, having previously taken an oath, as a member of Congress, or as an officer of the United States, or as a member of any State legislature, or as an executive or judicial officer of any State, to support the Constitution of the United States, shall have engaged in insurrection or rebellion against the same, or given aid or comfort to the enemies thereof. But Congress may by a vote of two-thirds of each House, remove such disability.

Restriction on previous state and federal officials convicted of treason

Section 4.

The validity of the public debt of the United States, author-

Public Debt

ized by law, including debts incurred for payment of pensions and bounties for services in suppressing insurrection or rebellion, shall not be questioned. But neither the United States nor any State shall assume or pay any debt or obligation incurred in aid of insurrection or rebellion against the United States, or any claim for the loss or emancipation of any slave; but all such debts, obligations and claims shall be held illegal and void.

Section 5.
The Congress shall have the power to enforce, by appropriate legislation, the provisions of this article.

(Ratified February 3, 1870) # Amendment XV

Section 1.
The Right to Vote The right of citizens of the United States to vote shall not be denied or abridged by the United States or by any State on
Changed by the
Nineteenth Amendment account of race, color, or previous condition of servitude —

Section 2.
The Congress shall have the power to enforce this article by appropriate legislation.

(Ratified February 3, 1913) # Amendment XVI

Federal Income Tax The Congress shall have power to lay and collect taxes on incomes, from whatever source derived, without apportionment among the several States, and without regard to any census or enumeration.

(Ratified April 8, 1913) # Amendment XVII

Direct Election
of Senators The Senate of the United States shall be composed of two Senators from each State, elected by the people thereof, for six years; and each Senator shall have one vote. The electors in each State shall have the qualifications requisite for electors of the most numerous branch of the State legislatures.

When vacancies happen in the representation of any State in the Senate, the executive authority of such State shall issue writs of election to fill such vacancies: Provided, That the legislature of any State may empower the executive thereof to make temporary appointments until the people fill the vacancies by election as the legislature may direct.

This amendment shall not be so construed as to affect the election or term of any Senator chosen before it becomes valid as part of the Constitution.

Amendment XVIII

(Ratified January 16, 1919)
Repealed by the Twenty-first Amendment

Section 1.

After one year from the ratification of this article the manufacture, sale, or transportation of intoxicating liquors within, the importation thereof into, or the exportation thereof from the United States and all territory subject to the jurisdiction thereof for beverage purposes is hereby prohibited.

Prohibition

Section 2.

The Congress and the several States shall have concurrent power to enforce this article by appropriate legislation.

Section 3.

This article shall be inoperative unless it shall have been ratified as an amendment to the Constitution by the legislatures of the several States, as provided in the Constitution, within seven years from the date of the submission hereof to the States by the Congress.

Amendment XIX

(Ratified August 18, 1920)

The right of citizens of the United States to vote shall not be denied or abridged by the United States or by any State on account of sex. Congress shall have power to enforce this article by appropriate legislation.

Right to vote extended to women

(Ratified January 23, 1933)

Amendment XX

Section 1.

Lame-Duck
Amendment
The terms of the President and the Vice President shall end at noon on the 20th day of January, and the terms of Senators and Representatives at noon on the 3d day of January, of the years in which such terms would have ended if this article had not been ratified; and the terms of their successors shall then begin.

Section 2.

The Congress shall assemble at least once in every year, and such meeting shall begin at noon on the 3d day of January, unless they shall by law appoint a different day.

Section 3.

If, at the time fixed for the beginning of the term of the President, the President elect shall have died, the Vice President elect shall become President. If a President shall not have been chosen before the time fixed for the beginning of his term, or if the President elect shall have failed to qualify, then the Vice President elect shall act as President until a President shall have qualified; and the Congress may by law provide for the case wherein neither a President elect nor a Vice President shall have qualified, declaring who shall then act as President, or the manner in which one who is to act shall be selected, and such person shall act accordingly until a President or Vice President shall have qualified.

Section 4.

The Congress may by law provide for the case of the death of any of the persons from whom the House of Representatives may choose a President whenever the right of choice shall have devolved upon them, and for the case of the death of any of the persons from whom the Senate may choose a Vice President whenever the right of choice shall have devolved upon them.

Section 5.
Sections 1 and 2 shall take effect on the 15th day of October following the ratification of this article.

Section 6.
This article shall be inoperative unless it shall have been ratified as an amendment to the Constitution by the legislatures of three-fourths of the several States within seven years from the date of its submission.

Amendment XXI

(Ratified December 5, 1933)

Section 1.
The eighteenth article of amendment to the Constitution of the United States is hereby repealed.

Repeal of Prohibition

Section 2.
The transportation or importation into any State, Territory, or Possession of the United States for delivery or use therein of intoxicating liquors, in violation of the laws thereof, is hereby prohibited.

Section 3.
This article shall be inoperative unless it shall have been ratified as an amendment to the Constitution by conventions in the several States, as provided in the Constitution, within seven years from the date of the submission hereof to the States by the Congress.

Amendment XXII

(Ratified February 27, 1951)

Section 1.
No person shall be elected to the office of the President more than twice, and no person who has held the office of President, or acted as President, for more than two years of a term to which some other person was elected President shall be elected

Limit on Presidential Terms

to the office of President more than once. But this Article shall not apply to any person holding the office of President when this Article was proposed by Congress, and shall not prevent any person who may be holding the office of President, or acting as President, during the term within which this Article becomes operative from holding the office of President or acting as President during the remainder of such term.

Section 2.

This article shall be inoperative unless it shall have been ratified as an amendment to the Constitution by the legislatures of three-fourths of the several States within seven years from the date of its submission to the States by the Congress.

(Ratified March 29, 1961)

Amendment XXIII

Section 1.

Presidential Electors for the District of Columbia

The District constituting the seat of Government of the United States shall appoint in such manner as Congress may direct:

A number of electors of President and Vice President equal to the whole number of Senators and Representatives in Congress to which the District would be entitled if it were a State, but in no event more than the least populous State; they shall be in addition to those appointed by the States, but they shall be considered, for the purposes of the election of President and Vice President, to be electors appointed by a State; and they shall meet in the District and perform such duties as provided by the twelfth article of amendment.

Section 2.

The Congress shall have power to enforce this article by appropriate legislation.

Amendment XXIV

(Ratified January 23, 1964)

Section 1.

The right of citizens of the United States to vote in any primary or other election for President or Vice President, for electors for President or Vice President, or for Senator or Representative in Congress, shall not be denied or abridged by the United States or any State by reason of failure to pay poll tax or other tax.

Prohibition of the
Poll Tax

Section 2.

The Congress shall have power to enforce this article by appropriate legislation.

Amendment XXV

(Ratified February 10, 1967)

Section 1.

In case of the removal of the President from office or of his death or resignation, the Vice President shall become President.

Presidential
Succession

Section 2.

Whenever there is a vacancy in the office of the Vice President, the President shall nominate a Vice President who shall take office upon confirmation by a majority vote of both Houses of Congress.

Vice Presidency

Section 3.

Whenever the President transmits to the President pro tempore of the Senate and the Speaker of the House of Representatives his written declaration that he is unable to discharge the powers and duties of his office, and until he transmits to them a written declaration to the contrary, such powers and duties shall be discharged by the Vice President as Acting President.

Incapacity to
perform duties
of office

THE FOUNDERS' ALMANAC
271

Section 4.

Whenever the Vice President and a majority of either the principal officers of the executive departments or of such other body as Congress may by law provide, transmit to the President pro tempore of the Senate and the Speaker of the House of Representatives their written declaration that the President is unable to discharge the powers and duties of his office, the Vice President shall immediately assume the powers and duties of the office as Acting President.

Thereafter, when the President transmits to the President pro tempore of the Senate and the Speaker of the House of Representatives his written declaration that no inability exists, he shall resume the powers and duties of his office unless the Vice President and a majority of either the principal officers of the executive department or of such other body as Congress may by law provide, transmit within four days to the President pro tempore of the Senate and the Speaker of the House of Representatives their written declaration that the President is unable to discharge the powers and duties of his office. Thereupon Congress shall decide the issue, assembling within forty-eight hours for that purpose if not in session. If the Congress, within twenty-one days after receipt of the latter written declaration, or, if Congress is not in session, within twenty-one days after Congress is required to assemble, determines by two-thirds vote of both Houses that the President is unable to discharge the powers and duties of his office, the Vice President shall continue to discharge the same as Acting President; otherwise, the President shall resume the powers and duties of his office.

Amendment XXVI

(Ratified July 1, 1971)

Section 1.

The right of citizens of the United States, who are eighteen years of age or older, to vote shall not be denied or abridged by the United States or by any State on account of age.

18-year-olds eligible to vote

Section 2.

The Congress shall have power to enforce this article by appropriate legislation.

Amendment XXVII

(Ratified May 7, 1992)

No law, varying the compensation for the services of the Senators and Representatives, shall take effect, until an election of representatives shall have intervened.

Proposed September 25, 1789 as part of the original Bill of Rights

Index to The Constitution and Amendments

A Note on
Slavery and the
American Founding

<hr/>

S lavery is the great exception to the rule of liberty proclaimed in the
Declaration of Independence and established in the United States
Constitution. From the beginning there has been intense debate
about slavery and America, precisely because it raises questions about this
nation's dedication to liberty and human equality. Does the continued
existence of slavery in the context of the American Founding, its motivat-
ing principles, and the individuals who proclaimed those principles,
make the United States or its origins less defendable as a guide for just
government?

At the time of the American Founding, there were about half a million slaves in the United States, mostly in the five southernmost states,
where they made up forty percent of the population. Many of the leading
American Founders — most notably Thomas Jefferson, George
Washington, and James Madison — owned slaves, but many did not.
Benjamin Franklin thought that slavery was "an atrocious debasement of
human nature" and "a source of serious evils." He and Benjamin Rush
founded the Pennsylvania Society for Promoting the Abolition of Slavery
in 1774. John Jay, who was the president of a similar society in New York,
believed that "the honour of the states, as well as justice and humanity, in
my opinion, loudly call upon them to emancipate these unhappy people.

To contend for our own liberty, and to deny that blessing to others, involves an inconsistency not to be excused." John Adams opposed slavery his entire life as a "foul contagion in the human character" and "an evil of colossal magnitude." James Madison called it "the most oppressive domin- ion ever exercised by man over man."

From his first thoughts about the Revolution to his command of the Continental army to his presidential administration, Washington's life and letters reflect a statesman struggling with the reality and inhumanity of slavery in the midst of the free nation being constructed. In 1774, Washington compared the alternative to Americans asserting their rights against British rule to being ruled "till custom and use shall make us as tame and abject slaves, *as the blacks we rule over with such arbitrary sway.*" When he took command of the Continental army in 1775, there were both slaves and free blacks in its ranks. (About 5,000 blacks served in the Continental Army.) Alexander Hamilton supported a general plan to enlist slaves in the army that would in the end "give them their freedom with their muskets," and Washington supported such a policy (with the approval of Congress) in South Carolina and Georgia, two of the largest slaveholding states.

In 1786, Washington wrote of slavery, "there is not a man living who wishes more sincerely than I do, to see a plan adopted for the abolition of it." He devised a plan to rent his lands and turn his slaves into paid labor- ers, and at the end of his presidency he quietly left several of his own house- hold slaves to their freedom. In the end, he could take it no more, and decreed in his will that his slaves would become free upon the death of his wife. The old and infirm were to be cared for while they lived, and the chil- dren were to be taught to read and write and trained in a useful skill until they were age 25. Washington's estate paid for this care until 1833.

During his first term in the House of Burgesses, Thomas Jefferson proposed legislation to emancipate slaves in Virginia, but the motion was soundly defeated. His 1774 draft instructions to the Virginia Delegates to the First Continental Congress, *A Summary View of the Rights of British*

America, called for an end to the slave trade: "The abolition of domestic slavery is the great object of desire in those colonies where it was unhappily introduced in their infant state." That same year the First Continental Congress agreed to discontinue the slave trade and boycott other nations that engaged in it. The Second Continental Congress reaffirmed the policy in 1776.

Jefferson's draft constitution for the state of Virginia forbade the importation of slaves, and his draft of the Declaration of Independence — written at a time when he owned about 200 slaves — included a paragraph condemning the British king for introducing slavery into the colonies and continuing the slave trade:

> He has waged cruel war against human nature itself, violating it's most sacred rights of life and liberty in the persons of a distant people who never offended him, captivating & carrying them into slavery in another hemisphere, or to incur miserable death in their transportation thither. This piratical warfare, the opprobrium of INFIDEL powers, is the warfare of a CHRISTIAN king of Great Britain. Determined to keep open a market where MEN should be bought & sold, he has prostituted his negative for suppressing every legislative attempt to prohibit or to restrain this execrable commerce.

These words were especially offensive to delegates from Georgia and South Carolina, who were unwilling to acknowledge that slavery went so far as to violate the "most sacred rights of life and liberty," and, like some of Jefferson's more expressive phrases attacking the king, were dropped in the editing process. Nevertheless, Jefferson's central point — that all men are created equal — remained as an obvious rebuke to the institution.

From very early in the movement for independence it was understood that calls for colonial freedom from British tyranny had clear implications for domestic slavery. "The colonists are by the law of nature free born, as indeed all men are, white and black," James Otis wrote in 1761. "Does it follow that it is the right to enslave a man because he is black?" In the wake of independence, state after state passed legislation restricting or banning the institution. In 1774 Rhode Island had already passed legislation providing that all slaves imported thereafter should be freed. In 1776 Delaware prohibited the slave trade and removed restraints on emancipation, as did Virginia in 1778. In 1779 Pennsylvania passed legislation providing for gradual emancipation; as did New Hampshire, Rhode Island, and Connecticut in the early 1780s; and New York and New Jersey in 1799 and 1804. In 1780, the Massachusetts Supreme Court ruled that the state's bill of rights made slavery unconstitutional. By the time of the U.S. Constitution, every state (except Georgia) had at least proscribed or suspended the importation of slaves.

Thomas Jefferson's 1784 draft plan of government for the western territories prohibited slavery and involuntary servitude after the year 1800. The final Northwest Ordinance of 1787, passed by the Confederation Congress (and repassed two years later by the First Congress and signed into law by President George Washington), prohibited slavery in the future states of Ohio, Indiana, Michigan, Illinois, and Wisconsin. That same year Jefferson published his *Notes on the State of Virginia*, which included this about slavery:

> And can the liberties of a nation be thought secure when we have removed their only firm basis, a conviction in the minds of the people that these liberties are the gift of God? That they are not to be violated but with his wrath? Indeed I tremble for my country when I reflect that God is just: that his justice cannot sleep for ever. ... I think a change already perceptible, since the origin of the present revolution. The spirit of the master is abating, that of the slave rising from the dust, his condition mollifying, the way I hope preparing, under the auspices of heaven, for a total emancipation, and that this is disposed, in the order of events, to be with the consent of the masters, rather than by their extirpation.

When delegates convened at Philadelphia to write a new constitution, however, strong sectional interests supported the maintenance of slavery and the slave trade. "The *real* difference of interests," Madison noted, "lay not between large and small states but between the Northern and Southern states. The institution of slavery and its consequences formed a line of discrimination." In order to get the unified support needed for the Constitution's ratification and successful establishment, the framers made certain concessions to the pro-slavery interests. The compromises they agreed to, however, were designed to tolerate slavery where it currently existed, not to endorse or advance the institution.

Consider the three compromises made by the Constitutional Convention delegates and approved as part of the final text:

1. On enumeration: apportionment for Representatives and taxation purposes would be determined by the number of free persons and three-fifths "of all other Persons" (Art. I, Sec. 2). The pro-slavery delegates wanted their slaves counted as whole persons, thereby according their states more representation in Congress. It was the anti-slavery delegates who wanted to count slaves as less — not to dehumanize them but to penalize slaveholders. Indeed, it was anti-slavery delegate James Wilson of Pennsylvania who proposed the three-fifths compromise. Also, this clause did not include blacks generally, as free blacks were understood to be free persons.

2. On the slave trade: Congress was prohibited until 1808 from blocking the migration and importation "of such Persons as any of the states now existing shall think proper to admit" (Art. I, Sec. 9). Although protection of the slave trade was a major concession demanded by pro-slavery delegates, the final clause was only a temporary exemption for existing states from a recognized federal power. Moreover, it did not prevent states from restricting or outlawing the slave trade, which many had already done. "If there was no other lovely feature in the Constitution but this one," James Wilson observed, "it would diffuse a beauty over its whole countenance. Yet the lapse of a few years, and Congress will have power to exterminate slavery from within our borders." Congress passed, and President Jefferson signed into law, such a national prohibition effective January 1, 1808.

3. On fugitive slaves: the Privileges and Immunities Clause (Art. IV, Sec. 2) guaranteed the return upon claim of any "Person held to Service or Labour" in one state who had escaped to another state. At the last minute, the phrase "Person *legally* held to Service or Labour in one state" was amended to read "Person held to Service or Labour in one state, *under the Laws thereof.*" This revision emphasized that slaves were held according to the laws of individual states and, as the historian Don Fehrenbacher has noted, "made it impossible to infer from the passage that the Constitution itself legally sanctioned slavery." Indeed, none of these clauses recognized slavery as having any legitimacy from the point of view of federal law.

It is significant to note that the words "slave" and "slavery" were kept out of the Constitution. Madison recorded in his notes that the delegates "thought it wrong to admit in the Constitution the idea that there could be property in men." This seemingly minor distinction of insisting on the use of the word "person" rather than "property" was not a euphemism to hide the hypocrisy of slavery but was of the utmost importance. Madison explained in Federalist No. 54:

> But we must deny the fact, that slaves are considered merely as property, and in no respect whatever as persons. The true state of the case is, that they partake of both these qualities: being considered by our laws, in some respects, as persons, and in other respects as property. In being compelled to labor, not for himself, but for a master; in being vendible by one master to another master; and in being subject at all times to be restrained in his liberty and chastised in his body, by the capricious will of another—the slave *may appear* to be degraded from the human rank, and classed with those irrational animals which fall under the legal denomination of property. In being protected, on the other hand, in his life and in his limbs, against the violence of all others, even the master of his labor and his liberty; and in being punishable himself for all violence committed against others—the slave is no less evidently regarded by the law as a member of the society, not as a part of

the irrational creation; *as a moral person, not as a mere article of property.*

Frederick Douglass, for one, believed that the government created by the Constitution "was never, in its essence, anything but an anti-slavery government." Douglass had been born a slave in Maryland, but escaped and eventually became a prominent spokesman for free blacks in the abolitionist movement. "Abolish slavery tomorrow, and not a sentence or syllable of the Constitution need be altered," he wrote in 1864. "It was purposely so framed as to give no claim, no sanction to the claim, of property in man. If in its origin slavery had any relation to the government, it was only as the scaffolding to the magnificent structure, to be removed as soon as the building was completed." This point is underscored by the fact that, although slavery was abolished by constitutional amendment, not one word of the original text was amended or deleted.

Judging by the policy developments of the previous three decades, the Founders could be somewhat optimistic that the trend was against slavery. At the Constitutional Convention Roger Sherman said that "the abolition of slavery seemed to be going on in the United States and that the good sense of the several states would probably by degrees complete it." In the draft of his first inaugural, George Washington looked forward to the day when "mankind will reverse the absurd position that the many were made for the few; and that they will not continue slaves in one part of the globe, when they can become freemen in another." And in one of his last letters, Jefferson wrote that "All eyes are opened, or opening, to the rights of man. The general spread of the light of science has already laid open to every view the palpable truth, that the mass of mankind has not been born with saddles on their backs, nor a favored few booted and spurred, ready to ride them legitimately, by the grace of God."

Nevertheless, there was plenty of reason for concern. In 1776, Adam Smith argued in *The Wealth of Nations* that slavery was uneconomical because the plantation system was a wasteful use of land and because slaves cost more to maintain than free laborers. But in 1793 Eli Whitney invented the cotton gin, making cotton production economical and leading to dramatic growth in the cotton industry, which greatly contributed to an increased demand for slave labor in the United States.

In 1819, during the debate over the admission of Missouri as a slave state, John Adams worried that a national struggle over slavery "might rend this mighty fabric in twain." He told Jefferson that he was terrified about the future and appealed to him for guidance. "What we are to see God knows, and I leave it to Him and his agents in posterity," he wrote. "I have none of the genius of Franklin, to invent a rod to draw from the cloud its thunder and lightning."

The Missouri crisis was "a fire bell in the night," wrote Jefferson in 1820. "We have the wolf by the ears and we can neither hold him, nor safely let him go. Justice is in one scale, and self-preservation in the other." But Jefferson gave no public support to emancipation and refused to free his own slaves. "This enterprise is for the young," he wrote.

Slavery was, indeed, the great flaw of the American Founding. Those who founded this nation chose to make practical compromises for the sake of establishing in principle a new nation dedicated to the proposition that all men are created equal. "The inconsistency of the institution of slavery with the principles of the Declaration of Independence was seen and lamented," John Quincy Adams readily admitted in 1837. Nevertheless, he argued, "no charge of insincerity or hypocrisy can be fairly laid to their charge. Never from their lips was heard one syllable of attempt to justify the institution of slavery. They universally considered it as a reproach fastened upon them by the unnatural step-mother country and they saw that before the principles of the Declaration of Independence slavery, in common with every mode of oppression, was destined sooner or later to be banished from the earth."

"In the way our Fathers originally left the slavery question, the institution was in the course of ultimate extinction, and the public mind rested in the belief that it was *in the course of ultimate extinction*," Abraham

Lincoln observed in 1858. "All I have asked or desired anywhere, is that it should be placed back again upon the basis that the Fathers of our government originally placed it upon."

Lincoln once explained the relationship between the Constitution and the Declaration of Independence by reference to Proverbs 25:11: "A word fitly spoken is like apples of gold in a setting of silver." He revered the Constitution, and was the great defender of the Union. But he knew that the word "fitly spoken" — the apple of gold — was the assertion of principle in the Declaration of Independence. "The *Union,* and the *Constitution,* are the *picture of silver,* subsequently framed around it," Lincoln wrote. "The *picture* was made *for* the apple — *not* the apple for the picture." That is, the Constitution was made to secure the unalienable rights recognized in the Declaration of Independence. As such, the slavery compromises included in the Constitution can only be understood — that is, can only be understood to be prudential compromises rather than a surrender of principle—in light of the Founders' proposition that all men are created equal. In the end, lamentably, it took a bloody civil war to reconcile the protections of the Constitution with that proposition and to attest that this nation, so conceived and dedicated, could long endure.

—MATTHEW SPALDING

Washington's Farewell Address is full of truths important at all times, and particularly deserving consideration at the present. With a sagacity which brought the future before him, and made it like the present, he saw and pointed out the dangers that even at this moment most imminently threaten us. I hardly know how a greater service of that kind could now be done to the community than by a renewed and wide diffusion of that admirable paper, and an earnest invitation to every man in the country to reperuse and consider it. Its political maxims are invaluable; its exhortations to love of country and to brotherly affection among citizens, touching; and the solemnity with which it urges the observance of moral duties, and impresses the power of religious obligation, gives to it the highest character of truly disinterested, sincere, parental advice.

Daniel Webster, *The Character of Washington,*
February 22, 1832, celebrating the centennial anniversary
of Washington's birthday.

INTRODUCTION TO WASHINGTON'S FAREWELL ADDRESS

———⟩◈⟨———

P hiladelphia's largest newspaper carried quite a momentous exclusive on September 19, 1796. The article was introduced, without
editorial comment, under the simple heading: "To the PEOPLE
of the United States" and then "Friends and fellow Citizens." The reader
discovered the lengthy article's author only at the end, where there
appeared the words: "G. Washington, United States." The first-of-its-kind
presidential statement — it was not communicated to Congress, delivered
on a grand occasion, or given an official fanfare — was reprinted by virtually every major newspaper in America, but only one, the *Courier of New
Hampshire,* can claim the credit for having reprinted it under the title for
which it is now known: "Washington's Farewell Address."

The practical purpose of the Address was to announce Washington's
unexpected decision to retire from public life and not seek a third term as
president. For a great leader to voluntarily relinquish political power and
retire from public life was itself unprecedented in the annals of history.
Washington used this occasion "to offer to your solemn contemplation
and to recommend to your frequent review, some sentiments which are the
result of much reflection, of no inconsiderable observation, and which
appear to me all important to the permanency of your felicity as a People."

It was an open letter of advice and warning to the American people about their long-term safety and happiness.

From the beginning, the Farewell Address was revered, along with the Declaration of Independence and the Constitution, as one of the great statements of American purpose. James Madison described it as one of "the best guides to the distinctive principles" of American government, and Thomas Jefferson made it primary reading at the University of Virginia. John Marshall described it as a "last effort to impress upon his countrymen those great political truths which had been the guides of his own administration," and argued that it contained "precepts to which the American statesman can not too frequently recur."

Today, the Farewell Address is primarily remembered for its recommendations concerning American involvement in international affairs. The first President sternly warned the nation to be constantly alert to the wiles of foreign influence and recommended as few political connections with other nations as possible. But the document also includes Washington's advice on national union, the Constitution and the rule of law, political parties, religion and morality, foreign influence in domestic affairs, and commercial policy.

President Washington had considered retiring at the end of his first term, and, in May 1792, went so far as to ask Representative James Madison for advice on the "mode and time most proper" for announcing his intention to step down and to prepare a "valedictory address" based on Washington's instructions. In the spring of 1796, Washington again thought of retirement and the preparation of a valedictory statement, and approached Alexander Hamilton to see if he would be interested in helping to revise the work. Washington sent Hamilton a rough draft of the address, made up of the paragraphs written by Madison in 1792 and an additional, lengthier section written by Washington himself. With Washington's direction, Hamilton skillfully produced a new, fuller draft, which Washington then reworked into the final manuscript. It was this manuscript, in Washington's handwriting, that Washington showed to his cabinet and then delivered to David Claypoole, the owner and editor of *Claypoole's American Daily Advertiser,* the largest newspaper in Philadelphia.

The timing of the publication of the document is important. Washington delivered the final manuscript, dated the original proof from the first printing, and recorded the Farewell Address in his letterbook as September 17. It was published for the first time on September 19. Just nine years earlier, on September 17, 1787, the draft Constitution had been approved by the Constitutional Convention which Washington had chaired. And it was published for the first time in David Claypoole's newspaper on September 19, 1787. Washington assuredly realized the great symbolic importance of these dates.

The general theme of the Farewell Address is the preservation of the Union as the core of American nationhood. The President thought that Americans could best achieve the material requirements of independence by being united rather than divided and predicted that if the people would assess the immense value of national Union not only to their collective but also their individual happiness, they would inevitably come to "cherish a cordial, habitual and immoveable attachment to it." He urged the people to discourage any hint of abandoning the Union and warned of those who sought to "enfeeble the sacred ties which now link together the various parts." The ties that linked the various parts — the foremost tie being the Union, the formal tie being the Constitution — must be cherished as *sacred* and must be *sacredly* maintained.

One potential source of division that Washington warned against was sectionalism. He was concerned that a strong preference for one's state or local section of the country might become prejudicial and destructive of the common interest and national character. Foreshadowing the conflict between Union and sectionalism in the mid-nineteenth century over the question of slavery, he spoke of designing men that might misrepresent and alienate other sections of the country as an expedient to their own political power.

Washington also warned of "the baneful effects of the Spirit of Party"—one of the two most famous recommendations of the Farewell Address. This was not surprising, as the question of party, and the more notorious problem of faction, was a dominant question of Washington's presidency and a prominent concern throughout the Founding period. By this he didn't mean what we mean by political parties but instead what we call special interest groups, pushing their single-issue agendas at the expense of the common good. In its worst form, excessive party spirit distracted the government, agitated the community and opened the door to foreign influence and corruption. "A fire not to be quenched; it demands a uniform vigilance to prevent its bursting into a flame, lest instead of warming it should consume."

For Washington, the most important opinion to encourage was a common understanding of the rights and responsibilities of constitutional government. Thus, in one of the most succinct paragraphs of the Address, he encouraged education as a requirement of good citizenship: "Promote, then, as an object of primary importance, institutions for the general diffusion of knowledge. In proportion as the structure of a government gives force to public opinion, it is essential that public opinion should be enlightened." By enlightened, Washington meant not only the basic parameters of liberal education but also knowledge of the rights of man and the obligations of citizenship.

Washington also believed that republican government was only possible if the virtues needed for civil society and self-government remained strong and effective. It is "substantially true that virtue or morality is a necessary spring of popular government," a rule that extends "to every species of free government." And the "great Pillars of human happiness" and the "firmest props of the duties of Men and citizens," he emphasized, were religion and morality. "Of all the dispositions and habits which lead to political prosperity, Religion and morality are indispensable supports." While there might be particular cases where morality did not depend on religion, Washington argued that this was not the case for the morality of the nation: "And let us with caution indulge the supposition, that morality can be maintained without religion."

Washington goes on to advise that the United States should "observe good faith and justice towds. all Nations." He noted that "it will be worthy of a free, enlightened, and at no distant period, a great Nation, to give to mankind the magnanimous and too novel example of a People always guided by an exalted justice and benevolence." Besides, proper conduct toward other nations served to elevate and distinguish the national character: "The experiment is recommended by every sentiment which ennobles human Nature."

Americans must be free from hatreds and allegiances to foreign nations if they were to become partisans of their own nation and the larger cause of human freedom it represented. Foreign influence, in addition to the "baneful effects" of party, was "one of the most baneful foes of Republican government." Washington recommended as the great rule of conduct that the United States primarily pursue commercial relations with other nations and have with them "as little political connection as possible." Binding the destiny of America to Europe would only serve to unnecessarily "entangle" the new nation's peace and prosperity with "the toils of European Ambition, Rivalship, Interest, Humour [and] Caprice."

Washington's other famous recommendation was against excessive ties with other countries: " 'Tis our true policy to steer clear of permanent Alliances, with any portion of the foreign world." (The infamous warning against "entangling alliances," often attributed to the Farewell Address, is in the 1801 Inaugural Address of Thomas Jefferson.) Washington warned of *political* connections and *permanent* alliances and added the hedge "So far, I mean, as we are now at liberty to do." Instead he favored harmony and liberal intercourse with all nations as recommended by "policy, humanity and interest" and recommended that the nation pursue a long-term course of placing itself in a position to defy external threats, defend its own neutrality, and, eventually, choose peace or war as its own "interest guided by justice shall Counsel."

In the end, Washington was reluctant to assume that his counsels would have the intended effect: "I dare not hope they will make the strong and lasting impression, I could wish." The first President was endeavoring to inculcate maturity and moderation in both domestic and international affairs, and hoped that his advice might lead Americans to "controul the usual current of the passions" and "prevent our Nation from running the course which has hitherto marked the Destiny of Nations." He also held out the prospect that his advice might "now and then" be remembered so as to "moderate the fury of party spirit, to warn against the mischiefs of foreign Intriegue, [and] to guard against the Impostures of pretended patriotism." If his words did not moderate the people, at least they might serve to moderate their leaders and representatives.

Nevertheless, despite his many warnings, Washington anticipated "the sweet enjoyment of partaking, in the midst of my fellow Citizens, the benign influence of good Laws under a free Government, the ever-favourite object of my heart, and the happy reward, as I trust, of our mutual cares, labours and dangers." Has America moved down the path that has previously "marked the Destiny of Nations"? Amidst the seemingly intractable problems of modern public policy, those looking for guidance would do well to look to the Farewell Address and its "counsels of an old and affecionate friend."

— MATTHEW SPALDING

WASHINGTON'S FAREWELL ADDRESS

To the PEOPLE of the United States:
Friends and Fellow-Citizens:

The period for a new election of a Citizen, to Administer the Executive government of the United States, being not far distant, and the time actually arrived, when your thoughts must be employed in designating the person, who is to be clothed with that important trust, it appears to me proper, especially as it may conduce to a more distinct expression of the public voice, that I should now apprise you of the resolution I have formed, to decline being considered among the number of those, out of whom a choice is to be made.

Declines Third Term

I beg you, at the same time, to do me the justice to be assured that this resolution has not been taken, without a strict regard to all the considerations appertaining to the relation, which binds a dutiful citizen to his country, and that, in withdrawing the tender of service which silence in my situation might imply, I am influenced by no diminution of zeal for your future interest, no deficiency of grateful respect for your past kindness; but am supported by a full conviction that the step is compatible with both.

Duty

The acceptance of, and continuance hitherto in, the office to which your suffrages have twice called me, have been a uniform sacrifice of inclination to the opinion of duty and to a deference for what appeared to be your desire. I constantly hoped, that it would have been much earlier in my power, consistently with motives, which I was not at liberty to disregard, to return to that retirement, from which I had been reluctantly drawn. The strength of my inclination to do this, previous to the last Election, had even led to the preparation of an address to declare it to you; but mature reflection on the then perplexed and critical posture of our Affairs with foreign Nations and the unanimous advice of persons entitled to my confidence, impelled me to abandon the idea.

I rejoice, that the state of your concerns, external as well as internal, no longer renders the pursuit of inclination incompatible with the sentiment of duty or propriety, and am persuaded, whatever partiality may be retained for my services, that in the present circumstances of our country you will not disapprove my determination to retire.

The impressions, with which I first undertook the arduous trust, were explained on the proper occasion. In the discharge of this trust, I will only say, that I have, with good intentions, contributed toward the Organization and Administration of the government the best exertions of which a very fallible judgment was capable. Not unconscious, in the outset, of the inferiority of my qualifications, experience in my own eyes, perhaps still more in the eyes of others, has strengthened the motives to diffidence of myself; and every day the encreasing weight of years admonishes me more and more, that the shade of retirement is as necessary to me as it will be welcome. Satisfied that if any circumstances have given peculiar value to my services, they were temporary, I have the consolation to believe, that while choice and prudence invite me to quit the political scene, patriotism does not forbid it.

In looking forward to the moment, which is intended

to terminate the career of my public life, my feelings do not
permit me to suspend the deep acknowledgment of that
debt of gratitude which I owe to my beloved country, for
the many honors it has conferred upon me; still more for
the steadfast confidence with which it has supported me;
and for the opportunities I have thence enjoyed of manifest-
ing my inviolable attachment, by services faithful and persevering, though in usefulness unequal to my zeal. If benefits
have resulted to our country from these services, let it always
be remembered to your praise, and as an instructive example
in our annals, that, under circumstances in which the
Passions, agitated in every direction, were liable to mislead,
amidst appearances sometimes dubious, vicissitudes of fortune often discouraging, in situations in which not infre-
quently want of Success has countenanced the spirit of
criticism, the constancy of your support was the essential
prop of the efforts, and a guaranty of the plans by which
they were effected. Profoundly penetrated with this idea, I
shall carry it with me to my grave, as a strong incitement to
unceasing vows that Heaven may continue to you the choicest tokens of its beneficence; that your union and brotherly
affection may be perpetual; that the free constitution which
is the work of your hands, may be sacredly maintained; that
its Administration in every department may be stamped
with wisdom and Virtue; that, in fine, the happiness of the
people of these States, under the auspices of liberty, may be
made complete, by so careful a preservation and so prudent
a use of this blessing as will acquire to them the glory of
recommending it to the applause, the affection, and adoption of every nation which is yet a stranger to it.

    Here, perhaps, I ought to stop. But a solicitude for your
welfare, which cannot end but with my life, and the appre-

Debt of Gratitude

Last Wishes

hension of danger, natural to that solicitude, urge me on an occasion like the present, to offer to your solemn contemplation, and to recommend to your frequent review, some **Sentiments and Warnings** sentiments; which are the result of much reflection, of no inconsiderable observation, and which appear to me all important to the permanency of your felicity as a People. These will be offered to you with the more freedom as you can only see in them the disinterested warnings of a parting friend, who can possibly have no personal motive to bias his counsel. Nor can I forget, as an encouragement to it, your indulgent reception of my sentiments on a former and not dissimilar occasion.

Love of Liberty Interwoven as is the love of liberty with every ligament of your hearts, no recommendation of mine is necessary to fortify or confirm the attachment.

The Unity of Government which constitutes you one people is also now dear to you. It is justly so, for it is a main Pillar in the Edifice of your real independence, the support of your tranquillity at home, your peace abroad; of your safety; of your prosperity; of that very Liberty which you so highly prize. But as it is easy to foresee, that from different causes and from different quarters, much pains will be taken, many artifices employed, to weaken in your minds the conviction of this truth; as this is the point in your political fortress against which the batteries of internal and external enemies will be most constantly and actively (though often covertly and insidiously) directed, it is of infinite moment, that you should properly estimate the immense value of your **National Union** national Union to your collective and individual happiness; that you should cherish a cordial, habitual and immovable attachment to it; accustoming yourselves to think and speak of it as of the Palladium of your political safety and prosperity; watching for its preservation with jealous anxiety; discountenancing whatever may suggest even a suspicion that it can in any event be abandoned, and indignantly frowning upon the first dawning of every attempt to alienate any portion of our Country from the rest, or to enfeeble the sacred ties which now link together the various parts.

For this you have every inducement of sympathy and interest. Citizens by birth or choice, of a common country, that country has a right to concentrate your affections. The name of AMERICAN, which belongs to you, in your national capacity, must always exalt the just pride of Patriotism, more than any appellation derived from local discriminations. With slight shades of difference, you have the same Religion, Manners, Habits, and political Principles. You have in a common cause fought and triumphed together. The independence and liberty you possess are the work of joint councils, and joint efforts, of common dangers, sufferings and successes.

Patriotism

But these considerations, however powerfully they address themselves to your sensibility, are greatly outweighed by those which apply more immediately to your Interest. Here every portion of our country finds the most commanding motives for carefully guarding and preserving the Union of the whole.

The North, in an unrestrained intercourse with the South, protected by the equal Laws of a common government, finds in the productions of the latter, great additional resources of Maritime and commercial enterprise and precious materials of manufacturing industry. The South, in the same Intercourse, benefiting by the same Agency of the North, sees its agriculture grow and its commerce expand. Turning partly into its own channels the seamen of the

Regional Interests

North, it finds its particular navigation invigorated; and while it contributes, in different ways, to nourish and increase the general mass of the National navigation, it looks forward to the protection of a Maritime strength, to which itself is unequally adapted. The East, in a like intercourse with the West, already finds, and in the progressive improvement of interior communications, by land and water, will more and more find, a valuable vent for the commodities which it brings from abroad, or manufactures at home. The West derives from the East supplies requisite to its growth and comfort, and what is perhaps of still greater consequence, it must of necessity owe the secure enjoyment of indispensable outlets for its own productions to the weight, influence, and the future Maritime strength of the Atlantic side of the Union, directed by an indissoluble community of Interest as one Nation. Any other tenure by which the West can hold this essential advantage, whether derived from its own separate strength or from an apostate and unnatural connection with any foreign Power, must be intrinsically precarious.

National Security   While then every part of our country thus feels an immediate and particular Interest in Union, all the parts combined cannot fail to find in the united mass of means and efforts greater strength, greater resource, proportionably greater security from external danger, a less frequent interruption of their Peace by foreign Nations; and, what is of inestimable value! they must derive from Union an exemption from those broils and Wars between themselves, which so frequently afflict neighboring countries, not tied together by the same government; which their own rivalships alone would be sufficient to produce, but which opposite foreign alliances, attachments and intriegues would stimulate and imbitter. Hence likewise they will avoid the necessity of those overgrown Military establishments, which under any form of Government are inauspicious to liberty, and which are to be regarded as particularly hostile to Republican Liberty: In this sense it is, that your Union ought to be considered as a main prop of your liberty, and that the love of the one ought to endear to you the preservation of the other.

These considerations speak a persuasive language to every reflecting and virtuous mind, and exhibit the continuance of the UNION as a primary object of Patriotic desire. Is there a doubt, whether a common government can embrace so large a sphere? Let experience solve it. To listen to mere speculation in such a case were criminal. We are authorized to hope that a proper organization of the whole, with the auxiliary agency of governments for the respective Subdivisions, will afford a happy issue to the experiment. 'Tis well worth a fair and full experiment. With such powerful and obvious motives to Union, affecting all parts of our country, while experience shall not have demonstrated its impracticability, there will always be reason, to distrust the patriotism of those, who in any quarter may endeavor to weaken its bands.

In contemplating the causes wch. may disturb our Union, it occurs as matter of serious concern, that any ground should have been furnished for characterizing parties by Geographical discriminations: Northern and Southern, Atlantic and Western; whence designing men may endeavor to excite a belief that there is a real difference of local interests and views. One of the expedients of Party to acquire influence, within particular districts, is to misrepresent the opinions and aims of other Districts. You cannot

Geographical Discriminations

shield yourselves too much against the jealousies and heart-burnings which spring from these misrepresentations. They tend to render Alien to each other those who ought to be bound together by fraternal affection. The Inhabitants of our Western country have lately had a useful lesson on this head. They have seen, in the Negotiation by the Executive, and in the unanimous ratification by the Senate, of the Treaty with Spain, and in the universal satisfaction at that event, throughout the United States, a decisive proof how unfounded were the suspicions propagated among them of a policy in the General Government and in the Atlantic States unfriendly to their Interests in regard to the Mississippi. They have been witnesses to the formation of two Treaties, that with G: Britain and that with Spain, which secure to them everything they could desire, in respect to our Foreign relations, toward confirming their prosperity. Will it not be their wisdom to rely for the preservation of these advantages on the Union by which they were procured? Will they not henceforth be deaf to those advisers, if such there are, who would sever them from their Brethren and connect them with Aliens?

To the efficacy and permanency of your Union, a Government for the whole is indispensable. No Alliances however strict between the parts can be an adequate substitute. They must inevitably experience the infractions and interruptions which all Alliances in all times have experienced. Sensible of this momentous truth, you have improved upon your first essay by the adoption of a **New Constitution** Constitution of Government, better calculated than your former for an intimate Union, and for the efficacious management of your common concerns. This government, the offspring of our own choice, uninfluenced and unawed, adopted upon full investigation and mature deliberation, completely free in its principles, in the distribution of its powers, uniting security with energy, and containing within itself a provision for its own amendment, has a just claim to your confidence and your support. Respect for its authority, compliance with its Laws, acquiescence in its measures, are duties enjoined by the fundamental maxims of true Liberty. The basis of our political systems is the right of the people to make and to alter their Constitutions of Government. But the Constitution which at any time exists, 'till changed by an explicit and authentic act of the whole People, is sacredly obligatory upon all. The very idea of the power and the right of the People to establish Government presuppos-es the duty of every Individual to obey the established Government.

All obstructions to the execution of the Laws, all com-binations and Associations, under whatever plausible char-acter, with the real design to direct, controul counteract, or awe the regular deliberation and action of the Constituted authorities are destructive of this fundamental principle and of fatal tendency. They serve to organize faction; to give it an artificial and extraordinary force; to put in the place of the delegated will of the Nation, the will of a party; often a small but artful and enterprising minority of the Community; and, according to the alternate triumphs of different parties, to make the public administration the Mirror of the illconcerted and incongruous projects of fac-tion, rather than the organ of consistent and wholesome plans, digested by common counsils and modified by mutual interests. However combinations or Associations of the above description may now and then answer popular ends, they are likely in the course of time and things, to become

Rule of law

Faction

potent engines by which cunning, ambitious, and unprincipled men will be enabled to subvert the Power of the People, and to usurp for themselves the reins of Government; destroying afterwards the very engines which have lifted them to unjust dominion.

Opposition to the Constitution

Towards the preservation of your Government and the permanency of your present happy state, it is requisite, not only that you steadily discountenance irregular oppositions to its acknowledged authority, but also that you resist with care the spirit of innovation upon its principles however specious the pretexts. One method of assault may be to effect, in the forms of the Constitution, alterations which will impair the energy of the system, and thus to undermine what can not be directly overthrown. In all the changes to which you may be invited, remember that time and habit are at least as necessary to fix the true character of Governments, as of other human institutions; that experience is the surest standard, by which to test the real tendency of the existing Constitution of a country; that facility in changes upon the credit of mere hypotheses and opinion exposes to perpetual change, from the endless variety of hypothesis and opinion: and remember, especially, that for the efficient management of your common interests, in a country so extensive as ours, a Government of as much vigor as is consistent with the per-

Liberty fect security of Liberty is indispensable. Liberty itself will find in such a Government, with powers properly distributed and adjusted, its surest Guardian. It is indeed little else than a name, where the Government is too feeble to withstand the enterprises of faction, to confine each member of the Society within the limits prescribed by the laws and to main-

Rights tain all in the secure and tranquil enjoyment of the rights of person and property.

I have already intimated to you the danger of Parties in
the State, with particular reference to the founding of them
on Geographical discriminations. Let me now take a more
comprehensive view, and warn you in the most solemn
manner against the baneful effects of the Spirit of Party,
generally.

This spirit, unfortunately, is inseparable from our
nature, having its root in the strongest passions of the
human Mind. It exists under different shapes in all
Governments, more or less stifled, controulled, or repressed;
but in those of the popular form it is seen in its greatest
rankness and is truly their worst enemy.

The alternate domination of one faction over another,
sharpened by the spirit of revenge natural to party dis-
sention, which in different ages and countries has perpetrat-
ed the most horrid enormities, is itself a frightful despotism.
But this leads at length to a more formal and permanent
despotism. The disorders and miseries, which result, gradually incline the minds of men to seek security and repose in
the absolute power of an Individual: and sooner or later the
chief of some prevailing faction, more able or more fortu-
nate than his competitors, turns this disposition to the purposes of his own elevation, on the ruins of Public Liberty.

Without looking forward to an extremity of this kind
(which nevertheless ought not to be entirely out of sight)
the common and continual mischiefs of the spirit of Party
are sufficient to make it the interest and duty of a wise
People to discourage and restrain it.

It serves always to distract the Public Councils and
enfeeble the Public administration. It agitates the
Community with ill founded jealousies and false alarms, kin-
dles the animosity of one part against another, foments occa-

sionally riot and insurrection. It opens the door to foreign influence and corruption, which find a facilitated access to the government itself through the channels of party passion. Thus the policy and the will of one country, are subjected to the policy and will of another.

There is an opinion that parties in free countries are useful checks upon the Administration of the Government and serve to keep alive the spirit of Liberty. This within certain limits is probably true, and in Governments of a Monarchical cast Patriotism may look with endulgence, if not with favour, upon the spirit of party. But in those of the popular character, in Governments purely elective, it is a spirit not to be encouraged. From their natural tendency, it is certain there will always be enough of that spirit for every salutary purpose. And there being constant danger of excess, the effort ought to be, by force of public opinion, to mitigate and assuage it. A fire not to be quenched; it demands a uniform vigilance to prevent its bursting into a flame, lest instead of warming it should consume.

Separation of Powers

It is important, likewise, that the habits of thinking in a free Country should inspire caution in those entrusted with its administration to confine themselves within their respective Constitutional spheres; avoiding in the exercise of the powers of one department to encroach upon another. The spirit of encroachment tends to consolidate the powers of all the departments in one, and thus to create whatever the form of government, a real despotism. A just estimate of

Love of Power

that love of power, and proneness to abuse it, which predominates in the human heart is sufficient to satisfy us of the truth of this position. The necessity of reciprocal checks in the exercise of political power; by dividing and distributing it into different depositories, and constituting each the

Guardian of the Public Weal against invasions by the others, has been evinced by experiments ancient and modern; some of them in our country and under our own eyes. To preserve them must be as necessary as to institute them. If in the opinion of the People, the distribution or modification of the Constitutional powers be in any particular wrong, let it be corrected by an amendment in the way which the Constitution designates. But let there be no change by usurpation; for though this in one instance may be the instrument of good, it is the customary weapon by which free governments are destroyed. The precedent must always greatly overbalance in permanent evil any partial or transient benefit which the use can at any time yield.

Constitutional Amendments

Of all the dispositions and habits which lead to political prosperity, Religion and morality are indispensable supports. In vain would that man claim the tribute of Patriotism, who should labor to subvert these great Pillars of human happiness, these firmest props of the duties of Men and citizens. The mere Politician, equally with the pious man ought to respect and to cherish them. A volume could not trace all their connections with private and public felicity. Let it simply be asked where is the security for property, for reputation, for life, if the sense of religious obligation desert the oaths, which are the instruments of investigation in Courts of Justice? And let us with caution indulge the supposition, that morality can be maintained without religion. Whatever may be conceded to the influence of refined education on minds of peculiar structure, reason and experience both forbid us to expect that National morality can prevail in exclusion of religious principle.

Religion and Morality

'Tis substantially true, that virtue or morality is a necessary spring of popular government. The rule indeed extends with more or less force to every species of free Government. Who that is a sincere friend to it can look with indifference upon attempts to shake the foundation of the fabric?

Education   Promote then as an object of primary importance, Institutions for the general diffusion of knowledge. In proportion as the structure of a government gives force to public opinion, it is essential that public opinion should be enlightened.

As a very important source of strength and security,

Public Credit   cherish public credit. One method of preserving it is to use it as sparingly as possible: avoiding occasions of expense by cultivating peace, but remembering also that timely disbursements to prepare for danger frequently prevent much greater disbursements to repel it; avoiding likewise the accu-

Debt   mulation of debt, not only by shunning occasions of expence, but by vigorous exertions in time of Peace to discharge the Debts which unavoidable wars have occasioned, not ungenerously throwing upon posterity the burden which we ourselves ought to bear. The execution of these maxims belongs to your Representatives, but it is necessary that public opinion should cooperate. To facilitate to them the performance of their duty, it is essential that you should practically bear in mind, that towards the payment of debts

Taxation   there must be Revenue; that to have revenue there must be taxes; that no taxes can be devised which are not more or less inconvenient and unpleasant; that the intrinsic embarrassment inseparable from the selection of the proper objects (which is always a choice of difficulties), ought to be a decisive motive for a candid construction of the Conduct of the Government in making it, and for a spirit of acquiescence in the measures for obtaining Revenue which the public exigencies may at any time dictate.

Observe good faith and justice towds. all Nations. **Foreign Relations**
Cultivate peace and harmony with all. Religion and morality enjoin this conduct; And can it be that good policy does
not equally enjoin it? It will be worthy of a free, enlightened, and, at no distant period, a great Nation to give to
mankind the magnanimous and too novel example of a
People always guided by an exalted justice and benevolence.
Who can doubt that in the course of time and things the
fruits of such a plan would richly repay any temporary
advantages wch. might be lost by a steady adherence to it?
Can it be, that Providence has not connected the permanent
felicity of a Nation with its virtue? The experiment, at least,
is recommended by every sentiment which ennobles human
Nature. Alas! is it rendered impossible by its vices?

In the execution of such a plan nothing is more essen- **Avoid Antipathies**
tial than that permanent, inveterate antipathies against particular Nations and passionate attachments for others
should be excluded; and that in place of them just and ami-
cable feelings toward all should be cultivated. The Nation
which indulges toward another an habitual hatred, or an
habitual fondness, is in some degree a slave. It is a slave to
its animosity or to its affection, either of which is sufficient
to lead it astray from its duty and its interest. Antipathy in
one Nation against another, disposes each more readily to
offer insult and injury, to lay hold of slight causes of
umbrage, and to be haughty and intractable, when acciden-
tal or trifling occasions of dispute occur. Hence frequent
collisions, obstinate envenomed and bloody contests. The
Nation, prompted by ill will and resentment sometimes
impels to War the Government, contrary to the best calcu-
lations of policy. The Government sometimes participates in
the national propensity, and adopts through passion what

reason would reject; at other times, it makes the animosity of the Nation subservient to projects of hostility instigated by pride, ambition and other sinister and pernicious motives. The peace often, sometimes perhaps the Liberty, of Nations has been the victim.

Avoid Passionate Attachments

So likewise, a passionate attachment of one Nation for another produces a variety of evils. Sympathy for the favorite nation, facilitating the illusion of an imaginary common interest, in cases where no real common interest exists, and infusing into one the enmities of the other, betrays the former into a participation in the quarrels and Wars of the latter, without adequate inducement or justification: It leads also to concessions to the favorite Nation of privileges denied to others, which is apt doubly to injure the Nation making the concessions; by unnecessarily parting with what ought to have been retained, and by exciting jealousy, ill will, and a disposition to retaliate, in the parties from whom equal privileges are withheld: and it gives to ambitious, corrupted, or deluded citizens (who devote themselves to the favorite Nation) facility to betray or sacrifice the interests of their own country, without odium, sometimes even with popularity; gilding with the appearances of a virtuous sense of obligation a commendable deference for public opinion, or a laudable zeal for public good, the base or foolish compliances of ambition corruption or infatuation.

As avenues to foreign influence in innumerable ways, such attachments are particularly alarming to the truly enlightened and independent Patriot. How many opportunities do they afford to tamper with domestic factions, to practice the arts of seduction, to mislead public opinion, to influence or awe the public Councils! Such an attachment of a small or weak, towards a great and powerful Nation, dooms the former to be the satellite of the latter.

Against the insidious wiles of foreign influence, (I con-jure you to believe me, fellow-citizens) the jealousy of a free people ought to be constantly awake; since history and experience prove that foreign influence is one of the most baneful foes of Republican Government. But that jealousy to be useful must be impartial; else it becomes the instru-ment of the very influence to be avoided, instead of a defense against it. Excessive partiality for one foreign nation and excessive dislike of another, cause those whom they actuate to see danger only on one side, and serve to veil and even second the arts of influence on the other. Real Patriots, who may resist the intriegues of the favourite, are liable to become suspected and odious; while its tools and dupes usurp the applause and confidence of the people, to surren-der their interests.

Foreign Influence

The Great rule of conduct for us, in regard to foreign Nations is in extending our commercial relations to have with them as little political connection as possible. So far as we have already formed engagements let them be fulfilled, with perfect good faith. Here let us stop.

Great Rule of Conduct

Europe has a set of primary interests, which to us have none, or a very remote relation. Hence she must be engaged in frequent controversies, the causes of which are essentially foreign to our concerns. Hence therefore it must be unwise in us to implicate ourselves, by artificial ties, in the ordinary vicissitudes of her politics, or the ordinary combinations and collisions of her friendships, or enmities:

Europe

Our detached and distant situation invites and enables us to pursue a different course. If we remain one People, under an efficient government, the period is not far off when we may defy material injury from external annoyance;

when we may take such an attitude as will cause the neutrality we may at any time resolve upon to be scrupulously
respected; when belligerent nations, under the impossibility
of making acquisitions upon us, will not lightly hazard the
giving us provocation; when we may choose peace or war, as
Interest, Guided   our interest, guided by justice shall Counsel.
by Justice   Why forego the advantages of so peculiar a situation?
Why quit our own to stand upon foreign ground? Why, by
interweaving our destiny with that of any part of Europe,
entangle our peace and prosperity in the toils of European
Ambition, Rivalship, Interest, Humour, or Caprice?

Alliances   'Tis our true policy to steer clear of permanent
Alliances with any portion of the foreign world. So far, I
mean, as we are now at liberty to do it, for let me not be
understood as capable of patronizing infidelity to existing
engagements, (I hold the maxim no less applicable to public
than to private affairs that honesty is always the best policy).
I repeat, therefore, let those engagements be observed in
their genuine sense. But in my opinion, it is unnecessary
and would be unwise to extend them.

Taking care always to keep ourselves, by suitable establishments, on a respectable defensive posture, we may safely
trust to temporary alliances for extraordinary emergencies.

Harmony, liberal intercourse with all Nations, are recommended by policy, humanity, and interest. But even our
Commercial Policy   Commercial policy should hold an equal and impartial
(Trade)   hand: neither seeking nor granting exclusive favors or preferences; consulting the natural course of things; diffusing
and diversifying by gentle means the streams of Commerce,
but forcing nothing; establishing with Powers so disposed;
in order to give trade a stable course, to define the rights of
our Merchants, and to enable the Government to support

them; conventional rules of intercourse, the best that present circumstances and mutual opinion will permit, but temporary, and liable to be from time to time abandoned or varied, as experience and circumstances shall dictate; constantly keeping in view, that 'tis folly in one Nation to look for disinterested favors from another; that it must pay with a portion of its Independence for whatever it may accept under that character; that by such acceptance, it may place itself in the condition of having given equivalents for nominal favours and yet of being reproached with ingratitude for not giving more. There can be no greater error than to expect, or calculate upon real favours from Nation to Nation. 'Tis an illusion which experience must cure, which a just pride ought to discard.

In offering to you, my Countrymen these counsels of an old and affectionate friend, I dare not hope they will make the strong and lasting impression, I could wish; that they will control the usual current of the passions or prevent our Nation from running the course which has hitherto marked the Destiny of Nations. But if I may even flatter myself, that they may be productive of some partial benefit, some occasional good; that they may now and then recur to moderate the fury of party spirit, to warn against the mischiefs of foreign Intrigue, to guard against the Impostures of pretended patriotism; this hope will be a full recompense for the solicitude for your welfare, by which they have been dictated.

Intended Effect

How far in the discharge of my Official duties, I have been guided by the principles which have been delineated, the public Records and other evidences of my conduct must Witness to You and to the world. To myself, the assurance of my own conscience is, that I have at least believed myself to be guided by them.

Neutral Policy   In relation to the still subsisting War in Europe my Proclamation of the 22d. of April 1793, is the index to my Plan. Sanctioned by your approving voice and by that of Your Representatives in both Houses of Congress, the spirit of that measure has continually governed me; uninfluenced by any attempts to deter or divert me from it.

After deliberate examination with the aid of the best lights I could obtain I was well satisfied that our Country, under all the circumstances of the case, had a right to take, and was bound in duty and interest to take, a Neutral position. Having taken it, I determined, as far as should depend upon me, to maintain it, with moderation, perseverance and firmness.

The considerations, which respect the right to hold this conduct, it is not necessary on this occasion to detail. I will only observe, that according to my understanding of the matter, that right, so far from being denied by any of the Belligerent Powers has been virtually admitted by all.

The duty of holding a Neutral conduct may be inferred, without anything more, from the obligation which justice and humanity impose on every Nation, in cases in which it is free to act, to maintain inviolate the relations of Peace and amity toward other Nations.

Predominant Motive   The inducements of interest for observing that conduct will best be referred to your own reflections and experience. With me, a predominant motive has been to endeavor to gain time to our country to settle and mature its yet recent institutions, and to progress without interruption to that degree of strength and consistency, which is necessary to give it, humanly speaking, the command of its own fortunes.

Though in reviewing the incidents of my Administration, I am unconscious of intentional error, I am nevertheless too sensible of my defects not to think it probable that I may have committed many errors. Whatever they may be I fervently beseech the Almighty to avert or mitigate the evils to which they may tend. I shall also carry with me the hope that my Country will never cease to view them with indulgence; and that after forty-five years of my life dedicated to its Service, with an upright zeal, the faults of incompetent abilities will be consigned to oblivion, as myself must soon be to the Mansions of rest.

Historical Judgment

Relying on its kindness in this as in other things, and actuated by that fervent love toward it, which is so natural to a Man, who views in it the native soil of himself and his progenitors for several Generations; I anticipate with pleasing expectation that retreat in which I promise myself to realize, without alloy, the sweet enjoyment of partaking, in the midst of my fellow Citizens, the benign influence of good Laws under a free Government, the ever-favourite object of my heart, and the happy reward, as I trust, of our mutual cares, labours and dangers.

G. WASHINGTON.
United States
September 19, 1796

&

GOOD **BOOKS** for
ADDITIONAL READING
AND A LIST of
RELIABLE SCHOLARS
ON THE
AMERICAN FOUNDING

&

Recommended Reading

BOOKS ON LEADING FOUNDERS

George Washington

Washington: The Indispensable Man
By James Thomas Flexner (Little, Brown and Co., 1984)

This is the best one-volume biography of Washington from his most accomplished biographer, who has also written a comprehensive four-volume biography for the more adventuresome reader. Not simply an abridged version of the larger work, it is an original and very readable biography written for a general audience.

Founding Father: Rediscovering George Washington
By Richard Brookhiser (Free Press, 1996)

This is not a life history of Washington but an analysis of his career and character as a soldier, founder, and statesman, presented in highly readable, thematic chapters. The author calls it a moral biography, intended to show how Washington navigated life and politics as a public figure.

A Sacred Union of Citizens: George Washington's Farewell Address and the American Character
By Matthew Spalding and Patrick Garrity (Rowman & Littlefield, 1997)

This work is a popular study of Washington's political thought as found in his major writings, arguing that Washington's project was not only to start a nation but to establish a national character. The book focuses on the Farewell Address of 1796, placing the writing in historical context and looking at how it has affected our political debate both past and present.

George Washington and American Independence
By Curtis Nettels (Little, Brown and Co., 1951)

This classic, well-written work looks at the political role played by General Washington in the fight for national independence over the course of the year preceding July 1776, and argues that the Declaration of Independence can be seen as a final ratification of earlier actions and events.

George Washington and American Constitutionalism
By Glenn Phelps (University Press of Kansas, 1994)

This book argues that George Washington was a committed and consistent constitutionalist throughout his life, and led — rather than followed — opinion concerning a continental government for the new nation. A more academic study, but readable nonetheless, it includes a good analysis of the Washington presidency.

Benjamin Franklin

Benjamin Franklin
By Carl Van Doren (The Viking Press, 1938)

This lengthy work is the classic, comprehensive biography of Franklin, written in the grand old style. It covers his life in Boston, Philadelphia, London, Paris, and back in the United States.

Franklin of Philadelphia
By Esmond Wright (Harvard University Press, 1986)

A solid, modern biography that is a bit more scholarly but highly readable. It includes a good closing essay on Franklin's continuing relevance.

Benjamin Franklin and American Foreign Policy
By Gerald Stourzh (The University of Chicago, 1954)

A scholarly study of Franklin's political thought, with a focus on his views concerning international security, national self-interest and the new diplomacy of the 18th century. It includes particular chapters on Franklin's opinions on the French Alliance and the peace settlement with Great Britain.

John Adams

John Adams
By David McCullough (Simon & Schuster, 2001)

This sweeping work of popular history covers all of Adams's life, with due prominence on his relationships with wife Abigail and fellow patriot Thomas Jefferson. The bestseller makes a strong case for Adams's importance, despite its weakness of neglecting Adams's intellectual contributions to the American Founding.

John Adams: A Life
By John Ferling (Henry Holt and Co., 1996)

A weighty but good biography that draws heavily on original texts. More academic than the McCullough biography, and perhaps less easy to read, but much more substantive and comprehensive.

John Adams and the Spirit of Liberty
By C. Bradley Thompson (University Press of Kansas, 1998)

This is a more academic work that focuses on Adams's major works to show how his political thought, particularly on constitutional development and political architecture, is relevant to the formation of American political ideals.

The Passionate Sage: The Character and Legacy of John Adams
By Joseph Ellis (W. W. Norton, 1993)

A good analysis of Adams's political thought, focusing on his post-presidential years, this is one of the first books to spark the recent revival in Adams's scholarship. It considers his mature ideas and character in order to assess his proper place in the Founding generation.

Thomas Jefferson

Thomas Jefferson and the New Nation: A Biography
By Merrill Peterson (Oxford University Press, 1970)

Though long, this is the standard — and most balanced — one volume Jefferson biography, providing a basic narrative and highlighting three dominant themes of Jefferson's career: democracy and popular government, the new American nationality, and philosophical enlightenment. Solidly grounded in Jefferson's writings, but intended more for the general reader than the scholar.

Jefferson the Virginian

By Dumas Malone (Little, Brown and Co., 1948)

This is the first volume of the majestic, multi-volume (and decidedly sympathetic) biography *Jefferson and his Time,* published between 1948 and 1977. The volumes deal with Jefferson's life through the American Revolution (Vol. 1), his time in Paris through the first Washington administration (Vol. 2), from then through the election in 1800 (Vol. 3), his first (Vol. 4) and second (Vol. 5) presidential terms, and his retirement (Vol. 6).

The Constitutional Thought of Thomas Jefferson

By David Mayer (University Press of Virginia, 1995)

Rather than the popular view of Jefferson as the champion of unrestrained democracy, this work focuses on Jefferson's philosophy of government, emphasizing his commitment to liberty, self-government, and written constitutions rigorously adhered to.

The Presidency of Thomas Jefferson

By Forrest McDonald (University Press of Kansas, 1987)

A brief but thorough and highly readable critical history of the politics and policies, both domestic and foreign, of Jefferson and his two terms as the nation's third president.

The Jefferson-Hemmings Matter: Report of a Commission of Scholars

Edited by Robert F. Turner (Carolina Academic Press, forthcoming)

A group of senior Jefferson scholars — several of them critics of Jefferson — consider and refute much of the DNA and historical evidence and conclude that the paternity allegations against Jefferson concerning his slave Sally Hemings are inconclusive.

Alexander Hamilton

Alexander Hamilton: A Biography

By Forrest McDonald (W. W. Norton, 1990)

An excellent political biography explaining Hamilton's greatest contributions in finance, economics, and law. It convincingly makes the case for the first secretary of the treasury's importance to the political economy of the early American Republic.

Alexander Hamilton, American
By Richard Brookhiser (Simon and Schuster, 2000)

This thematic, popular biography by the author of *Founding Father: Rediscovering George Washington* captures the dynamic Hamilton and credits him with originating American capitalism.

Alexander Hamilton and the Idea of Republican Government
By Gerald Stourzh (Stanford University Press, 1970)

A scholarly book on Hamilton's political thought in the context of his and his contemporaries' understanding of republican government and its application to American politics in light of the great ideas — revolution, popular sovereignty, the public good, foreign policy — confronting the Founders between 1760 and 1800.

Republican Empire: Alexander Hamilton on War and Free Government
By Karl Walling (University Press of Kansas, 1999)

This academic study argues that Hamilton sought to combine the strength necessary for war with the restraint required by the rule of law, popular consent, and individual rights to help found the world's most durable republican empire.

James Madison

James Madison: A Biography
By Ralph Louis Ketchum (The MacMillan Company, 1971)

This comprehensive and lengthy volume is one of the best Madison biographies, and it is accessible to general readers and scholars alike. It is a very thorough historical narrative and distillation of both the ideas and the man, with a good emphasis on his role in the Continental Congress and at the Constitutional Convention.

James Madison and the Creation of the American Republic
By Jack Rakove (Scott, Foresman, 1990)

This relatively short but solid biography focuses on Madison's public life, as a skillful leader and a brilliant political thinker, to emphasize how he successfully combined serious ideas and practical politics to the benefit of the new nation.

American Compact: James Madison and the Problem of the Founding

By Gary Rosen (University Press of Kansas, 1999)

This academic consideration of Madison's political thought argues that his understanding of the social compact, the nature of the Founding and the origins of the Constitution are not just of historical significance but can shed light on current issues such as diversity, constitutional interpretation, and federalism.

The Last of the Founders: James Madison and the Republican Legacy

By Drew R. McCoy (Cambridge University Press, 1989)

This highly readable yet scholarly work focuses on Madison's years of retirement from 1817 to his death in 1836. It is a consideration of his later political thought looking back on the earlier Founding period, dealing with his views on questions such as nullification, political economy, and slavery.

THE AMERICAN REVOLUTION

A History of the American Revolution

By John Alden (Alfred Knopf, 1969)

Perhaps the best single-volume history of the American Revolution, it covers the period from 1763 to 1789, and considers the political, military, social, economic, and constitutional aspects of the time, taking a balanced look at all of the parties and issues involved.

Angel in the Whirlwind: The Triumph of the American Revolution

By Benson Bobrick (Simon and Schuster, 1997)

A sweeping narrative of the American Revolution that takes the reader from Lexington Green to the Battle of Yorktown, describing in novel-like fashion the major battles and the main characters, juxtaposing the patriot George Washington and the traitor Benedict Arnold.

Paul Revere's Ride

By David Hackett Fischer (Oxford University Press, 1995)

This compelling book retells the common tale of Paul Revere's famous midnight ride and the ensuing skirmishes at Lexington and Concord in a narrative that is at the same time readable and scholarly. It argues that the conflict was not the spontaneous uprising of legend but an organized and active resistance.

The War of American Independence:
Military Attitudes, Policies, and Practice 1763-1789

By Don Higgenbotham (The MacMillan Company, 1971)

This is the best military history of the colonial and Founding era. It follows battles and campaigns as well as military policy and popular attitudes toward war, tracing the interaction between warfare and society and how that affected civil and military institutions in the United States.

Patriots: The Men Who Started the American Revolution

By A.J. Langguth (Simon and Schuster, 1988)

A wonderful work that brings the American Revolution to life through important vignettes along the way, highlighting those who fought it in the political and military arenas, from James Otis in 1761 to George Washington at Yorktown in 1783.

The Glorious Cause: The American Revolution, 1763-1789

By Robert Middlekauff (Oxford University Press, 1982)

This narrative traces the Revolution's origins from the end of the Seven Years War, emphasizing the common soldiers' views of the American War of Independence to how they came to see it as a glorious cause not just for independence but to form a new nation. It focuses on questions of governance, politics, constitutionalism, and war; and ties popular convictions about rights and politics to the colonists' religious convictions.

Decisive Day: The Battle of Bunker Hill
The Winter Soldiers: The Battles for Trenton and Princeton
Saratoga: Turning Point of America's Revolutionary War

By Richard M. Ketchum (Henry Holt and Co., 1999)

These three charming narrative histories read like novels. Drawing on an enormous range of sources, including diaries and letters by officers and common soldiers, and vivid descriptions and arresting portraits of participants, each book in the series (originally published in the 1970s) tells the story surrounding a decisive battle of the American Revolutionary War.

THE CONSTITUTIONAL CONVENTION

1787: The Grand Convention
By Clinton Rossiter (MacMillan Company, 1966)

Rossiter, the editor of the most widely read edition of the *Federalist Papers,* examines the meeting that created the Constitution in this very readable (and trustworthy) work, focusing on the setting, men, events, and consequences of the federal convention through the early years of the new Republic. A number of related documents are also included.

Miracle at Philadelphia: The Story of the Constitutional Convention, May to September 1787
By Catherine Drinker Bowen (Little, Brown and Company, 1966)

This popular (but less authoritative) narrative of the Constitutional Convention focuses narrowly on the participants and the day-to-day convention debate in almost novel-like form.

The Framing of the Constitution
By Max Farrand (Yale University Press, 1913)

This is a more succinct and charming version of the Rossiter book on the events surrounding the Constitutional Convention, written by the scholar who compiled the definitive collection of the notes and records of the meeting.

THE CONSTITUTION

The Framing and Ratification of the Constitution
Edited by Leonard Levy and Dennis Mahoney (MacMillan, 1987)

A nice collection of 21 essays on the framing and ratification of the Constitution, addressing various topics ranging from our colonial background and the events leading up to the Constitutional Convention to questions of original intent and organization of the new government.

From Parchment to Power: How James Madison Used the Bill of Rights to Save the Constitution
By Robert Goldwin (American Enterprise Institute, 1997)

A clear and convincing historical study of the constitutional issues surrounding the creation of the Bill of Rights, looking at the philosophical arguments behind these guarantees and how Madison crafted the first 10 amendments and then shepherded them through the First Congress.

Commentaries on the Constitution
By Joseph Story (Carolina Academic Press, 1987)

A classic and substantive work on the meaning of the U.S. Constitution by one of its early scholars and one of the greatest justices of the Supreme Court. This reprint of the 1833 edition includes histories of various colonies, of the Revolutionary and of the Confederation periods; it also includes straight-forward commentaries on the clauses of the Constitution.

What the Anti-Federalists Were For: The Political Thought of the Opponents of the Constitution
By Herbert J. Storing (The University of Chicago, 1981)

A brief introduction to the thought of the anti-Federalists, who opposed the ratification of the Constitution and wanted a small republic, more federalism, and a bill of rights, among other things. It also considers their affect on enduring themes of American political life such as a concern for big government and the infringement of personal liberty.

GENERAL HISTORIES

The Colonial Wars: 1689-1762
By Howard H. Peckman (The University of Chicago Press, 1964)

A good explanation of the four major military conflicts that were spin-offs of European wars and that dominated the American continent — thus contributing to a want of independence — in the years before the Founding era: King William's War (1689-97), Queen Anne's War (1702-13), King George's War (1744-48) and the French and Indian War (1755-62).

Origins of the American Revolution
By John C. Miller (Little, Brown and Company, 1943)

An older, but still useful history of the events leading up to the American Revolution that chronicles the various British acts against the colonials from the beginning of the French and Indian War to the Declaration of Independence.

The Birth of the Republic, 1763-89
By Edmund Morgan (University of Chicago Press, 1956)

The story of the American Revolution told in a concise, readable manner, explaining how 13 colonies came together over British tax policy and established their own constitutional principles to protect their freedom. The best, short history of the era.

Setting the World Ablaze: Washington, Adams, Jefferson and the American Revolution
By John E. Ferling (Oxford University Press, 2000)

This comparative biography reconstructs the lives of three of the greatest Founders from their youths through their participation in the American Revolution, providing a wide view of their participation in the Revolution as well as more intimate looks at their individual struggles.

Founding Brothers: The Revolutionary Generation
By Joseph Ellis (Alfred A. Knopf, 2000)

This work views the American Founding though the intertwined experiences of seven leaders of the period, looking at six discrete moments that exemplify the time.

The Age of Federalism: The Early American Republic, 1788-1800
By Stanley Elkins and Eric McKitrick (Oxford University Press, 1993)

This lengthy work traces the development of the new nation from the time after the Constitutional Convention through its first three presidents. A comprehensive analysis of the early national period, including all the achievements and fights of the chief figures.

The Slaveholding Republic: An Account of the United States Government's Relations to Slavery
By Don E. Fehrenbacher (Oxford University Press, 2001)

This detailed study, stretching from the First Continental Congress to the Civil War, argues persuasively that early trends in the colonies were against slavery and that the U.S. Constitution is not a pro-slavery document, despite later policies that supported the institution.

Colonies Into Nation: American Diplomacy, 1763-1801
By Lawrence S. Kaplan (The MacMillan Company, 1972)

An interpretative history of American diplomacy from the Treaty of Paris in 1763 to the inauguration of Thomas Jefferson, showing how pre-Revolutionary and post-Revolutionary diplomacy developed consistently over time to reinforce — and play a vital role in creating — a united country seeking independence in a hostile world.

The American Presidency: An Intellectual History
By Forrest McDonald (University Press of Kansas, 1994)

This work examines the creation and history of the presidency and looking at the political theorists who influenced the Founders, at the Constitutional Convention, the precedent-setting terms of Washington and Jefferson and the evolution of the office's expressed and implied powers.

RELIGION AND THE FOUNDING

On Two Wings: Humble Faith and Common Sense at the American Founding
By Michael Novak (Encounter Book, 2001)

This nicely written book argues that from the very beginning the American Founders not only believed that they were acting reasonably but also believed that they were carrying out God's commandment. A counterbalance to the popular emphasis on secular history, it also includes an appendix on several forgotten Founders.

Christians in the American Revolution
By Mark A. Noll (Baker Books, 1991)

This short work examines the revolution that occurred in the hearts and minds of the colonists by examining the interaction between religious convictions and political thought in the Founding era. A look at the topic in broad strokes; the work is a good overview of the subject.

Religion and the New Republic: Faith in the Founding of America
Edited by James H. Hutson (Rowman & Littlefield, 2000)

A collection of seven compelling essays on church-state relations in the early Republic, conveying the variety of accommodations that existed between religion and public order in the formative period of American history.

The American Founding as the Best Regime: The Bonding of Civil and Religious Liberty

By Harry V. Jaffa (The Claremont Institute, 1990)

This brief but forceful booklet is a powerful argument for the significance of America as the first regime in Western civilization to provide for the coexistence of the claims of reason and of revelation, through the establishment of religious liberty, thus making possible the blessings of free government.

The Politics of Reason and Revelation: Religion and Civic Life in the New Nation

By John G. West, Jr. (University Press of Kansas, 1996)

This work argues that the Founders and their immediate successors wanted religion to play a dynamic, positive role in American politics, and examines religious political activism from 1800 to 1835 to show the success of an earlier understanding of church-state relations in conformity with their intent.

INTERPRETATION AND ASSESSMENT

The Reinterpretation of the American Revolution

Edited by Jack P. Greene (Harper & Row, 1968)

A very good anthology of 24 interpretative essays by earlier scholars — such as Bernard Bailyn, Perry Miller, Forrest McDonald, Douglas Adair, and Martin Diamond — that provides a broad introduction to the leading (and disagreeing) schools of modern scholarship on the American Founding.

Essays on the Making of the Constitution

Edited by Leonard Levy (Oxford University Press, 1987)

A strong collection of essays that bring together differing viewpoints on the roles and motivations of the framers of the Constitution. Includes a selection from Charles Beard's historic An Economic Interpretation of the Constitution as well as essays attacking and essays defending Beard's thesis.

The American Founding: Essays on the Formation of the Constitution

Edited by J. Jackson Barlow, Leonard W. Levy, and Ken Masugi (Greenwood Publishing, 1988)

This is a collection of 11 short but scholarly essays on the political thought of the American Founding by authors such as Merrill Peterson, Jack Rackove, Harry V.

Jaffa, and Henry Steele Commager. The essays address topics such as classical political thought, John Locke, equality, natural rights, and the Enlightenment in relation
to American thought.

Saving the Revolution: The Federalist Papers and the American Founding
Edited by Charles Kesler (New York: Free Press, 1987)

A very approachable collection of 14 essays by foremost scholars explaining and
interpreting the *Federalist Papers* on topics such as republicanism, federalism, foreign
policy, the separation of powers, executive power, and the original purposes of the
Constitution.

Vindicating the Founders: Race, Sex, Class, and Justice in the Origins of America
By Thomas West (Rowman & Littlefield, 1997)

This popular work seeks to debunk widely held, politically-correct opinions about
the Founders by addressing their views on the controversial issues of slavery, property rights, women, the family, welfare, and immigration.

Taking the Constitution Seriously
By Walter Berns (Simon and Schuster, 1987)

This brief work makes a defense of the original intent of the Framers by relating
the Constitution back to the principles of the Declaration of Independence and
considering how the Founding dealt with various challenges to the idea of
constitutionalism.

PRIMARY SOURCES AND WRITINGS

The Federalist Papers
Alexander Hamilton, John Jay, and James Madison (Mentor Books edition, 1999)
Published as a series of newspaper articles intended to sway New Yorkers in the
debate over ratification, this famous collection of essays in defense of the
Constitution remains the greatest work of American political philosophy. The classic
edition, edited by the late Clinton Rossiter, has now been published with a fine
introduction by Charles Kesler, as well as an historical glossary and other supple-
mentary materials.

George Washington: A Collection

Edited by William B. Allen (Liberty Press, 1995)

A marvelous collection of Washington's correspondence and writings from his early, middle, and later years. Reading through the well-chosen selections provides a clear perspective on Washington's life and statesmanship. Includes all of Washington's major writings, as well as "The Rules of Civility and Decent Behavior" and his Last Will and Testament.

Franklin: Writings

Edited by J.A. Leo Lemay (Library of America, 1987)

A good collection of Franklin's many writings, including his charming essays under various pseudonyms such as Silence Dogood, the Busy-Body and Richard Saunders, the "author" of *Poor Richard's Almanack*. It also includes Franklin's autobiography, based on the original manuscript, and his speeches in the Constitutional Convention.

The Revolutionary Writings of John Adams

Edited by C. Bradley Thompson (Liberty Fund, 2000)

This collection focuses on Adams's pre-Revolutionary and Revolutionary writings, including *A Dissertation on the Canon and Feudal Law*, his *Novanglus* letters, the influential *Thoughts on Government* and various writings recounting the Anglo-American dispute.

Jefferson: Collected Writings

Edited by Merrill Peterson (Library of America, 1984)

A very complete selection of Jefferson's writings, containing all Jefferson's main works (*Autobiography, A Summary View of the Rights of British America, Notes on the State of Virginia*), his major speeches, and public papers (including the original and revised drafts of the Declaration of Independence) and a wide variety of private letters.

Selected Writings and Speeches of Alexander Hamilton

Edited by Morton J. Frish (American Enterprise Institute, 1985)

A nice collection of Hamilton's most important letters, speeches, and essays from 1775 to 1803, including his opinion on the national bank and his Report on Manufactures. An excellent overview of Hamilton's political thought, complemented with introductions and commentary.

The Mind of the Founder: Sources of the Political Thought of James Madison

Edited by Marvin Meyers (Brandeis University Press, 1981)

A very nice collection of Madison's essays, letters, and speeches between 1774 and 1836, including numerous writings that illuminate his central role in the Constitutional Convention and the creation of the Bill of Rights. It shows his part in the rise of party opposition during the Washington administration. Its virtue is a great explanatory essay on Madison, section introductions, and brief note with each entry.

Paine: Collected Writings

Edited by Eric Foner (Library of America, 1995)

This collection includes Paine's Revolutionary writings *Common Sense* and *The American Crisis,* and many other pamphlets, articles and, letters, as well as the full text of his later works *Rights of Man* and *The Age of Reason.*

COLLECTED DOCUMENTS

American Political Writing During the Founding Era

By Charles Hyneman and Donald Lutz (Liberty Press, 1983)

This two-volume set includes pamphlets, articles, sermons and essays written by various political authors between 1762 and 1805. It is a gold mine of 76 less well-known but equally colorful and highly reasoned popular writings of the Revolutionary era. Each entry is introduced by a brief note on the author.

The Founders' Constitution

Edited by Philip B. Kurland and Ralph Lerner (Liberty Fund, 2000)

Originally published by the University of Chicago Press to commemorate the bicentennial of the Constitution, this extensive work consists of extracts from the leading works on political theory, history, law, and constitutional arguments on which the Framers and their contemporaries drew and which they themselves produced. Liberty Fund has prepared a paperback edition of the entire work in five volumes. It is also available online at *http://press-pubs.uchicago.edu/founders.*

Colonies to Nation, 1763-1789: A Documentary History of the American Revolution

By Jack P. Greene (W. W. Norton, 1975)

This collection tells the story of the American Founding using documents ranging from government papers and popular pamphlets to diary accounts and personal letters. Each section has a full introduction and each entry is prefaced by an introductory note, thus placing all the documents in a coherent framework.

Debates on the Constitution

Edited by Bernard Bailyn (The Library of America, 1993)

A very nice two-volume collection of Federalist and anti-Federalist speeches, articles, and letters during the struggle over ratification of the Constitution, focusing on debates in the press and correspondence between September 1787 and August 1788, as well as on the debates in the state ratifying conventions of Pennsylvania, Connecticut, Massachusetts, South Carolina, Virginia, New York, and North Carolina.

The Records of the Federal Convention of 1787

Edited by Max Farrand (Yale University Press, 1986)

This definitive work, originally published in 1937, gathers into three volumes all the records written by participants of the Constitutional Convention of 1787, including the extensive, official notes taken throughout by James Madison.

Documents of American History

By Henry Steele Commager (Prentice Hall, 1988)

This two-volume set is the definitive collection of the most important official and quasi-official documents in American history. The first volume alone contains 345 documents from 1492 up to 1898. A good source for Founding era documents — from the Mayflower Compact and several colonial charters to resolutions of the Continental Congress, documents of the Constitutional Convention and important diplomatic writings — although some have been condensed.

Political Sermons of the American Founding Era, 1730-1805

Edited by Ellis Sandoz (Liberty Fund, 1998)

This is a superb collection of 55 religious sermons from a range of denominational and theological viewpoints, which bear on the politics of the day. All told, the sermons (each averages about twenty pages) display the religious seriousness of the time, as well as the importance of the pulpit to the American Revolution.

The Essential Antifederalist
Edited by William B. Allen and Gordon Lloyd (University Press of America, 1985)

This volume of essays offers an accessible selection of leading anti-Federalist opinion. After a nice interpretative essay by the editors, the selections are grouped to focus on the origins of anti-Federalist thought, then later views on federalism, republicanism, capitalism, and democracy.

Our Sacred Honor: Words of Advice from the Founders in Stories, Letters, Poems and Speeches
Edited by William J. Bennett (Broadman & Holman Publishers, 1997)

A charming, readable book of material collected and edited with lively commentary by the author of *The Book of Virtues*. Not surprisingly, the book is divided into sections on Patriotism and Courage, Love and Courtship, Civility and Friendship, Education of the Head and Heart, Industry and Frugality, Justice, and Piety.

USEFUL WEBSITES

U.S. Congressional Documents and Debates 1774-1873
www.memory.loc.gov/ammem/amlaw/lawhome.html

(Sponsored by the Library of Congress)

An extensive site that includes the Journals of the Continental Congress, detailing the First Continental Congress (September 5 to October 26, 1774) and the Second Continental Congress (May 10, 1775 to March 2, 1789); Farrand's Records of the Federal Convention of 1787, the single best source of notes and correspondence during the Constitutional Convention; and Elliot's Debates, the record of the constitutional ratifying conventions in various states. It also includes the Journals of Congress, Maclay's Journal (one of the few accounts of Senate activity before the chamber was opened to the public in 1795) and the debates in Congress as recorded in Annals of Congress, Register of Debates and The Congressional Globe.

Fundamental Documents of the American Founding
www.nara.gov/exhall/charters/

(Sponsored by the National Archives and Records Administration)

The Declaration of Independence, U.S. Constitution, and Bill of Rights in transcription form, as well as high-resolution images of the full original documents. In addition, there are articles detailing the creation of the Declaration and the Constitution, and useful biographies of the 55 delegates to the Constitutional Convention. There is also a readable text and a high-resolution version of the Magna Carta, the charter of English liberties.

The Founders' Constitution
press-pubs.uchicago.edu/founders/
(Sponsored by the University of Chicago Press and the Liberty Fund)

The online version of a work first published in 1986 in five oversized volumes with more than 3,200 double-column pages. Edited by University of Chicago scholars Ralph Lerner and Philip Kurland, the documents included range from the early 17th century to the 1830s, from the reflections of philosophers to popular pamphlets, from public debates in ratifying conventions to the private correspondence of the leading political actors of the day. They are arranged, first, according to broad themes or problems to which the Constitution of 1787 has made a significant and lasting contribution. Then they are arranged by article, section, and clause of the U.S. Constitution, from the Preamble through Article Seven and continuing through the first twelve Amendments.

A User's Guide to the Declaration of Independence
www.founding.com
(Sponsored by the Claremont Institute)

An in-depth discussion of various fundamental concepts in the Declaration of Independence, such as equality, natural rights, the meaning of "self-evident" truths, and the Declaration's theory of man. In addition, this site offers a line-by-line analysis of the Declaration, with easy links to particular words and phrases allowing for a closer inspection and understanding of the reasoning and intent of Thomas Jefferson and other framers. Finally, there is an examination of a variety of issues within the context of the American Founding, such as race, property rights, religion, immigration restrictions, and property requirements and voting, as well as on the debates in the state ratifying conventions of Pennsylvania, Connecticut, Massachusetts, South Carolina, Virginia, New York, and North Carolina.

The Founders' Almanac Online
www.foundersalmanac.org
(Sponsored by The Heritage Foundation)

The complete content of the Founders' Almanac is made available to researchers, students — anyone at anytime. In addition to the chronology of notable events, collection of essays, and the full text of the Declaration of Independence and Constitution, the interactive calendar enables users to find important dates and events according to a given criteria, and the quotation database is searchable by name, topic or date. The regularly updated site also features resources as well as links to other, related sites.

EXPERTS ON THE
AMERICAN FOUNDING

Allen, Dr. William B.
Professor of Political Science
Michigan State University
303 South Kedzie
East Lansing, MI 48824-1032
Phone: 517-432-9967
E-mail: allenwi@pilot.msu.edu

Arkes, Dr. Hadley
Edward N. Ney Professor of
   Jurisprudence and American
   Institutions
Amherst College
206 Converse Hall
Political Science Department
Amherst, MA 01002-5000
Phone: 413-542-2293
E-mail: hparkes@amherst.edu

Arnn, Dr. Larry P.
President
Hillsdale College
33 East College Street
Hillsdale, MI 49242
Phone: 517-437-7341
E-mail: larry.arnn@hillsdale.edu

Belz, Dr. Herman
Professor of History
University of Maryland, College Park
2137 Francis Scott Key Hall
Department of History
College Park, MD 20742
Phone: 301-405-4287
E-mail: hb5@umail.umd.edu

Bennett, Dr. William J.
Distinguished Fellow
The Heritage Foundation
Co-Director, Empower America
1701 Pennsylvania Avenue,
   Suite 900
Washington, DC 20006
Phone: 202-452-8200
E-mail: bennett@empower.org

Berns, Dr. Walter
Professor of Government Emeritus
Georgetown University
Resident Scholar, American
   Enterprise Institute
1150 17th Street, NW
Washington, DC 20036
Phone: 202-862-5859
E-mail: wberns@aei.org

Bork, Robert H.
John M. Olin Scholar in Legal
  Studies
The American Enterprise Institute
1150 17th Street, NW
Washington, DC 20036
Phone: 202-862-5800
E-mail: rbork@aei.org

Carey, Dr. George
Professor of Government
Georgetown University
Government Department
Box 571034
Washington, DC 20057-1034
Phone: 202-687-5613
E-mail: careygw@georgetown.edu

Ceaser, Dr. James
Professor of Government
The University of Virginia
Charlottesville VA 22904-4787
Cabell Hall, Rm 243
Phone: 804-924-7903
E-mail: jwc2g@virginia.edu

Forde, Dr. Steven
Professor of Political Science
University of North Texas
P. O. Box 305340
Denton, TX 76203-5340
Phone: (940) 565-4999
Email: forde@unt.edu

Forte, Dr. David
Professor of Law
Cleveland-Marshall College of Law
Cleveland State University
1801 Euclid Avenue
Cleveland, OH 44115
Phone: 216-687-2342
E-mail: david.forte@law.csuohio.edu

Franck, Dr. Matthew J.
Professor of Political Science
Radford University
P.O. Box 6945
Radford, VA 24142
Phone: 540-831-5854
E-mail: mfranck@runet.edu

Gaziano, Todd
Senior Fellow in Legal Studies
The Heritage Foundation
214 Massachusetts Avenue, NE
Washington, DC 20002
Phone: 202-608-6182
E-mail: todd.gaziano@heritage.org

George, Dr. Robert P.
McCormick Professor of
  Jurisprudence
Princeton University
Corwin Hall
Department of Politics
Princeton, NJ 08544
Phone: 609-258-3270
E-mail: rgeorge@princeton.edu

Goldwin, Dr. Robert A.
Resident Scholar
The American Enterprise Institute
1150 17th Street, NW
Washington, DC 20036
Phone: 202-862-5912
E-mail: bobgoldwin@
  compuserve.com

Greve, Dr. Michael
John G. Searle Scholar
American Enterprise Institute
1150 17th Street, NW
Washington, DC 20036
Phone: 202-862-4874
E-mail: mgreve@aei.org

Kesler, Dr. Charles R.
Professor of Government
Director, Henry Salvatori Center
Claremont McKenna College
Pitzer Hall 114
Claremont, CA 91711
Phone: 909-621-8201
E-mail: charles_kesler@mckenna.edu

Kmiec, Dr. Douglas W.
Dean and St. Thomas More
  Professor of Law
The Catholic University of America
  School of Law
620 Michigan Avenue, NE
Columbus School of Law
Washington, DC 20064
Phone: 202-319-5140
E-mail: kmiec@cua.edu

Lund, Dr. Nelson
Professor of Law
The George Mason University
  School of Law
3401 North Fairfax Drive
Arlington, VA 22201
Phone: 703-993-8045
E-mail: nlund@gmu.edu

Mayer, Dr. David N.
Professor of Law and History
Capital University Law School
303 East Broad Street
Law and Graduate Center
Columbus, OH 43215-3200
Phone: 614-236-6561
E-mail: dmayer@law.capital.edu

McClay, Dr. Wilfred M.
Sun Trust Chair of Excellence in
  Humanities
The University of Tennessee,
  Chattanooga
615 McCallie Avenue
Chattanooga, TN 37403
Phone: 423-755-5202
E-mail: mcclay@mindspring.com

McConnell, Dr. Michael W.
Presidential Professor of Law
The University of Utah College of
  Law
332 South 14000 East Front
Salt Lake City, UT 84112
Phone: 801-581-6342
E-mail: mcconnellm@law.utah.edu

McDonald, Dr. Forrest
Distinguished University Research
  Professor
The University of Alabama
P. O. Box 155
Coker, AL 35452
Phone: 205-339-0317

Meese, Edwin, III
Ronald Reagan Distinquished Fellow
  in Public Policy
The Heritage Foundation
214 Massachusetts Avenue, NE
Washington, DC 20002
Phone: 202-608-6180

Owens, Dr. Mackubin Thomas
Associate Dean of Academics for
Electives and Directed Research
U.S. Naval War College
686 Cushing Road
Newport, Rhode Island 02841
Phone: 401-841-2015
Email: owensm@nwc.navy.mil

Pilon, Dr. Roger
B. Kenneth Simon Chair in
  Constitutional Studies
Cato Institute
1000 Massachusetts Avenue, NW
Washington, DC 20001
Phone: 202-789-5233
E-mail: rpilon@cato.org

Rabkin, Dr. Jeremy
Associate Professor of Government
Cornell University
McGraw Hall
Ithaca, NY 14853
Phone: 607-255-4915
E-mail: jar11@cornell.edu

Schramm, Dr. Peter W.
Executive Director
John M. Ashbrook Center for Public
  Affairs
Ashland University
401 College Avenue
Ashland, OH 44805
Phone: 419-289-5411
E-mail: pschramm@ashland.edu

Sheehan, Dr. Colleen
Assistant Professor of Political
  Science
Villanova University
800 Lancaster Ave.
St. Augustine Center 254
Villanova, PA 19085-1699
Phone: (610) 519-7421
Email: colleen.sheehan@villanova.edu

Spalding, Dr. Matthew
Director, B. Kenneth Simon Center
  for American Studies
The Heritage Foundation
214 Massachusetts Avenue, NE
Washington, DC 20002
Phone: 202-608-6171
E-mail: matthew.spalding
  @heritage.org

Stoner, Dr. James R.
Associate Professor of Political
  Science
Louisiana State University
208-B Stubbs Hall
Department of Political Science
Baton Rouge, LA 70803
Phone: 225-388-2142
E-mail: poston@lsu.edu

Thompson, Dr. Bradley
Associate Professor of History and
  Political Science
Ashland University
401 College Ave.
Ashland, Ohio 44805
Phone: (419) 289-5946
Email: cthompso@ashland.edu

West, Dr. Thomas G.
Professor of Politics
The University of Dallas
1845 East Northgate Drive
Department of Politics
Irving, TX 75062
Phone: 972-721-5278
E-mail: tomwest@acad.udallas.edu

Williams, Dr. Walter E.
Professor of Economics (Chair)
George Mason University
4400 University Drive, MSN 3G4
Fairfax, VA 22030
Phone: 703-993-1148
E-mail: wwilliam@gmu.edu

Wolfson, Dr. Dorothea
Fellow at the Johns Hopkins
  University
Center for the Study of American
  Government
10009 Crestwood Road
Kensington, MD 20895
Phone: (301) 493-5035
Email: Diw8@aol.com

CONTRIBUTORS

Steven Forde is Professor of Political Science at the University of North Texas. He is the author of *The Ambition to Rule: Alcibiades and the Politics of Imperialism in Thucydides* and several articles on classical and modern political philosophy including American political thought.

Mackubin Thomas Owens is Professor of Strategy and Force Planning at the Naval War College in Newport, Rhode Island, where he also teaches courses on the American Founding and U.S. civil-military relations. He is a regular columnist for *The Providence Journal.*

Colleen Sheehan is Assistant Professor of Political Science at Villanova University, and has served in the Pennsylvania House of Representatives. She is the co-editor of *Friends of the Constitution: Writings of the Other Federalists 1787-1788,* and is currently working on a book exploring the political thought of James Madison.

Matthew Spalding is Director of the B. Kenneth Simon Center for American Studies at The Heritage Foundation in Washington, D.C. He is the co-author of *A Sacred Union of Citizens: George Washington's Farewell Address and the American Character* and co-editor of *Patriot Sage: George Washington and the American Political Tradition.*

C. Bradley Thompson is an Associate Professor and Chairman of the Department of History and Political Science at Ashland University, in Ashland, Ohio. He is the author of *John Adams and the Spirit of Liberty* and the editor of *The Revolutionary Writings of John Adams.*

Dorothea Wolfson is a Fellow at the Johns Hopkins University Center for the Study of American Government. She has taught at Loyola University in Baltimore, Maryland, and collaborated with William J. Bennett on *Our Sacred Honor: Words of Advice from the Founders in Stories, Letters, Poems and Speeches.*

THE HERITAGE FOUNDATION

The Heritage Foundation is committed to
building an America where freedom, opportunity,
prosperity and civil society flourish

F ounded in 1973, The Heritage Foundation is a research and educational institute — a think tank — whose mission is to formulate and promote conservative public policies based on the principles of free enterprise, limited government, individual freedom, traditional American values, and a strong national defense.

Heritage's staff pursues this mission by performing timely, accurate research on key policy issues and effectively marketing these findings to our primary audiences: members of Congress, key congressional staff members, policymakers in the executive branch, the nation's news media, and the academic and policy communities. Heritage's products include publications, articles, lectures, conferences, and meetings.

Governed by an independent Board of Trustees, The Heritage Foundation is a nonpartisan, tax-exempt institution. Heritage relies on the private financial support of the general public — individuals, foundations, and corporations — for its income, and accepts no government funds and performs no contract work. Heritage is one of the nation's largest public policy research organizations. More than 200,000 contributors make it the most broadly supported think tank in America.

For more information, or to support our work, please contact The Heritage Foundation at (800) 544-4843 or visit www.heritage.org.

Note on Type

This book was set in Adobe Caslon. Designed for the Adobe Corporation by Carol Twombly, the typeface is based on a 17th-century type by English typefounder William Caslon (1692-1766). During the 18th century the fonts were hugely popular among printers throughout Europe and the American colonies. It was Benjamin Franklin's favorite typeface, and the first printings of the Declaration of Independence and the U.S. Constitution were set in Caslon.